Typing Politics

Typing Politics

The Role of Blogs in American Politics

Richard Davis

OXFORD
UNIVERSITY PRESS

2009

OXFORD
UNIVERSITY PRESS

Oxford University Press, Inc., publishes works that further
Oxford University's objective of excellence
in research, scholarship, and education.

Oxford New York
Auckland Cape Town Dar es Salaam Hong Kong Karachi
Kuala Lumpur Madrid Melbourne Mexico City Nairobi
New Delhi Shanghai Taipei Toronto

With offices in
Argentina Austria Brazil Chile Czech Republic France Greece
Guatemala Hungary Italy Japan Poland Portugal Singapore
South Korea Switzerland Thailand Turkey Ukraine Vietnam

Published by Oxford University Press, Inc.
198 Madison Avenue, New York, New York 10016

www.oup.com

Oxford is a registered trademark of Oxford University Press

Library of Congress Cataloging-in-Publication Data
Davis, Richard, 1955–
Typing politics : the role of blogs in American politics / Richard Davis.
   p.   cm.
ISBN 978-0-19-537376-9; 978-0-19-537375-2 (pbk.)
1. Political participation—Technological innovations—United States.   2. Blogs—Political aspects—United
States.   3. United States—Politics and government—Blogs. I. Title.
JK1764.D375 2009
320.9730285'6752—dc22   2008051392

9 8 7 6 5 4 3 2 1

Printed in the United States of America
on acid-free paper

*To the many colleagues in the field of political communication
who have shaped and refined my views over the years*

Acknowledgments

Only one name appears on the front cover of this book, but without the help of many people there would be no book. I'm grateful for the assistance of those who helped conduct the research and offered support to complete this study.

Several research assistants contributed to parts of this book. They are listed in alphabetical order: Mackenzie Ackerson, Eric Buell, Janae Card, Bethany Davis, William Jackson-Buchanan, Mansi Mehan, Jeanine Plamondon, Adriel Pond, Allison Seil, Phil Singer, Holly Howington Sweetwood, Kathryn Toone, Chelsea Wheeler, and Kaylie Whittemore.

I appreciate the support and editorial direction of David McBride, my editor at Oxford University Press, as well as the work of the editorial and production team at Oxford. This is my fifth book with Oxford. Their professionalism and commitment to their authors is unsurpassed, which has made working with the Oxford team such a joy.

I want to thank several entities that helped me in the data collection and writing stages of this project. The Joan Shorenstein Center on the Press, Politics and Public Policy gave me a fellowship to complete this book. The other fellows and faculty at the Shorenstein Center provided helpful suggestions during that semester. I appreciate their interest in this project. In addition, the College of Family, Home, and Social Sciences gave me a much appreciated leave to complete my research. Grants for this research were provided by the John S. and James L. Knight Foundation, the Carnegie Foundation, and the College of Family, Home, and Social Sciences at Brigham Young University. In addition, the college provided a semester leave, allowing me to focus my efforts on completing this book.

Contents

Typing Politics

Introduction

It was a time of intense partisanship across the nation. The United States was divided between two political parties with sharply divergent ideologies. The closeness of elections meant that the outcomes sometimes remained inconclusive for a long time after the people had voted. Essayists spent much of their time reviewing media accounts and then writing polemics attacking their opponents, including launching personal attacks on presidential candidates and other politicians in the opposition. Many of them did so under pseudonyms to hide their identity. Their essays circulated widely among the political elite of the day.

This was the state of American politics and media just over 200 years ago, when Republicans and Federalists dominated the political scene and partisan newspaper editors supported or attacked them. But it could just as easily describe our own age. Today those essayists are called "bloggers," short for "webloggers." They are people who maintain online journals that discuss politics. Like their early counterparts, they spend many hours each day collecting information and writing commentary; instead of publishing their essays in broadsheets circulated in taverns and other public places, though, they post them on their Web sites. Bloggers thrive on commentary, rumor, gossip, and satire. And, similar to the partisan press of that earlier day, they also collaborate with politicians who know their writing can be instrumental in reaching a politically interested and potentially active audience.

There is both old and new in the blog phenomenon. The use of writing to make political points to a broader audience is an ancient practice, but this particular form—"blogs," short for "weblogs"—is a wholly new medium. Blogs are so new that *Webster's Dictionary* didn't include a definition for the term until 2005. The term weblog itself did not originate until 1997, and the shorter version, blog, came two years later.[1]

Blogging was not an activity ordinary people engaged in until 1999, when a user-friendly software by Pyra Labs for blogging could be downloaded for free.

This software provided a tool for easily updating Web sites.[2] Suddenly, anyone with a computer and an e-mail address could become a blogger within a few minutes. And many people have done just that. Blog growth has been astounding. In 2000, blogs could be numbered in the thousands, but four years later there were an estimated 4.3 million blogs.[3] In 2008, an estimated 133 million blogs had been created, and approximately 120,000 new blogs are started each day.[4]

Not only are the numbers of blogs growing, but so is the audience for blogs. By 2008, according to the Pew Internet and American Life Project, 73 percent of Americans were online. That was up from 71 percent a year before and 61 percent five years earlier.[5] This means there is a rapidly expanding potential audience for blog reading. When people were asked in 2004 what a blog was, 62 percent of Internet users did not know.[6] In 2003, 2 percent of adult Internet users said they had blogs, and 11 percent said they had read the blogs of others. Eighteen months later, 27 percent of adult Internet users said they had read someone else's blog, and 7 percent said they had set up a blog.[7] By 2008, an estimated 22 million American adults, or 12 percent of Internet users, had a blog, and 50 percent of Internet users said they had read someone else's blog.[8]

The blog audience is not necessarily a political audience, however. Political blogs are a small subset of the total *blogosphere*, the term used to describe the world of blogs.[9] Many blogs discuss entertainment and technology.[10] According to one classification, more than 70 percent of blogs are personal journals.[11] In a survey of Internet users in California, 9 percent of Internet users said they read political blogs "almost every day."[12]

Political blog reading has become a daily activity for a small minority of political activists. One former State Department spokesperson said, "They're the first thing I read when I get up in the morning and the last thing I read at night."[13] A reporter for the *New Republic* said he reads ten to fifteen blogs daily.[14] One likely reason for the increased public awareness of blogs is news media coverage of the blogging phenomenon. Coverage mushroomed in only five years: there were three newspaper stories about blogs in 1999, 209 in 2001, 1,442 in 2003, and 3,212 in 2004.[15]

A medium that acquires a significant audience and discusses politics constantly is bound to be considered of some political importance. The claims of blogging's role, present and future, are hardly modest, and the most vocal advocates are bloggers themselves. Liberal bloggers believe they already have altered electoral outcomes. They claim they defeated Senator Joe Lieberman (D-Connecticut) in the 2006 senatorial primary, although Lieberman, as an Independent, defeated blogger favorite Ned Lamont in the general election that year. Another claimed victory was the Democratic takeover of the U.S.

Senate and House of Representatives in 2006. Liberal bloggers take credit for making possible the U.S. Senate wins of senators Sherrod Brown (D-Ohio), Jon Tester (D-Montana), Jim Webb (D-Virginia), and other Democratic candidates that year.[16] Conservative bloggers point to their own victories as well. They argue that they were instrumental in causing the withdrawal of U.S. Supreme Court nominee Harriet Miers. They also point to the early retirement of CBS News anchor Dan Rather after an embarrassing *60 Minutes II* scandal as a blog triumph.

But these events are small potatoes compared to what many foresee as the broader role of the blogosphere. Specifically, news stories about blogs have emphasized the medium as a new tool for personal empowerment. One journalist opined that blogs have "given the average Jane the ability to write, edit, design, and publish her own editorial product—to be read and responded to by millions of people, potentially—for around $0 to $200 a year."[17] They emphasize how "Joe Average Blogger" can revolutionize politics through blogging.[18]

The blogosphere is trumpeted because it will revolutionize journalism by stripping away the advantages of the media elite. One blogger argued, "It has made the price of entry into the media market minimal. In days gone by, you needed a small fortune to start up a simple magazine or newspaper. Now you need a laptop and a modem."[19] Newspaper columnist Walter Mossberg has praised blogs because they "introduce fresh voices into the national discourse."[20] Others suggest that blogs will reinvigorate public journalism, which was a movement designed to reengage the American citizenry in public life.[21]

The change, proponents argue, has empowered average people. Matt Drudge, although technically not a blogger, told the National Press Club, "Every citizen can be a reporter, can take on the powers that be....Now, with a modem, anyone can follow the world and report on the world—no middle man, no Big Brother."[22] A political scientist explained, "To blog is to declare your presence; to disclose to the world that you exist and what it's like to be you."[23]

Blogging also has been seen as the salvation of the Internet. Originally the Internet was viewed as an unsullied world where individuals could communicate beyond the reach of established organizations. That utopia has long since vanished. Yet as the World Wide Web has become inundated with commercial messages, the blogosphere has been perceived as the area of the Internet that is still untouched by commercialization, the place where the real revolution is happening.[24]

Blogs have been viewed as possible tools in the promotion of democracy. Former Virginia governor Mark Warner said that bloggers are "potentially creating a new public square for democracy."[25] Indeed, the blogosphere has arrived at a time of growing public cynicism about politicians and government.[26] Bloggers may have stoked that cynicism by attacking political elites. Markos Moulitsas, founder of the popular blog Daily Kos, decried the political establishment: "The media elite has failed us. The political elite has failed us. Both parties."[27] Simultaneously blogger proponents view blogs as the opposite of stale elite politics, as an opportunity for fresh democratic expression. Political consultant Joe Trippi claims that the revolution will not be televised; instead it will be blogged.[28] The blogosphere, it has been suggested, might even be able to overthrow dictatorships.[29]

The nature of the blogosphere facilitates its role as a tool for promoting democracy, bloggers contend. It is a vehicle for average citizens to participate as never before. Blogging has been seen as a "mark of emancipation" because it allows average people who have been marginalized in the past to express their views in the public square.[30] Because it is average people who are blogging, one scholar called the blogging phenomenon "the worship of the ordinary."[31] A political scientist contended that although the Internet has failed to diversify news and information sources available to individuals, "political blogs have the potential to break out of this reality," and a communications scholar praises blogs because "they enrich the information mix."[32] One blogger promises that bloggers "will no longer remain passive and meek....We, the people, are coming to power slowly and indefatigably."[33]

Blogs, some predict, will challenge existing political institutions and organizations by placing power in the hands of the people. Stephen Coleman, a British political scientist, argued, "Blogs diminish people's need to be spoken for by others."[34] According to Democratic blogger and author Jerome Armstrong, "No longer will people rely on conventional wisdom to dictate how campaigns are waged. Instead, millions of online activists will guide the campaign strategies of progressives to succeed from this point forward."[35] Bloggers believe that the rise of the blogosphere will shake up politics as we know it. "There's no doubt," claimed blogger Moulitsas, "we're turning the political world upside down."[36]

To some extent, the assertion that the blogosphere is a vehicle for expression by the common person is quite true. The vast majority of blogs are places where ordinary people express themselves about their own lives, primarily to friends or family.[37] Many are attracted to the allure of writing down their personal views and seeing those views disseminated throughout the world. The fact that, in nearly all cases, very few people are paying attention does not seem to matter.

The act of writing fulfills a need: a need to speak, if not necessarily to be heard. One Washington lobbyist compared the blogosphere to "the guys who gather around the counter at the local diner. Everyone's got an opinion and an audience who will listen."[38] A political blogger expressed the appeal of blogs when he said, "If you're gonna pay any attention at all…, you find yourself yelling at the television, and wanting to respond to stuff you see that you regard as outrageous." Another attributed it to the illusion of being able to publish worldwide without having to be a famous writer.[39]

For the vast majority of bloggers, the act of blogging has little or nothing to do with politics. Indeed, relatively few blogs actually focus on politics or government. Only 11 percent of bloggers in one survey said that the primary topic of their blogs is politics or political issues.[40] A few political blogs, however, have become among the most widely read on the Internet. Daily Kos, Instapundit, Michelle Malkin, and The Huffington Post are titles of blogs that did not exist a decade ago, and still are unknown to many Americans. Nevertheless they have acquired a role in politics in and out of the blogosphere. They provide information and commentary on a wide range of topics. One scholar termed them "veritable *Time* magazines of the Internet."[41]

Those elite blogs have earned large audiences (some larger than the audiences for regional newspapers) that turn to them on a daily basis for news and commentary. They and other blogs have caught the attention as well of elites: journalists, interest group leaders, candidates, and elected officials. And they have become the embodiment of a predicted movement of power from elites to ordinary citizens. Blogging has inspired a new term, "netroots," to describe individuals who are using the blogosphere to shape politics. One blogger has predicted the netroots will grab power from elites and use it to move politics away from "politicians that adhere to a say-nothing poll-tested message designed not to offend."[42]

The growth of blogs and their embrace by millions of Americans raise questions about how blogs are affecting American politics. Are they reshaping democracy by empowering millions of Americans? Are they changing the face of politics? Are they replacing traditional journalism?

This book is an examination of the political role of blogs today. It is not a how-to book on blogging; my intent is not to explain the nuts and bolts of running a political blog. Nor is it an encouragement to blog or a polemic on how blogging will revolutionize the world. Rather, the thesis of this book is that political blogs affect politics through a transactional relationship with other agenda seekers (politicians, groups, political organizations, etc.), journalists, and the audience. This thesis is significant because it contradicts the conventional wisdom that blogs represent both a distinction from and a reform of the existing communications and political systems. Bloggers make this claim and trumpet it incessantly. However, this book is intended to offer a counter-thesis: that not only have political players adapted to the blogosphere, but the blogosphere has in turn been mainstreamed in order to acquire relationships with other players.

To test this thesis, we will review briefly the role of agenda setting, specifically the transactional nature of agenda setting. Chapter 1 examines traditional agenda setters and introduces blogs as another player in those transactional relationships. In chapter 2 we analyze the recent intersection between political blogs and American political life, including a discussion of incidents of blogs' role in scandals, campaigns and elections, and governmental processes. These events help explain how bloggers have entered the political landscape. Chapter 3 turns to the political blogosphere. How did it get started? What types of political blogs are out there? What are the best-known blogs? Who runs them? Who reads them? This chapter continues the mainstreaming theme by demonstrating how political bloggers already are, or are becoming, mainstream players in political processes such as policy making and electoral campaigns.

Chapter 4 goes inside blogs to examine their content. What are blogs like? What topics do they discuss? What is the nature of discussion of the political blogosphere? In chapter 5, we turn to bloggers' relations with other players, beginning with an examination of their relationship with other agenda seekers. How do bloggers and other agenda seekers interact? How has the blogosphere been incorporated into media strategies of these agenda seekers? Then we study how political players themselves have been transformed into bloggers. Then we turn to the intersection of blogs and traditional journalists in chapter 6 to explore the development of a symbiotic relationship between these two entities. Have news organizations adapted to the blogosphere? If so, in what ways? Do journalists use blogs for newsgathering? If so, why and how do they do so? The topic of chapter 7 is the audience. Who is the audience for bloggers? How do audience and bloggers interact with each other? What are the gratifications of blog reading for the audience?

Finally, we summarize and speculate on the future. Will blogs displace traditional journalism? Will blogs supplement traditional media by providing specialized information that traditional news providers can't? Will blogs become a form of niche journalism? Does the future of blogs mean the integration of the culture of the blogosphere into public discourse and news dissemination, or will the blogosphere adapt to the norms of traditional media and become increasingly a mainstream venue?

1

Agenda Setting

On September 26, 2006, President George W. Bush signed a bill that created a searchable database of federal grants and contracts designed for citizens, groups, and the press to track federal spending. The bill seemed unremarkable except that it was strongly opposed by two senior senators who did not want public disclosure of the pork barrel projects they supported. They placed a secret hold on the bill to prevent a vote.[1] Other members of Congress found it difficult to press these more senior members.

Then several political bloggers joined the battle. Glenn Reynolds, N. Z. Bear, and others used their blogs to urge readers to contact their senators and see who was blocking the bill. One congressional aide admitted, "Bloggers mobilized Congress, Congress did not mobilize bloggers."[2]

Under scrutiny from blogs and their audiences, the two senators relinquished their hold. Congress passed the bill, and the White House even acknowledged the role of bloggers by inviting several to join the bill-signing ceremony. This was a first. Bloggers were gaining official recognition for setting the agenda and helping to shape legislation.[3]

Two years earlier, in July 2004, a newly formed group called Swift Boat Veterans for Truth began running ads attacking Senator John Kerry's war record. Kerry's presidential campaign initially ignored the ads, which were designed to undermine his claims to heroism. The news media followed suit. But the blogosphere aired the charges extensively. Eventually the traditional media could not ignore the story any longer and by August began to cover the charges. The Kerry campaign went on the defensive.[4]

Attempts to set policy and political agendas are hardly novel. Everyone in national politics seeks to do so: presidents, members of Congress, interest groups, bureaucratic agency heads, and the press. But bloggers are new participants in the agenda-setting process. Their role as agenda seekers—those who work to shape policy agendas—is a far cry from the personal journal writing origins of the blogosphere. It is an indication of the blogosphere's new status as a player in the agenda-setting process.

The Nature of Agenda Setting

Agenda setting, according to political scientist Bernard Cohen, is the ability to affect what people think about.[5] It refers to the power to determine public priorities. Because the news media's audience reach is vast, and attention is regular and sometimes intense, studies of agenda setting usually focus on the traditional media's ability to affect others' agendas, both policy makers and the press.

Agenda-setting research found such an impact. Initially agenda setting focused on the correlation between issue salience in media content and the public's attitudes.[6] However, media agenda setting goes beyond issue salience to specific attributes of issues or candidates.[7] For example, voters are more likely to focus on particular attributes of candidates when those attributes also have been emphasized in media campaign coverage.[8]

Agenda-setting effects are not limited to ordinary citizens. Policy makers, too, can be affected by media agendas.[9] That conclusion may seem obvious because policy makers are a highly attentive public. They are constantly seeking job-related information, and, because their positions depend on the continued support of the public, they are also concerned about what the public is thinking. The effect on policy makers can sometimes be far-reaching; for example, President Ronald Reagan called the prime minister of Israel to complain about Israel's bombing of Beirut after watching television news stories of the destruction of the city, and President George H. W. Bush responded to news coverage of Kurdish refugees following the Persian Gulf War.[10]

However, the effects of agenda setting on the mass public are mitigated by various factors.[11] The characteristics of the individual or group as well as the latent concerns people already have affect the media's ability to set issue priorities.[12] For example, skeptics of the media are less likely than other citizens to be affected by media agenda setting.[13] One limitation is time. Media agenda-setting effects are not necessarily long term.[14]

Transactional Agenda Setting

These cases suggest that, even though there are restrictions in effects, agenda setting is unidirectional: the mass media transmits messages to the audience generally, or policy makers specifically, and the recipients accept such messages. In fact, the process is much more complex. Rather than a linear relationship in which other players are merely the receivers of media agendas, the agenda-setting process is more transactional in nature. Elites, the public, and the media all join in agenda setting.[15] During political campaigns, candidates and media interact in agenda setting, responding to each other's words and actions.[16] Even candidate advertising can affect the agenda of the news media.[17] Presidents especially are powerful agenda setters for the public, not just the press.[18]

In terms of audience role, the transactional nature of the process seems obvious. For example, the media cannot set an agenda that does not appeal to the audience.[19] In fact, media agenda-setting efforts have failed when the audience is uninterested in the media's agenda. For example, CBS News once sent news anchor Dan Rather to the Midwest for a week to broadcast about the farm problem, but CBS's emphasis was preempted by regime change in the Philippines and Rather quickly returned to New York.[20]

Agenda setting becomes crucial during an election campaign, when voters have decisions to make about candidates and policy.[21] Agenda seekers—primarily candidates—attempt to focus voters' attention on issues helpful to their candidacy, emphasizing their strengths and their opponent's weaknesses. These agenda items include both policy issues (national security, economy, education, etc.) and non-policy issues (leadership qualities, competence, experience, etc.). The candidates battle each other for control of the media and the public agenda. Whoever controls the agenda controls the information that voters are getting, and thus is likely to be the election winner. For example, in 2004 one of the most important issues for voters was terrorism, and those voters who considered terrorism the most important issue cast their votes overwhelmingly for the candidate who emphasized fighting terrorism—President George W. Bush.[22]

However, the candidates are not alone in their struggle to set the public agenda. The news media also carry their own agendas into campaigns, particularly presidential races. That agenda is to cover what journalists consider the more newsworthy aspects of an electoral campaign, such as the horse race aspects, candidate mistakes, and campaign strategies.[23] Still another player is the audience, whose relationship to media is active, not passive. The audience determines what information they access through selective exposure and attention. They also use media for their own purposes. In an election campaign, an important aspect of the audience's agenda is to glean enough information to make intelligent decisions about matters that are relevant to them.[24]

These three sets of players—candidates, media, audience—interact to shape agendas in an electoral campaign. As political scientist Russell J. Dalton et al. explain, "Candidates attempt to define the election in terms of their preferred issues, but they are constrained by political events and the interests of the public. The media are important intermediaries in this information process, although they largely report on the events and activities of the campaigns. Citizens enter an election with preexisting concerns that may be modified or reinforced by the candidates' statements about what issues are important....Furthermore, the candidates, the public, and the media are responding to ongoing events in the world."[25]

Blog Agenda Setting

In one sense, the emergence of bloggers as a new player in these relationships does not recast the agenda-setting process. That is because bloggers act much like the other players. Like the others, they possess agendas. Like the others, they seek to place those agendas before the public and compel other players to address them. One case is the conservative blogosphere's attempt to set the agenda in reaction to a statement by Senator Dick Durbin during a debate over the U.S. detention camp at Guantanamo, Cuba. Durbin said that someone reading about treatment of prisoners at the detention camp might think these were acts "done by Nazis, Soviets in their gulags, or some regime—Pol Pot or others—that had no concern for human beings." Conservative bloggers immediately shifted the agenda from the substance of Durbin's remarks to the connection between totalitarian regimes and the U.S. military. Despite the attempt by liberal bloggers to defend Durbin and turn the agenda back to abuses at Guantanamo, Durbin accepted the conservative bloggers' new agenda and apologized for his statement.

The Durbin case and others lead bloggers to claim that, even though they are the new kids on the block, they are successful at agenda setting. Some even claim they do it better than other political players. Blogger Andrew Sullivan argued that "blogs now really do play a role in leading and directing the national conversation."[26]

Yet there is a difference. Bloggers straddle the roles performed by others. For example, they are like news media in the sense that they possess their own networks of communication for disseminating information to the general audience, or at least a subset of that audience. And like the news media they deliver daily (or even more frequent) messages through that network. Moreover, their audience has come to rely on bloggers for information that supplements what they get from other sources. That distinctive relationship with an audience, along with the role of news and information source, means that unlike other players, such as members of Congress and interest groups, bloggers need not rely on the news media to reach a national audience.

On the other hand, they are similar to other agenda seekers, although unlike traditional news media, in the sense that they support specific agendas that are directly related to policy outcomes. Unlike news media organizations that intervene primarily when media interests are threatened, bloggers openly take sides and form alliances with other players who also are seeking to shape the public agenda on a wide range of topics. They advocate clearly for one candidate or policy outcome over another. And although one could argue that traditional news media do the same through editorials, currently bloggers dismiss the distinction between news and editorial functions that is the journalistic standard in today's traditional news media product.

Despite the fact that the blogosphere is its own world, and bloggers may well be highly influential in that world, bloggers still attempt to go beyond the blogosphere. They know that, despite occasional rhetoric to the contrary, the blogosphere is a confined sphere of influence that may well never touch the vast majority of Americans who pay little or no attention to it. And without that expanded influence, public officials may dismiss the blogosphere as mere rantings by fringe groups. Therefore bloggers must go beyond the realm of blogging to influence the larger political environment. They must engage with other players—journalists, agenda seekers, and the audience—in the transactions that set broader agendas than those of the blogosphere's.

Bloggers and Journalists

The relationship between bloggers and journalists is not quite equal in terms of the attention each pays to the other. Whereas journalists occasionally mention blogs in their news stories, bloggers constantly draw from and play off of traditional news content. It seems that the most common source of information on blogs is the morning's newspaper or a breaking news story from a television news Web site such as CNN or Fox. The evidence for journalists' role in setting blog agendas seems self-evident. But is the same true in the opposite direction? Do bloggers have the capability to set news agendas? Is the relationship transactional?

If journalists read blogs, then agenda setting is possible. Journalists don't seem to be quick to cite blogs as sources, if they are indeed using them. Even when blogs may be the source, journalists are reticent to acknowledge them. Instead, they may use the euphemism "Internet buzz," meaning that something circulating on the Internet has become newsworthy. For example, during the 2008 campaign, a photograph appeared showing Senator Barack Obama wearing a turban and dressed as a Kenyan tribal elder. The photograph reinforced the rumor that Obama was a Muslim. News stories attributed the first news of the photo to the Drudge Report but did not mention the blogs that not only repeated the news of the photo but reproduced the photo itself.[27] Not mentioning blogs specifically helps distance journalists from the blogosphere, which is both a competitor and widely viewed as a source of conspiracy theories, shrillness, and extremism.

Yet there are ways the blogosphere could set media agendas. One is directly: journalists turn their attention to a topic raised by a single blog or the blogosphere generally. Another is more indirect: blogs could affect policy makers' agendas, and media coverage would then reflect the policy makers' actions and statements initially influenced by blogs. Another indirect method is blog influence on other players, such as interest groups that use blog agendas in their own agenda-setting efforts; in this way, blog influence on the agenda is felt, but not directly.

In order to set the agenda, blogs have to either obtain information the news media do not possess or use information jointly shared in a way that captures attention from other players, including the press. The former is possible, but infrequent. But the latter could be more common. And it could occur in reaction to media coverage (or the lack thereof) of a story reporters know about but initially dismiss as not worthy of inclusion in the news product.

Reaction offered by the blogosphere can contribute to a story frame. Framing refers to the process of placing a story within a context.[28] Blogs have the potential to frame in cases where they are the first to disseminate a story. By commenting on the information they provide, they potentially frame the information in a certain way that conforms to their (and presumably their readers') worldviews. Framing by blogs becomes important particularly when blogs serve as the first analysis of and commentary on an event. When journalists provide a description of an event, blogs may become valuable in offering a context for the event before others weigh in. In turn, if a blog's frame is what journalists see first, then that frame may influence subsequent news coverage. One reporter said that he reads a particular blog because it "poses important questions that we might not have thought of on our own."[29]

One example of blog framing is reaction to a dramatic and tragic event. The initial event—a bomb blast, a plane crash, a refinery explosion—typically lacks immediate explanation as to why the event occurred. Only after a terrorist group takes credit or authoritative sources weigh in with a judgment does a frame begin to take shape. With a blog, however, a frame can be established quickly. Bloggers responding within minutes can create a frame, such as the role of Middle Eastern terrorists or the failure of the administration to protect against terror. The initial frame may not prove to be the accurate one; nevertheless that first frame may be repeated by journalists who are seeking some context for the event but don't have the time to research it themselves or who feel that that their sources, not themselves, need to determine the meaning of the event. However, the initial frame may be transitory, disappearing when journalists' more authoritative sources contradict it.

The original question is whether blogs can set agendas. Bloggers attempt to do so. Blog content is not just using traditional media as a springboard, as we will see later. Sometimes bloggers tout stories that traditional media miss. They point to stories passed on from readers or acquired from other blogs, Internet sites, or local media that national media have ignored or downplayed. The story then becomes the blogger's own. Bloggers provide their readers with details that the traditional media missed. They challenge traditional media to pick up the story and follow their agenda. The challenge often is accompanied by insinuation that the story has been ignored for political reasons. One example is the story of the suicide of a student at the University of Oklahoma who was blown up on campus. Police, campus officials, and the student's family explained the death as a suicide. Some bloggers attributed it to an attempted terrorist bombing. Charles Johnson of the Little Green Footballs blog claimed the event had been "determinedly ignored by mainstream media" and touted the story along with other conservative blogs such as Michelle Malkin and Power Line.[30]

Despite bloggers' attempts to set agendas, the traditional media maintain an advantage in agenda setting due to their historical role as the source of news. Bloggers still rely on newspapers and broadcast media for news, although hardly exclusively. The news media's ability to acquire news and disseminate it broadly, in addition to the audience's expectations that they do so, give the news media advantages in agenda setting. Also, the news media's active reporting capability transcends that of the blogosphere. News media are actively seeking new information to pass on to the audience and have a staff to do so. Bloggers claim the same role: they seek information from readers and pass that information on in posts. But news media possess both the professional staff for newsgathering and greater access to sources of power, such as White House staff, members of Congress, foreign leaders, and the like.

Bloggers' reliance on journalists establishes conditions for agenda setting from news media to blogs. Yet the potential for bidirectional agenda setting exists as well. Blogs and journalists interact, albeit from a distance, in the transmission of information. Moreover, bloggers possess incentives to set media agendas. Many seek to shape politics and policy outcomes outside the realm of the blogosphere. Such incentives usually result in attempts to affect how other players act and react.

Bloggers and the Agenda Seekers

The journalist-blogger relationship also predicts another association, one between other agenda seekers and bloggers. Many of those who seek to shape agendas and policy believe the blogosphere now can affect that process. A survey of congressional public relations staffers found that half of them believe blogs are more useful than the traditional media in identifying future national political issues.[31]

Because bloggers may affect press agendas, as other agenda seekers also attempt to do, they become the object of attention of those agenda seekers. The attention of those who seek to shape agendas—would-be policy influencers—would seem to add yet another layer to the policy agenda process. Agenda seekers hope to affect policy by using the press to reach the public, who in turn will demand action on the part of policy makers. More directly, the press also reaches policy makers without the intervention of the public. With blogs, the route becomes more convoluted: from blog to news media to audience to policy makers. The longer the trail and the greater the number of carriers (or filters) along the way, the more likely the final message will not be the same one that initially entered the blogosphere.

Nevertheless there are good reasons for other agenda seekers and bloggers to interact with each other. With intense competition for the attention of the news media, blogs become a new avenue for catching the notice of journalists and initiating the agenda-setting process. Given the potential that journalists will pay attention to blogs, many agenda seekers have decided that affecting blog content carries the potential of acquiring journalist notice as well.

Unlike journalists, who are accustomed to public relations efforts, bloggers relish the attention paid them by policy makers, candidates, interest groups, political parties, and others seeking to shape agendas. After years of following the actions of these agenda seekers, bloggers appreciate receiving acknowledgment in return. The attention is heady.

Yet as bloggers become part of the public relations and lobbying machinery of groups, candidates, and politicians, their willingness to play a role as transmitter of favorable information for others may diminish. Already some A-list bloggers are becoming skeptical of their newfound celebrity in the lobbying process. Glenn Reynolds of Instapundit said he gets 1,500 e-mails a day but doesn't read most of them. Another blogger said, "The very best way to get me not to cover a story is to have a PR [public relations] firm contact me."[32]

Nevertheless the lobbying for blog attention continues, and blogs will be part of PR strategies as long as the perception exists that such efforts work. The attention is partly directed at the blogosphere itself, but blog content is also a way to get journalists' attention without pleading directly with journalists for it.

For agenda seekers, one important distinction between bloggers and journalists is the former's overt partisanship. That makes reaching out to them easier because the agenda seeker begins with a potentially sympathetic recipient. Ideologically driven agenda seekers and their soul mates in the blogosphere begin with a shared open agenda that not only makes bloggers receptive to information from such sources, but improves the likelihood that the agenda seeker's efforts will be rewarded.

Interestingly, however, ideology is not necessarily a barrier to agenda seekers' relations with bloggers. A new trend is to cross the ideological divide in the blogosphere in order to broaden the reach of an agenda-seeking campaign. For example, a lobbyist for merit-based education reform started blogging on The Huffington Post in order to reach liberals.[33]

Another means of interaction for agenda seekers is circulating existing blog content that is favorable to their cause. The agenda seeker will cull blog posts that reinforce the seeker's message and disseminate them to the press, as well as their supporters. The blog's attention to the issue offers some form of legitimacy for the press that might move the story beyond the blogosphere and out into the mainstream media and the public sphere. One example of this process occurred during the 2008 presidential campaign. The Huffington Post criticized Senator Barack Obama for a planned appearance with a minister who some people perceived as hostile to gays. The Clinton campaign forwarded the blog post to journalists to make sure they saw it.[34]

This route of blog to media to public to policy maker is not the only one involving the blogosphere. Another route completely bypasses the press and the general public; in this case, the object of direct attention is the blog audience, who then become the source of grassroots lobbying of policy makers. The blog audience may seem a minuscule component of the general audience and therefore insignificant in influencing policy makers, but the nature of that audience is the source of its power. It consists of people who are more politically interested and active. The example at the beginning of this chapter is a case of the perceived power of the blogosphere itself, minus any appeal to the broader public.

Placing items on blogs can have the same effect as leaking to the press. Bloggers say they get much of their material from readers,[35] who send them items they have seen from various online sources. But those readers may be insiders—agenda seekers themselves—who attempt to use the blogosphere to shape press coverage.

Others, however, are open about their intent to use blogs to shape agendas and policy. One U.S. senator admitted that he used blogs by coordinating conference calls with bloggers and passing on information intended to stimulate grassroots action against an immigration bill.[36] The U.S. Chamber of Commerce used bloggers to try to get blog readers in the grassroots to weigh in with members of Congress on legislation to raise taxes on hedge fund managers. Chamber publicists worked with bloggers who posted appeals to readers to contact the chair of the Senate Finance Committee to express opposition to the legislation.[37]

However, it would be a mistake to suggest that bloggers have become an important vehicle for affecting legislation. By far the most common approach is still the traditional method of going directly to the mainstream media. A survey of Washington insiders found that a majority did not read blogs, or did so only when they heard about blog content through word of mouth.[38] Capitol Hill staffers were more likely to read blogs; one-third said they read blogs regularly, although 28 percent said they never read blogs.[39] But their bosses are likely not to be blog readers, and interest groups are not much involved in blogs; a little more than a third said they have staff members monitor blogs, and more than half said they did nothing with blogs.[40]

One explanation for the reticence to use blogs is the perception that, despite hype about the blogosphere, it is a medium with little influence on the political environment. It is still perceived as a self-contained unit of individuals who are merely reinforcing each other. One lobbyist wondered whether "they help to build support among anyone other than core activists already engaged on an issue."[41]

Bloggers and the Blog Audience

Still another interaction occurs between a blogger and his or her audience. Bloggers are not immune to the reaction of their audience to blog content. In fact, the interaction with the audience and the effect of that interaction on the transmitter of information is more apparent with bloggers than in traditional media. Most political bloggers allow comments on what they post, and they receive them; much of the space on a blog is taken up by the comments of blog readers. And many news media Web sites today allow site readers to post comments on stories, although the practice is not universal. By contrast, a national newsmagazine or daily newspaper may print a sample of letters to the editor.

Because readers' comments on blogs are frequent and pointed, interaction is practically inherent in the relationship between blogger and reader. Moreover, because comments usually are transparent for both blogger and the blog audience, it is difficult for bloggers to ignore them. In fact, they are not likely to ignore them. In their own posts, bloggers often make reference to the reactions of readers to information that has been posted. Bloggers are aware that, with intense competition in the blogosphere, readers can go elsewhere; failure to acknowledge readers' needs will lead to readers abandoning the blog. By potentially affecting blog content, the audience is another player in the transactional relationship of blogs in agenda setting.

Conditions for Blog Agenda Influence

Various attributes of blogging suggest that blogs have the potential to be active participants in agenda setting. One is the bloggers' ability to get a story out first. Increasingly, journalists turn to blogs for fast-breaking news. One syndicated columnist called blogs "a kind of early warning system" for him.[42] As mentioned earlier, blogs may get it wrong, or at least offer an incomplete account, but because blogs also sometimes get it right, they draw the attention of journalists checking for news.

Even when bloggers do not release a story first, they can offer the first reaction to an event covered by the press.[43] This is particularly true in the case of an unexpected event such as a terrorist attack, a natural disaster, or the untimely death of a prominent individual. That response may be in the form of an individual blogger discussing a news event, or a collection of bloggers gravitating around a story and adding to it with commentary. Due to the nature of blogging compared to traditional media, reaction to an event will be disseminated more rapidly than journalistic coverage of public reaction, particularly in the print media.

Another trait of the blogosphere that suggests power is its record of agenda setting. Blogger-initiated stories occasionally have impacted news content. For example, in July 2004 an airline passenger posted an account of suspicious activity by Syrian passengers onboard a U.S. airline flight. The post was discussed in the blogosphere and eventually was picked up by the *New York Times* and other traditional media.[44] In another case, the blog Talking Points Memo broke a story about a sweetheart real estate deal involving Alaska senator Lisa Murkowski; three days later the *Anchorage Daily News* published a story on the suspicious transaction and issued an editorial denouncing it. The reporter credited the blog for the story.[45]

Like most other agenda seekers, bloggers succeed only sporadically at agenda setting. One example is the story of a purported affair involving Democratic presidential candidate John Edwards in the *National Enquirer*. The story was picked up by several blogs, but traditional media largely ignored it or mentioned it only on their blogs.[46]

Another factor, and one closely related to the perception of blog success, is the increasing attention blogs have been accorded by other players. The more attention paid to the medium, the greater the probability that stories from blogs will be noticed, repeated, and eventually find their way beyond the blogosphere. This attention comes not only from policy makers, journalists, and other agendas seekers but also from the public. Audience figures suggest that blogs possess the potential to shape audience agendas because people read them. Moreover, the audience for political blogs, although not large within the blogosphere or in the general public, is a highly attentive public consisting of individuals who are more likely to be local opinion leaders.[47]

Other factors make agenda setting by blogs difficult. Policy makers probably pay much less attention to blogs than they do to traditional media sources, and policy makers are likely to be unresponsive to a medium they ignore. However, those barriers may be reduced over time. As support staff and assistants become policy makers they may bring with them to key policy positions a familiarity with blogs and a reliance on them for information. Blog use then may grow over time with generational replacement.

Another barrier, one that also may change, is lack of trust in blogger information. The absence of blogger standards similar to those the press adheres to means that blog readers may not be able to rely on blog content for accuracy. If blogs become more like traditional media, a topic to be discussed further, then blog content may become more credible and widely accepted.

But do blogs actually shape media agendas? Bloggers claim they do. Blogger Glenn Reynolds said that when blogs work together they "can put things on the agenda."[48] But working together is not a common practice among bloggers, who have their own agendas and usually do not act in concert. The blogosphere's own divisions and autonomy may well limit its ability as an agenda setter. Blog cooperation on agenda setting would place a common theme before a large audience of blog readers as well as heighten the importance of such a topic for others who play significant roles in agenda setting.

Conditions exist for bloggers to shape agendas of other players and, in turn, to be affected by those same players. But before answering the question of whether they actually do, it is important first to explain why political blogs have become new players in the first place.

2

Blogs and Politics

It was an incongruous moment for the dawn of the power of new technology: the center of attention was an icon from the past. Strom Thurmond, longtime South Carolina politician and former segregationist third-party presidential candidate, was being feted by his colleagues as he closed his nearly half-century career in the U.S. Senate. Among the 500 guests were many Washington notables, including four Supreme Court justices.[1] Several politicians spoke, including former Senate Majority Leader Bob Dole. They noted Thurmond's role in American history and praised him for his accomplishments over a long life.

But Senate Majority Leader Trent Lott, Republican of Mississippi, went further. Lott said that his state had voted for Thurmond when the former segregationist ran for president as a third-party candidate in 1948. Lott went on: "I want to say this about my state: When Strom Thurmond ran for president we voted for him. We're proud of it. And if the rest of the country had followed our lead we wouldn't have had all these problems over all these years, either."[2]

The statement elicited some gasps from the attendees but no reaction from the press who covered the event. Major newspaper stories the next day, a Friday, reported the birthday party but made no reference to Lott's comments.[3] Nor did the comments appear on television—with one exception. ABC News included the incident in a story on an early morning broadcast, but it did not run on *Good Morning, America*. The story also received some attention in an online column on the ABC News Web site, where the quote was placed in the middle of other news. The story was picked up later that morning by a journalist for *Slate* and another for *Salon*. By early afternoon, the story appeared on the blog Eschaton. Another blog, Talking Points Memo, followed in midafternoon. Both added historical material about Thurmond that put the Lott quote in a critical context of advocating segregation and opposing civil rights.

Senator Lott was not slow in responding to the growing criticism of his remarks, particularly when his office got a call from a *Washington Post* reporter writing a story on his comment and the nascent blog response. Lott's office countered that day with a statement clarifying his words as merely an attempt to "pay tribute to a remarkable man who led a remarkable life. To read anything more into these comments is wrong."[4] The statement did not quell the story.

But the extent of attention to the story was not immediately apparent. It was almost as if politicians, the media, and bloggers were attempting to sort out how significant this incident was. It took three days following the event for the story to gain traction with bloggers. Prominent bloggers such as Andrew Sullivan and Glenn Reynolds began to chide Lott for his statements. As the weekend passed, both bloggers and traditional media picked up the story. Their coverage was fed by Lott's repeated statements unsuccessfully trying to put the incident behind him. As the story grew other politicians joined the fray, offering criticism of Lott's comments. After Republican senators and then the White House distanced themselves from Lott, the isolated Senate majority leader finally relinquished his post.

The incident became the sign that the political blogosphere had come of age, even though it was only a couple of years old. Bloggers praised each other for bringing down a high government official. One blogger called the incident the first time blogs showed "the very positive role they could play."[5]

Credit even came from outside the blogosphere. The *Guardian*, a Manchester, England, newspaper, called the Lott incident "a defining moment for the vibrant online culture of weblogs."[6] Political commentator John Podhoretz concluded that the "drumbeat that turned this story into a major calamity for Lott...was entirely driven by the Internet blogosphere."[7] Remarkably, Trent Lott joined the praise, once stating, "Bloggers claim I was their first pelt, and I believe that."[8]

Trent Lott was only the first pelt claimed by the political blogosphere. Another one, three years later, involved an institution that seemed far removed from the rough-and-tumble atmosphere of political blogs: the U.S. Supreme Court. It was the fall of 2005 and President George W. Bush was seeking a replacement for retiring Justice Sandra Day O'Connor. When the announcement came that the president had chosen White House counsel Harriet Miers, bloggers pounced.

Unlike in the Trent Lott case, the blogosphere wasted no time in weighing in on Miers's suitability for the role of associate justice of the Supreme Court. Within minutes of the Oval Office ceremony, the blogosphere panned Miers. Surprisingly, the harshest attacks came from President Bush's conservative base rather than the liberal bloggers who had been itching for a fight. Former Bush White House speechwriter David Frum used his blog to question Miers's allegiance to conservative principles. Another conservative blogger highlighted Miers's refusal to join the premier conservative legal group, the Federalist Society. Several conservative blogs who had been geared up to support the president's Supreme Court nominees, such as RedState, ConfirmThem, and National Review Online, led the charge against the nomination.[9]

The battle was one the White House immediately began losing. Republican politicians started to hear from their base. Conservatives, some of whom must have read the blogs, contacted their senators and urged them not to rush to support Miers and the White House. The conservative blogosphere's reaction attracted media attention because of the rarity of conservative shock troops turning against their own leadership. The White House responded by tapping the chair of the Republican National Committee to calm bloggers through a telephone conference call, although the tactic ultimately failed.[10]

The blogosphere helped doom Miers's nomination in a couple of ways. One was by framing the debate. Rather than a simple contest between Democrats and Republicans, the fight was among Republicans over the nature of her conservatism. It also highlighted her middling legal background, which was a far cry from the shining ideological standard-bearer the conservative movement had expected. Moreover, the blogosphere sent messages to Republican senators that killing the Miers nomination was a priority for them. One conservative blogger wrote that he saw "no reason—none, nada, zilch—for conservatives who care about the courts to lift a finger to support this candidate."[11] That effort likely helped stop the rush of support presidents expect from their political base when they make such an appointment.

Immediate opposition to a Supreme Court nominee is nothing new. Senator Edward Kennedy responded on the day of the Robert Bork nomination in 1987 with an intense speech castigating Bork for his past votes and predicting a dire future for the country if Bork were nominated.[12] Nor is opposition from within a political party new to the nomination process; conservatives decried the nomination of fellow conservative Judge Douglas Ginsburg after revelations that he had smoked marijuana as a Harvard Law School professor and that his wife had performed abortions.[13]

But the difference in the Miers case was the speed with which the White House's image machine was challenged by conservative bloggers. The White House never recovered from the onslaught. The incident suggested the blogs' potential agenda-setting power even in the area of Supreme Court nominations.

The blogosphere's role in the downfall of Trent Lott and Harriet Miers emboldened bloggers to report scandals involving public officials in the opposition camp. For example, in early 2007 the blog Talking Points Memo repeatedly posted about a potential scandal involving political firings of U.S. attorneys by the attorney general's office. The posts finally got the notice of the House Judiciary Committee and led to subsequent committee hearings. In 2008 a blog titled Shame on Elaine targeted Secretary of Labor Elaine Chao with accusations of corruption and incompetence in her department. The spokesperson for the labor group running the blog said that the group wanted to "make sure [Chao's] legacy is told in the correct light."[14]

Blogs and Elections

The examples of Trent Lott and Harriet Miers suggest that political blogging primarily is about defeating high-profile establishment figures.[15] Yet that suggestion misses the broader reach of the blogosphere. Perhaps the most talked-about role for blogs is as players in electoral campaigns. The use of blogs in the 2004 Howard Dean presidential campaign spurred interest in blogs and, along with other developments that year, led PC Magazine to predict that "blogs are positioned to have an even greater impact during the next election cycle."[16]

Strategies for interacting with bloggers have become part of presidential campaign management and shape the candidates' campaign style.[17] In 2008 a video from 1994 circulated on the Internet that showed Republican presidential candidate Mitt Romney taking a pro-choice position on abortion and asserting he was supportive of gay rights. The campaign quickly created a video of Romney rebutting the online video. Among others, it was sent to conservative blogs with the expectation that they would post the new video and spread it across the blogosphere. The tactic helped blunt the effect of the attack video.[18]

In an age of sound bites and diminished media coverage of campaigns and politics, blogs allow campaigns to bypass traditional media to reach a politically astute audience. Like talk radio and television talk shows before them, blogs offer an alternative venue for getting news out that traditional media outlets will not cover and that political activists want to read. According to a Republican National Committee spokesman, "[Blogs] provide another vehicle for operatives like myself to get out a message. They help further a story line."[19] Campaigns are diversifying their communications effort by turning to new media forms that will carry their messages more effectively than traditional media.[20]

Blogs' influence is not at the level of determining outcomes of presidential elections. However, blogs are helping candidates win, particularly at lower levels. Blogs were cited in the victory of Ned Lamont over Senator Joseph Lieberman in the Democratic senatorial primary in 2006. Lamont received strong support from liberal bloggers, although he lost the general election when Lieberman entered the campaign as an Independent. The political blogosphere asserted that, in 2006, it helped make a difference in the election of several congressional candidates and two successful U.S. Senate candidates in Montana and Virginia. Bloggers claimed they influenced elections that year by raising money and encouraging activists to support selected candidates.[21]

Presidential candidates acknowledge the role of blogs in elections. In 2008 presidential candidates early on added political bloggers to their staffs to help them understand and relate to the blogosphere. During the 2008 presidential primaries, Governor Mike Huckabee even thanked bloggers for keeping his campaign alive when he had relatively little money.[22]

Senator Hillary Clinton learned about blogs the hard way. She skipped the annual convention of liberal bloggers called Yearly Kos in 2006, but then showed up in 2007. A 2007 presidential preference poll on the Daily Kos blog found that she came in a distant third (9 percent) behind former senator John Edwards (36 percent) and Senator Barack Obama (27 percent). At first, Clinton paid little attention to blogger criticism. Ultimately she responded by hiring a prominent blogger, Peter Daou, as her liaison to the political blogosphere in order to blunt the blogosphere's attacks on her. But the liberal blogosphere never warmed to Clinton.[23]

Bloggers also have taken on the role of candidate recruiter. Retired general Wesley Clark said that blogs propelled him to run for president in 2004.[24] Proponents of a campaign to draft Al Gore for the 2008 presidential race used the blogosphere to gain support, as did supporters of Fred Thompson prior to his entry into the campaign.[25] Two Virginia bloggers pressed James Webb to run for the U.S. Senate against George Allen. When Webb started his campaign, he hired the two bloggers to work for him.[26]

Blogs have not been merely supportive of candidates. They also have used their position to expose and embarrass candidates. Because the blogosphere includes tens of thousands of people who post comments and blog themselves, a candidate's offhand remark meant to appeal to a small group in an obscure place can become a widespread news event. For example, Democratic presidential candidate Joe Biden joked during a campaign appearance, "You cannot go to a 7-Eleven or Dunkin' Donuts unless you have a slight Indian accent. I'm not joking." The comment was broadcast on C-SPAN and then was circulated through political blogs. Biden's office quickly released a statement saying the Delaware senator respected the Indian American community.[27]

A more direct example of blogs' role occurred on April 11, 2008, when The Huffington Post posted audio of Senator Barack Obama saying that Pennsylvania voters, who would be voting in the upcoming presidential primary, are "bitter" and "cling to guns and religion." The blog post of Obama's remark, which was made at a fund-raiser, spread from the blogosphere to traditional media and resulted in Obama's apologizing for his comment.[28]

The most famous incident, however, concerned 2008 Republican vice-presidential running mate Sarah Palin and her family. Immediately following Palin's selection by McCain, liberal blogs such as Daily Kos and Comments from the Left Field circulated the rumor that Palin's teenage daughter was the real mother of Palin's newborn son. In order to blunt the rumors spreading throughout the blogosphere, Palin made the surprise announcement that her teenage daughter was five months pregnant, which would have made it impossible for her to have given birth to a four-month-old infant.[29]

In other cases, blog content may have affected decisions not to run for office. A potential Ohio Republican candidate in a special congressional election was outed as a homosexual on a state political blog. The candidate withdrew, saying that his sexual orientation would become more important than other issues. A potential Republican candidate for Congress in San Diego withdrew amid allegations posted on a local blog that he had a business association with a pedophile.[30]

Blogs and Policy

With blog audiences collectively numbering in the millions and politicians and journalists paying attention to blogs, blog influence on public policy would seem to be a given. Various players in American politics assume that. They view blogs as potentially influential in mobilizing grassroots voters. New Mexico governor Bill Richardson called bloggers "agents of advocacy."[31]

Politicians already give credit to the blogosphere for affecting the policy process. For example, Senator Harry Reid credited blogs for helping Democrats win the debate over the privatization of Social Security.[32] Indeed, blogs offered the talking points Democrats used to oppose the president's plan.[33] Blogs also became a forum for groups that seek to end the war in Iraq. The role of blogs in protesting the war came early, and at a time when opposition came from few other places.[34] The Dean for America blog was one example of a forum for such criticism. Policy makers may call for an explicit role for blogs in shaping political outcomes. At the Yearly Kos Convention, Senator Harry Reid asked bloggers to help dispel the myth that Democrats don't stand for anything: "We don't have a bully pulpit, but we have you. We need you to be our megaphone."[35]

Pulling to the Fringe?

If blogs are affecting policy, the logical question is whether a particular type or direction of policy is the result of blog influence. Some blog observers fear that political blogs are pulling policy makers, candidates, and parties to the extremes. There is evidence that blogs urge lawmakers to take hard stances and eschew compromise. For example, bloggers pressured Democratic senators to support a filibuster of Judge Samuel Alito's nomination to the Supreme Court even though party leaders knew they lacked the votes. With an eye to the liberal blogosphere, Senator John Kerry blogged on Daily Kos and issued a call to his colleagues to support the filibuster. Kerry himself was in Switzerland, suggesting the filibuster was a last-minute effort spurred by criticism of Senate Democrats by the blog community and Kerry's need to satisfy this group in order to avoid losing their support during a potential presidential run.[36]

Bloggers also have lambasted presidential candidates who move to the center. Bloggers attacked Senator Hillary Clinton as a presidential candidate because she was hewing to centrist policy stances attractive to Independents and moderate Republican voters. They also criticized her vote to authorize the war in Iraq in 2002 and the fact that she would not apologize for the vote.[37]

The Iraq war caused continued tension between liberal bloggers and congressional Democrats. Bloggers on the left applied constant pressure on Democratic leaders in Congress to do more to stop the war. The MyDD blog used an ad watch series to criticize Democratic candidates for not being partisan enough or not attacking President Bush strongly enough.[38] Liberal bloggers also identified Democratic candidates worthy of the public's support, but not necessarily using the same criteria as the national party organizations. For blogs, the more important criterion was whether the candidate opposed the Iraq war early on or would run on a platform of economic populism.[39]

Liberal bloggers have even proposed punishing Democratic lawmakers when they take positions bloggers oppose. In 2007 Senator Chuck Schumer of New York announced his support for the nomination of Michael Mukasey for U.S. attorney general as a replacement for the beleaguered Alberto Gonzales. Mukasey was a native of New York, a highly respected judge in New York City, and, according to Schumer, a vast improvement over Gonzales. But some liberal bloggers were upset with Schumer's endorsement. One liberal blog urged readers to call the Democratic Senatorial Campaign Committee (DSCC), which Schumer chaired, and "tell them you will not give one penny to his committee."[40]

The pressure is not only from the left. Conservative bloggers criticized the Bush administration when it sought accommodation with Democrats. Bloggers were particularly harsh on Senator John McCain, who was perceived as not conservative enough to be the Republican presidential nominee.[41] In fact, similar to Moulitsas's effort to punish the DSCC, Hugh Hewitt and other bloggers on the right started a campaign in 2005 to punish the National Republican Senatorial Committee because some Republicans compromised with Democrats on the judicial filibuster issue.[42]

Bloggers respond that they are not extremists. Markos Moulitsas and Jerome Armstrong argue that their objective has been to turn power away from single-issue groups in favor of a broader populist economic agenda.[43] Moulitsas said that bloggers were not "these far-leftist, naïve and young political extremists," but "actually a fairly representative cross-section of the Democratic Party." He emphasized, "We don't have an agenda other than seeking strong Democratic voices."[44] Some liberal bloggers point to the fact that they have supported conservative Democrats such as Tester in Montana and Webb in Virginia and avoided criticizing conservative Democrats who reflect their particular regions where Democrats struggle to gain popular support.[45] Bloggers also note that they have been highly supportive of traditional candidates. Some liberal blogs have included links to ActBlue, the Democratic fund-raising Web site, where readers could donate to the candidate they've just been reading about. The links helped raise an estimated $2.3 million for Democratic candidates in 2006.[46] Similarly, conservative blogs promote donations through Slate Card, the Republican equivalent of ActBlue.

Bringing Down "Big Media"

Not only are politicians fair game to bloggers, but so are the journalists whom bloggers often deride as part of "big media." Traditional journalists often become the object of intense criticism by bloggers. One conservative blogger said that journalists see themselves as "some kind of a priesthood that sets them apart from the rest of the country and makes them a kind of transnational elite, separate and apart from the citizens of the United States."[47]

Bloggers enjoy pointing out the mistakes of traditional journalists. The most famous example was the embarrassment of Dan Rather in the midst of the 2004 presidential campaign. Rather hosted a *60 Minutes II* segment revealing documents showing that President Bush received special treatment allowing him to join the Texas Air National Guard during the Vietnam War. The documents, purportedly written by Bush's squadron leader at the time, were immediately challenged by conservative bloggers. A reader on a blog called Free Republic asserted that the documents were fake because they came from a word processor that would not have been available in the 1970s, as suggested by the date on the documents. At the same time, Power Line, a conservative blog run by John Hinderaker, Scott Johnson, and Paul Mirengoff, discussed the CBS story and urged readers to go to the CBS site and inspect the documents. A reader directed Scott Johnson to the Free Republic post and Johnson responded with a Power Line post that included the Free Republic post as well as reactions from other readers pointing out errors in the CBS story.[48]

Reaction to the Power Line post spread across the blogosphere. Within twenty-four hours of the broadcast, the blogosphere's questioning of the credibility of the CBS News story had reached CBS and prompted them to issue a statement standing by the validity of the documents and the legitimacy of the story. Eventually, however, CBS admitted that the network could not verify the authenticity of the documents. Rather apologized to viewers and two months later announced his retirement from the anchor chair, even though two years remained on his contract.[49]

Rather's retirement was viewed as a major victory for the blogosphere. It proved, as many bloggers claimed, that the blogosphere had the power to check the mainstream media. Bloggers were not shy about celebrating Rather's retirement and claiming responsibility for bringing down one of the icons of broadcast journalism. Andrew Sullivan concluded that the deed was "not bad for a bunch of slackers in their nightclothes."[50] A blogger for Power Line gave the credit to "the power of the Internet."[51] Some outside the blogosphere claimed that bloggers did not in fact bring down Rather because the news media eventually would have picked up the story themselves. Even if that were true, the blogosphere did disseminate the story faster and beat the news media at its own watchdog role.[52]

Blogs' focus on uncovering journalistic faults has worried journalists. One former newspaper editor called bloggers "salivating morons who make up the lynch mob."[53] But the Rather story showed that blogs could become powerful forces in shaping the decision-making process within traditional media organizations.

Despite unease about blogs by some in the journalist community, journalists' respect for the new medium rose. One gauge of journalist interest in blogs is the amount of news coverage accorded the blogosphere. Initially the theme of coverage was the novelty of blogs in politics. For example, when bloggers covered their first national party conventions in 2004, they, too, became part of the story. Traditional journalists interviewed them as well as the politicians attending the convention.[54] Bloggers became new media stars. Within a few months of launching her Wonkette blog, Ana Marie Cox was featured in the *Washington Post* and on MSNBC, toured the talk show circuit, and was asked to cover the Democratic National Convention for MTV.[55]

But the novelty angle faded for some news organizations and transformed into a different approach: the blogosphere as regular news maker. News organizations began to cover the blogosphere as a regular beat. CNN instituted an "Inside the Blog" segment that reviews discussion on the blogosphere. A CNN executive said, "We want to…do a reading of the blogs that our audience doesn't have time to do."[56] CNN also invited bloggers to be a part of their election night coverage.[57] *Time* magazine instituted a regular feature called "Blog Watch," reporting on the latest blogosphere happenings. The *Minneapolis Star Tribune* carries a regular feature on current blog coverage.

Now blog content as it touches on the news media, which it often does, is taken seriously by news organizations. News media professionals understand that blog stories can become big enough to warrant attention by traditional media. For example, in September 2006 blogger Michelle Malkin accused the Associated Press for failing to report that one of its news photographers had been found five months earlier by the U.S. military with an Al Qaeda leader and an Al Qaeda ammunitions cache. In an earlier day, the AP would have ignored such a claim. But the AP responded to Malkin's statements with a strongly worded statement accusing her of "innuendo, distortion, and factual error," and sent e-mails to bloggers to assert its side of the story.

Journalists may even contribute to bloggers' efforts to diminish existing news organizations. In 2003 the *New York Times* was hit by a scandal involving manufactured stories by reporter Jayson Blair. Executive editor Howell Raines and managing editor Gerald Boyd survived the controversy until a blog leaked insider memos and descriptions of staff meetings intended to discredit Raines. The information, which came from staff members who were disgruntled over the editorial leadership at the paper, was damaging to Raines. When Raines was subsequently fired, bloggers claimed victory even though others concluded that the blog reports constituted only part of the story. Nevertheless, journalistic insiders' own contributions to a blog that resulted in the embarrassment of their own editor, and possibly his resignation, was a sign that journalists perceived blogs as a vehicle for expressing their frustrations.[58]

New Player?

When the Trent Lott story first broke in 2002, blogs were unknown to the vast majority of Americans. Few had read a blog, much less a political blog. Since then the blogosphere has carved out a niche in American political life. It is a factor in public relations strategies. It is catered to by national policy makers. Blog stories break into national news media topics. Occasionally blogs have played a role in dramatic events in American politics, such as the retirement of Dan Rather, the withdrawal of Harriet Miers's name as a Supreme Court nominee, and the resignation of Trent Lott as Senate majority leader.

Whether the blogosphere is a permanent fixture in political life is debatable. Online discussion has undergone various forms in the life span of the Internet, and, for the most part, online forums have lacked the transformative powers once predicted for them. Bulletin boards, Usenet, and chat rooms are examples of political communication forms that at one time were touted as capable of transforming politics and reshaping the way political communication is conducted. However, each faded as a force on the Internet, much less in the larger political environment. E-mail is one forum that has outlasted the others and has the strongest potential of operating as a grassroots mobilizing tool, although even it has not achieved that potential.[59]

Blogs could be different. Their history is short, but during their brief existence they have affected a few key events. They possess the potential of affecting more in the future. Perhaps the greatest hope for a long-lasting role for blogs is the attention they receive from journalists, which will be discussed later. The present task is to answer some questions about this newly influential medium: Who are these bloggers, particularly the most influential ones who receive media attention and attract relatively large numbers of readers? How did they get to be influential in the blogosphere, as well as in American politics? What are their blogs about? How do they operate, and what do they say on those blogs that impacts other political players?

3

Bloggers

In 2007 the Democratic Leadership Council, a centrist group within the Democratic Party, held its annual convention in Nashville, Tennessee. In the past, the convention had attracted presidents and presidential candidates. Bill Clinton, Al Gore, and Hillary Clinton belonged to the group. But the Nashville convention attracted no presidential candidates.[1]

A few days later, the Yearly Kos Convention of liberal political bloggers formed through the Daily Kos blog opened in Chicago. The convention attracted 1,400 bloggers and, unlike the DLC meeting, five of the 2008 Democratic presidential candidates.

The new role of the political blogosphere could not have been more starkly demonstrated than by the decision five presidential candidates made concerning which event to attend. Candidate snubbing of the premier Democratic Party organization over the past two decades in favor of a meeting of bloggers derisively dubbed the "pajamadeen" seemed emblematic of a cataclysmic shift in the Democratic Party. But it also was a sign of the arrival of the political blogosphere as a force to be reckoned with by candidates.

If the political blogosphere had arrived, it wasn't because it had traveled very far in the first place. As mentioned earlier, the blogosphere is not very old; as a mass medium, it is clearly a creature of the 21st century. And political blogging as a genre of the blogosphere is even newer. The first recognized political blog was created by Mickey Kaus, a journalist who started blogging on *Slate*.[2] Kaus had written for *Newsweek* and the *New Republic* before starting his own blog. Then he moved the blog to *Slate* and gained an audience.

Other political bloggers, such as Markos Moulitsas, Glenn Reynolds, and Jerome Armstrong, quickly followed. They came from different backgrounds, but they all adopted blogs as a means for expressing themselves as political opinion leaders. Because blogging was new and the audience small, the idea of becoming nationally recognized writers with hundreds of thousands of daily readers was far-fetched, if even imagined.

However, blogging, including political blogging, caught on. The phenomenon acquired a niche audience of readers who relied on bloggers for daily (or more frequent) updates on news and opinion. Simultaneously, a loose association of political bloggers formed. These bloggers linked to each other and promoted their new community as an alternative to the media establishment.

In 2003, in the early days of blogging, journalists began to pay attention to a little-known former Vermont governor who was running for president. No one expected Howard Dean to win because he had minimal name recognition and few resources. However, a novelty of his campaign was the fact that he was tapping the support of a new Internet community called bloggers. In addition, the Dean campaign had its own blog, Dean for America, that captured the attention of the blogging community as well as the press.[3] The Dean campaign even gave the impression that they were integrating their blog into the campaign in a way that was novel for online political communication. The campaign encouraged a prominent role for blogs in campaign decisions, such as whether or not the candidate should opt out of public financing.

The reality was something different. The Dean campaign created the illusion that the blog was an interactive forum, but actual dialogue was rare. Two scholars of the Dean campaign's blog concluded, "The weblog was used as a way to relay information to citizens, but was not used as a forum to dialogue with citizens."[4]

Nevertheless the Dean campaign gave blogging a measure of public exposure that it had not previously enjoyed, and it led to others jumping on the blog bandwagon. The other Democratic candidates as well as the Bush campaign also started blogs on their campaign Web sites. However, the approaches differed significantly. During the general election campaign, the Kerry campaign blog included apparently uncensored comments. The Bush campaign blog, however, excluded comments and only Bush campaign officials and activists blogged.[5]

The usage of blogs by presidential candidates and the growth in the number of blogs as well as the size of the audience contributed to rising press interest in the new blogging phenomenon. The blogosphere suddenly became a hot news story. News coverage of blogs more than doubled between 2003 and 2004.[6] PC Magazine declared 2004 the year of the blog.[7]

A recurring theme of news coverage of the newly emergent political blogosphere was the medium's potential for enhancing political participation. The political blogosphere was termed the "netroots," that is, the home of online activists who are using their newfound power to revolutionize politics.[8] The term also suggested that the blogosphere was a highly democratic and inclusive medium that reflected the public's opinion rather than that of elites. One political scientist has called blogs the "sophisticated listening posts of modern democracy."[9] Markos Moulitsas termed his blog "basically our little Democratic living room," suggesting that, rather than the halls of power, blogs are the province of ordinary people.[10]

Two Levels of the Blogosphere

Despite the rhetoric of a new democratic medium that reflects the views of average people, the blogosphere, particularly the visible blogosphere seen by the press and the public, is a hierarchical medium. It is not a grouping in which the various blogs are essentially equal to one another. In fact, the blogosphere actually consists of two highly distinct levels of blogs: influentials and common blogs.[11] The influentials are the blogs that have been discussed so far in this book and are the main focus of discussion throughout. However, before continuing on in that discussion, it is worth noting briefly the other type, the common blogs. They deserve mention because of their size: in sheer numbers they dominate the political blogosphere. Moreover, they actually reflect the democratic elements of the blogosphere touted by pundits and journalists.

Common Blogs

The vast majority of blogs, the common blogs, are written in public obscurity. They are read by small audiences, and most last for only brief periods, many never maintained by their authors. According to a 2004 survey, out of 2.7 million blogs, 1.6 million were no longer active four months after their creation, and 1 million lasted only one day.[12] For a majority of bloggers, the costs of maintaining a blog become excessive given the low return for the time invested. One journalist wrote that his blog could best be described as being like a Labrador retriever: "friendly, fun, not all that bright, but constantly demanding your attention."[13] Those bloggers who gave up on maintaining their blog may have concluded that the constant demand on their attention was not worth the opportunity to express views to a limited number of readers.

Even those common blogs that continue are read by diminutive audiences, typically family and friends. They are written by people who update them in their spare time; 84 percent of bloggers said their blog is a hobby or occasional interest. Nor are they updated daily or even weekly; 59 percent of bloggers said they spend just one to two hours weekly maintaining their blog.[14] Nor are the vast majority of common bloggers sanguine about the influence of their blogs; only 27 percent said they keep a blog "to influence the way other people think."[15]

The two groups of bloggers are different from each other in another sense. Common blogs have remained largely untouched by the blogosphere's integration with mainstream politics and journalism. That is true because traditional players have no interest in the content of common blogs. They know common blogs have limited audiences and influence in the blogosphere. The two types also differ in content, reflecting the effects of mainstreaming. A case in point is the divergence in coverage of the Trent Lott resignation at the end of 2007. On November 26, 2007, the Mississippi senator and former Senate majority leader announced suddenly that he would retire by the end of the calendar year.[16] The announcement caught Washington by surprise; Lott had just been reelected to a six-year term in 2006. News accounts repeated Lott's statement that he wanted to spend more time with his family and that he had wanted to leave before Hurricane Katrina but stayed in response to constituent pressure. The news coverage also mentioned, but did not emphasize, a point that Lott himself did not make. This was the fact that if Lott left before January 1, 2008, he would not be subject to new rules on lobbying.[17]

The two types of blogs differed in treatment of this event. Like the traditional press, A-list blogs such as Daily Kos, Talking Points Memo, and MyDD noted Lott's departure. They differed somewhat from the journalistic explanation, which was largely reflective of Lott's own statements. Instead these bloggers stressed financial reasons for Lott's retirement, despite Lott's denial of those motivations.[18] But blogs not on the A-list, such as Tennessee Guerilla Women, Slot—The Stranger, and TruthDig, were quick to repeat a rumor spread by Big Head BC, a Washington, D.C., blog, that Lott was leaving before a sex scandal involving a purported relationship with a male escort broke in the press. When Lott made his announcement, *Hustler* magazine publisher Larry Flynt disclosed that he had been investigating potentially scandalous information about Lott. The Flynt announcement implied that the magazine had been behind the surprise resignation.

However, A-list blogs such as The Huffington Post and MyDD barely mentioned the rumor or included a denial by the escort that diminished the credibility of the story. The story of a conservative Republican Senate leader being exposed in a sex scandal would seem to be a natural for the political blogosphere, particularly if traditional media ignored the story. For many blogs, it was. But the A-list blogs either ignored it or treated it as an unbelievable rumor.

Their similarity to traditional journalists reflected the A-list blogs' closer proximity to journalists than to their fellow bloggers.

Common blogs differ significantly from A-list blogs in the sense that the former really are closer to the democratic notion of the blogosphere. They are far more likely to be the writings of average people expressing themselves politically online.[19] Common blogs proliferate because the start-up costs for a blog are minimal; they are no greater than the cost of having an Internet connection. Anyone can create a place for himself or herself in the blogosphere.

But having a presence and being influential are worlds apart. Common bloggers rarely can compete with A-list bloggers. Few ordinary citizens with jobs and families can devote full time to political blogging. A-list bloggers, by contrast, receive an income from advertising or donations that allow them to devote large blocks of time to their blogs. A-list bloggers post throughout the day, keeping track of and responding to new events. For example, on September 4, 2006, Crooks and Liars began posting at 1:10 a.m. and continued posting, more or less continuously, until 7:03 that evening. Those who work in 9–5 jobs would find it difficult to maintain that kind of blogging schedule day after day. One would-be influential blogger admitted that he was unwilling and unable to blog for four or five hours each day in order to attract a constant audience.[20]

Common bloggers also differ in their relationship with their audience. For example, they enjoy a degree of freedom that A-list bloggers have lost. Common bloggers need not worry that what they say will offend advertisers. They need not cater to a large audience, particularly an audience of elites such as congressional and campaign staffers, party officials, journalists, or pundits. A comment they make will not be criticized by other A-list bloggers because it will not be seen by them. On the other hand, they don't get the favored treatment outside the blogosphere that goes to A-list bloggers. They are not invited to conferences or receptions by elites. They do not get press credentials. Politicians and celebrities don't post on their blogs.

That doesn't mean that common blogs may not each have a political influence over a small group of individuals. Nor does it mean that the mass of common blogs might not unite in some way to offset the power of the influentials and shape politics directly. That may be the utopian vision of advocates of the blogosphere, that is, that the medium serves as a vehicle for fostering democracy, perhaps even direct democracy.

But it is an unlikely scenario. One reason is the fact that journalists, who are the gatekeepers of information moving from the political blogosphere to the broader public, pay attention almost exclusively to the small number of influentials. As Matthew Hindman noted, "While press coverage has emphasized the success stories—particularly the unlikely success stories—it has often ignored the other million political bloggers who receive no traffic at all."[21] Another reason is that common bloggers themselves point their own attention to the influentials rather than each other. Some dream that they, too, will move into the A-list and attract a large audience and political influence equal to that enjoyed by Moulitsas, Sullivan, or Reynolds. But the leap is not easy. One tactic for making the jump is to get mentioned on an A-list blog. Bloggers frequently include links to other blogs from whom they've received information. Sometimes those posts will be made in the form of comments on other bloggers' posts, potentially increasing exposure to the blogger making the comment. Commenters also may include a hyperlink to their own blog within their comment to an A-list blog. They hope the link will drive traffic to their blog.[22] Indeed, links to other blogs embedded in blog posts facilitate readers' blog jumping. The conventional wisdom of the blogosphere is that blog links are coveted because they enhance influence and bring new readership.[23]

The blog link then becomes an opportunity for common bloggers who are A-list wannabes to get noticed by the A-list bloggers' audience. Those common bloggers pass on information to the A-list blogs with the hope that the more prominent blog will post the item and then link back to their blog, the original blog.[24] The A-list blog's readers may follow the link to the common blog, save the blog as a favorite or bookmark, and then return to the blog subsequently.

Another tactic is to become part of an A-list blogger's blog roll. A blog roll is a set of links to other blogs. Usually bloggers place blog rolls on the side of their home page. The blog roll is a way for bloggers to promote each other and for readers to view other blogs they may be interested in. Blog rolls enhance the reach of any particular blog because another set of blog readers can easily become aware of and access a new blog. Bloggers usually include blogs close to their own interests.[25] Listed blogs typically share the same partisan stance as the host blog.[26] By including a common blog on their blog roll, A-list blogs can provide exposure and legitimacy to a blog that otherwise would remain obscure in the blogosphere.

The transition from common blog to A-list (or perhaps B-list) is not impossible. Nearly all A-list blogs started out with small audiences. Markos Moulitsas was an unknown political activist and recent Army veteran when he started Daily Kos. Bloggers for Power Line admitted that at first they were blogging for their immediate families.[27] Glenn Reynolds, founder of Instapundit, was an occasional blogger on a *Slate* readers' forum, and Ana Marie Cox ran a little-known blog and attempted to hold down a job as a journalist.[28] Each moved from common blog to the A-list. However, Cox's transition to the A-list was more representative of how the A-list will be created in the future. She was approached by a corporate blog owner to start a political gossip blog.

Another example of near instant movement to the A-list is The Huffington Post, run by Arianna Huffington. The syndicated columnist and former independent California gubernatorial candidate initiated her blog with seven staff members and $2 million in capital. That amount subsequently was supplemented by several million dollars for blog maintenance.[29] Capital of that size is available only to well-known individuals who are expected to attract a sizable audience and a significant revenue base in quick succession, or to corporate blogging networks such as Gawker that can afford a substantial investment and absorb initial losses for ultimate long-term capital gain.

The jump from common blog to influential will become increasingly difficult in the future as blogging becomes more commercialized. A few bloggers will possess the financial backing to become A-list blogs, but common bloggers will find the move to the A-list nearly impossible. The gap between influential and common blog will grow larger. Common blogs will become the equivalent of mimeographed flyers, while influentials will resemble corporate media giants.

However, even if common bloggers do not become influentials, there is still a sense of satisfaction for many in being a political blogger, albeit below the radar. Political bloggers still seek to influence others, and likely do so to a greater extent than bloggers who do not discuss politics. And they care about the reputation they acquire as political bloggers and sometimes even seek to adjust their writing to serve their audience, however small.[30]

In summary, common blogs are the most numerous and democratic elements of the blogosphere, but they also are the least influential in affecting politics or policy. Therefore they receive little attention from politicians, journalists, or academics. It may be disturbing that the political blogosphere spends so little time on more than 99 percent of political blogs. However, any other approach would miss the locus of power currently in the political blogosphere.

Influentials

The other group of blogs, which constitutes a tiny segment of the political blogosphere in number, consists of the influentials. These are the blogs read by a relatively large daily audience, sometimes up to hundreds of thousands of people. One study of political blogs found that one, Daily Kos, accounted for 10 percent of all the political blog traffic, and the top ten political blogs had 48 percent of all political blog traffic.[31]

The influentials are the ones who appear on blog rolls of other influentials. They also appear on the blog rolls of many blogs that are not so influential. When a new blog goes up, the blog roll, if there is one, is likely to include links to existing influential blogs. As a result, influential blogs become even more influential.[32] Unlike other bloggers, influentials are the ones who are invited to attend political conventions, speak to various groups, and meet with prominent politicians. Their blogs are read by journalists and occasionally even mentioned in news stories. They are the ones who are viewed as worthy of attention by those who seek to shape agendas. One U.S. senator opined, "Several pretty significant blogs are becoming a direct line between elected officials here in Washington and the American people."[33]

To those outside the blogosphere, the influentials *are* the blogosphere. They are bloggers who are covered by the news media. They are the public face of political blogging to the majority of Americans who do not blog nor read blogs. When people think of the political blogosphere, they think of bloggers they read about in the press: Glenn Reynolds, Markos Moulitsas, and Andrew Sullivan. These are the influentials.

Bloggers, both influentials and common bloggers, usually share a common view, however. Both perceive themselves to be closer to the public than is the traditional press. Bloggers have been described as "both more distanced from the Washington scene and much closer to being 'average' people."[34] The rhetoric of the blogging movement suggests that ordinary people are driving blogs and therefore reshaping politics. For example, in the wake of the 2006 midterm elections, Jerome Armstrong, MyDD blogger, argued, "People-powered politics is what won this election for the Democratic Party. With this victory, power is returning to where it belongs in a democracy—with the people."[35] Moulitsas of Daily Kos attributed the appeal of the blogs to the longing of Americans to be part of the media rather than passive consumers: "Now we have a medium that allows them to be part of that conversation."[36] Clearly, the rhetoric applies to the vast majority of political bloggers: the common bloggers. But does it apply to the influentials? Are A-list bloggers merely common bloggers who have acquired a large audience and suddenly have been thrust into political prominence?

The most commonly read political blogs are not written by ordinary individuals. There are four general occupational groups among the writers of the top blogs: college professors, lawyers, journalists, and political consultants and activists. Instapundit, Hugh Hewitt, and Eschaton belong in the first group; Power Line is in the second; Andrew Sullivan, Talking Points Memo, The Huffington Post, and Michelle Malkin are in the third; the fourth includes Daily Kos and

MyDD. This is not to say that there aren't individual bloggers with different backgrounds; for example, Charles Johnson of Little Green Footballs was a Web designer. But these are occupations that allow individuals the flexibility of time to devote to blogging, and they are writing-intensive professions similar to blogging. The A-list bloggers also differ from average Americans in the level of their educational backgrounds. They are well educated. A study of the top ten political bloggers found that seven have doctoral degrees, and eight of the ten went to an Ivy League or an elite private or public school.[37]

The A-list bloggers may not be the only ones who are unrepresentative of the public. Even B-list bloggers look more like A-list bloggers than they do the general public. According to a survey of seventy-five political bloggers who had at least 2,000 daily visitors, 25 percent were current or former college professors and 37 percent were current or former business executives. Six of ten had a master's or doctoral degree.[38] Top political bloggers are far better educated than journalists or the blog audience.

Matthew Hindman, the author of the study, also compared bloggers with op-ed columnists. He found that bloggers were far more likely than op-ed columnists to have a doctoral degree (more than 50 percent versus 20 percent) and also were more likely to have attended elite schools. Hindman concluded that "almost all bloggers in our sample are elites of one sort or another."[39]

Why is the upper class overrepresented among top political blogs? One answer is the time commitment required to maintain such a blog. Top political blogs become that way because they attract repeat visitors. And they attract a steady audience because they are updated frequently—several times daily. That kind of schedule can be maintained only by someone who blogs full time or who has a flexible work schedule, such as a professional in business or academe. A blue-collar worker on an assembly line or a plumber making house calls would have a difficult time updating a political blog throughout the day. Moreover, bloggers need to spend large chunks of time becoming informed about issues and current events in order to write material that is informative for their audience. Information gathering is time consuming and something the common person is unlikely to have time to engage in unless it is already part of his or her professional life as a teacher or writer or political consultant. Another explanation lies with the nature of blogging as a writing-intensive activity. Those who are most skilled at and familiar with constant writing, such as academics, writers, journalists, and pundits, are most likely to gravitate successfully to blogging.

One glaring unrepresentative characteristic of blogs is the dearth of women among top political bloggers.[40] Wonkette, one of the most popular political blogs, originally was written by Ana Marie Cox, although she left the blog in 2006. Michelle Malkin also is a notable exception as a popular female blogger, as is Arianna Huffington of The Huffington Post. But the community of influential blogs is male-dominated.

Another underrepresented group is racial and ethnic minorities. In Hindman's study, he identified one African American political blogger in his sample of seventy-five top political bloggers.[41] Nor are bloggers likely to be Hispanic. Markos Moulitsas is half-Salvadoran and half-Greek, but generally Hispanic bloggers also have not broken into the ranks of top political blogs.[42] However, that finding is not true for common bloggers, who tend to be more racially diverse than the general population.[43] Race is not necessarily a conscious issue in the blogosphere. When Steven Gilliard Jr., an influential liberal blogger, died at the age of forty-two, many blog readers learned for the first time that he was African American.[44] Additionally, one survey of African American bloggers found that they did not perceive they were excluded by others in the blogosphere because of race.[45] However, other barriers besides race explicitly may have an indirect effect on the inclusion of minorities among the ranks of A-list bloggers. These include Internet access, educational background, and underrepresentation of minorities in professional occupations that are more likely to produce political bloggers.

In summary, influential blogs are run by well-educated white male professionals. That fact is a far cry from the rhetoric that the blogosphere has become the venue for common people to compete with political elites. As Hindman noted, "It is…difficult to conclude that blogging has changed which sorts of citizens have their voices heard in politics."[46] Common bloggers exist, and they have an opportunity to express their views across the Internet. But that is not the same as being heard. For the most part, those who are heard within and beyond the blogosphere are those who would have been heard had they chosen other avenues for involvement in politics, such as lobbying, donating money, and running for office. Those who would not have been influential without blogs remain that way as bloggers.

Two Blogospheres

Although some bloggers are political centrists and others lie at the extremes, the influentials in the blogosphere generally fall into two camps based on broad ideology: liberal and conservative. Discussing these ideological camps separately is important because they are polar opposites in many ways. The ideological separation between liberals and conservatives has been compared to the appearance of "two warring nations, divided and uncommunicative save for a no-man's land between them."[47] Yet they are better described as separate but overlapping spheres rather than two halves of one. In fact, the two are alike in many ways: they both critique the media, and at times they unite on issues of importance to them that cross ideological lines. For example, both liberals and conservatives condemned Trent Lott's statements, discussed earlier.[48] They also work together to criticize bloggers who engage in unacceptable behavior, such as plagiarism.[49] They even collaborate on issues that unite them. As mentioned earlier, both liberal and conservative bloggers supported the federal spending database President Bush signed into law in 2006.[50] Daily Kos, a liberal blog, and RedState, a conservative, joined forces to lobby Senate Democratic and Republican leaders to support a bill required electronic filing of campaign reports to the Federal Election Commission.[51] Both liberals and conservatives are defensive of the role of the blogosphere and critical of traditional media.

The liberal/conservative dichotomy is not stark. The Huffington Post, a well-known liberal blog, hosts conservative bloggers. Individual bloggers take positions on some issues that contradict the conventional issue stances of their camp. For example, a former Bush White House aide started a blog called Terra Rossa, which is written for conservatives who are concerned about the environment.[52] Also, politicians may cross over and pay attention to blogs outside of their own sphere. Senator Hillary Clinton advertised on conservative political blogs during her presidential campaign, and Senator Dick Durbin, the Senate minority leader, blogged on RedState.[53] In the blogosphere's early years, the liberal blogosphere held the countercultural role of critic of administration policies of a conservative president. However, conservative bloggers also expressed their differences with George W. Bush on topics such as the Iraq war, the federal deficit, and the Harriet Miers nomination.

Nevertheless, in many other ways they are separate and distinct; one indication of this is the blog rolls. Blogs primarily touts other blogs in the same ideological camp. As will be seen later, their treatment of topics also differs across the two camps. But first, we examine what these two blogospheres are like. Who are the bloggers who occupy them? How do they differ from one another?

The Liberal Blogosphere

The liberal blogosphere is inhabited by bloggers who loosely use their blogs to support Democratic candidates or at least left-leaning political positions. The level of their allegiance to the Democratic Party per se varies across the blogo-sphere. For some, such as Jerome Armstrong and Markos Moulitsas, the liberal blogosphere is explicitly a medium to support the party. It offers a forum for Democrats to mobilize and elect candidates. Through channeling support to particular candidates and prodding Democratic leaders, bloggers can help the party elect candidates and create an energetic, vocal party organization. For them, blogging is a means to influence candidates' campaign strategies and help establish the direction of the party and its campaign messages. In addition to content, they want to change campaign style by urging less reliance on broad-cast television and more on niche media like blogs and the Internet.

Others, however, are less committed to the party organization or even par-ticular candidates. Bloggers such as Arianna Huffington (The Huffington Post) and Duncan Black (Eschaton) view blogging as an entity separate from tradi-tional political players. Rather than political activism, they use blogging primar-ily to espouse liberal views and criticize the traditional media.

The liberal blogosphere may have become more readily embraced by the left than the conservative blogosphere has been by the right because there has been no such leftist alternative to traditional media. Talk radio essentially has been dominated by conservative talk show hosts, leaving the left without a medium for expression and organization. And Fox News has provided another venue for conservatives, reducing the need for a conservative blogosphere.

Even the existence of a blogosphere where the left potentially can gather does not make liberals feel they have a voice as powerful as the right's. Moulitsas compared Daily Kos with its half-million readers to Rush Limbaugh and Sean Hannity, who have millions of listeners and viewers, and concluded, "They have a lot of people reaching a lot of people, and we have blogs."[54] Moreover, the blogosphere is not a liberal blogosphere, but one liberals share with a host of conservative blogs. Nevertheless, the liberal blogosphere has developed into a haven for the political left. This has been facilitated by the existence of less com-mercial pressure than exists for traditional media. Jerome Armstrong of MyDD called the liberal blogosphere "a rapid-response mechanism for Democrats we didn't have before."[55]

To understand the liberal blogosphere, it is important to discuss the most prominent blogs, who writes them, how they came to be, and what distin-guishes them from other blogs. Any such list begins with Daily Kos.

Daily Kos   The most established blog in the liberal blogosphere is Daily Kos. Along with The Huffington Post, Daily Kos tops the audience numbers among political blogs generally.[56] It is run by Markos Moulitsas, a former devotee of

Ronald Reagan. Moulitsas, whose mother is Salvadoran, lived in El Salvador for five years as a child before the family moved to Chicago, where Moulitsas grew up. He enlisted in the army at seventeen, an act he said radically changed his political views.[57] After leaving the army, he attended Northern Illinois University and Boston University, earning two bachelor's degrees and a law degree. He worked as a Web design project manager and occasionally blogged for MyDD, a liberal blog run by Jerome Armstrong.[58] By 2002 Moulitsas had decided to start his own blog. Daily Kos was born in May 2002, after he decided he needed "an outlet to discuss the issues that [he] cared about."[59] By 2004 Moulitsas had achieved wide recognition within the blogosphere as Daily Kos acquired the largest political blog audience and appeared on numerous political blog rolls. Moreover, he became a force in Democratic Party politics as a fund-raiser. In 2004 he raised approximately $1 million for Democratic candidates.[60]

Daily Kos is a domestic-oriented blog, as opposed to blogs that focus on foreign affairs generally or specific areas of the world. Moreover, Moulitsas's main interest is not policy, but elections. He once called himself "an election-focused blogger."[61] He began working as a political consultant with his partner, Jerome Armstrong. He was asked early on in the Dean campaign to advise them on blogs, and later in 2004 he consulted for the congressional campaigns.[62] Moulitsas has been involved in key electoral campaigns. For example, in 2006 he worked for the campaign of Sherrod Brown, a U.S. Senate candidate in Ohio who beat incumbent Mike DeWine.

Moulitsas has been a spokesperson for the blogging movement and a forceful advocate of blogging influence in mainstream politics. He and Armstrong cowrote the book *Crashing the Gates: Netroots, Grassroots, and the Rise of People-Powered Politics* and advocate individual Democrats taking back control of the Democratic Party from established interests. Moulitsas also participates in an annual blogger convention that promotes the power of political blogging. Devoted readers and bloggers on Daily Kos, as well as other bloggers, meet together each year in an annual blogger convention called Yearly Kos.[63] Moulitsas did not initiate the convention, nor does he run it, but he did allow his site's name to be connected to the event. It has become a major forum for liberal bloggers to congregate. In 2006, 1,000 people attended; a year later, the attendance was 1,400. As mentioned at the beginning of this chapter, the convention has attracted more than just bloggers. Democratic political leaders, such as Senator Harry Reid, the Senate majority leader, DNC chair Howard Dean, and Speaker Nancy Pelosi have attended. It also has become a forum for bloggers to meet presidential candidates.[64]

Yet the relationship between Moulitsas and Democratic Party leaders has been somewhat strained. Moulitsas has put himself at odds with these same high-profile Democrats as he wrestles with them over control of the party's message. When a Democratic political consultant said that bloggers were not representative of the electorate, Moulitsas urged his readers to punish the leader: "Not one dime, ladies and gentleman, to anything connected with" the consultant.[65]

Moulitsas's mission is to reform the Democratic Party. He has been critical of the Democratic National Committee and the Democratic Senatorial Campaign Committee and has stated that both parties have failed the people. "Republicans failed us because they can't govern. Democrats failed us because they can't get elected."[66] At the same time, his own vision of the liberal blogosphere is as a uniter of the party. "Blogs are uniting the left of the party with the center of the party to the right of the party, and I don't think any other institution in the Democratic Party can even remotely boast of that kind of power."[67]

Moulitsas has had his own controversies. He was criticized by other bloggers when he commented on the killing of four American civilian contractors by a crowd in Iraq, saying, "I feel nothing over the death of mercenaries." He also has been accused of ethical violations, such as that he chooses which candidate to support on his blog based on who hires his political consultant partner, Jerome Armstrong.[68] However, he has weathered this criticism and maintained a devoted base of readers.

The distance Moulitsas has come in a short period of time is nothing short of remarkable. In 2002 he was an unknown who ran a blog that was a read by a few thousand people. Now he has become an acknowledged voice in Democratic politics whom powerful party leaders must take into consideration.

MyDD   Like Markos Moulitsas, Jerome Armstrong, the founder of MyDD, is a political activist. In addition to blogging, Armstrong is a political consultant for Democratic candidates, including the 2004 presidential candidate Howard Dean and the potential presidential candidate and U.S. Senate candidate Mark R. Warner from Virginia.[69] Armstrong joined with Senator John Kerry, the former Democratic presidential nominee, to initiate a netroots effort to end the war in Iraq.[70]

Armstrong started one of the early political blogs in 2001 and is sometimes called the "blogfather." He is a proponent of using the blogosphere to challenge traditional political processes and institutions. Even the title of Armstrong's blog reflects his approach to the blogosphere. MyDD stands for My Direct Democracy. His philosophy is that new technologies such as blogs offer a fresh kind of democracy that broadens public participation in politics.[71] And he has not been shy to take credit for political change. Armstrong attributed the Democratic congressional victory in 2006 to the netroots, the activists for the Democratic Party who use the Internet, including blogs, to further their agenda. Armstrong sees a connection between blogs and the Democratic Party in the politics of the future, claiming that the main issue of the future "is not the size or the role of government, but instead the role that people play in our political process."[72]

The Huffington Post   Another popular blog in the liberal blogosphere is The Huffington Post, which is sometimes referred to as HuffPo. The blog is written by a staff headed by the blog's namesake, Arianna Huffington. Once married to a conservative member of Congress from California who ran for the U.S. Senate in 1994, Huffington moved dramatically from the right to the left during the late 1990s. She became a nationally syndicated columnist, an author, and, briefly, an independent candidate for California governor against Arnold Schwarzenegger in the 2003 gubernatorial recall election.[73]

Huffington launched her blog in May 2005 and touted it as a 300-person blog. The blog's initial contributors featured a who's who of the left, including Gary Hart, Arthur Schlesinger Jr., Vernon Jordan, and Robert Kennedy Jr., as well as entertainers such as Jamie Lee Curtis and Bill Maher. To give voice to minority views, however, The Huffington Post even includes conservative commentary.[74] At the launch, Huffington likened the blog to a big dinner party and predicted it would be "about politics and books and art and music and food and sex."[75] The blog initially received severe criticism for being uneven. But Huffington found her niche, and The Huffington Post soon became a popular political blog on the A-list, as well as a reliably leftist critic of the policies of the Bush administration.[76]

Huffington's blog has become a one-stop source for constantly updated news and commentary, with up to eighty posts per day. Much like the Drudge Report, The Huffington Post has become a news update service with the help of partners such as Yahoo, TMZ.com, and *People* and *Variety* magazines. It has ventured into original reporting as well by hiring traditional journalists to report and write for the blog.[77]

Eschaton   Like many other bloggers, Duncan Black, the founder of Eschaton (atrios.blogspot.com), long used a pseudonym, Atrios, when blogging. A former economics professor at the London School of Economics and the University of California, Irvine, Black started Eschaton in April 2002. The site eventually caught on. In two years he had 40,000 daily visitors.[78] Black acquired notoriety both within and beyond the blogosphere when he spotted Trent Lott's comment on Strom Thurmond and posted it on his blog the day after the event. Black also took a step beyond other bloggers when he connected Lott's statements at the Thurmond birthday party to the former segregationist's 1948 presidential platform on race.[79]

Unlike Moulitsas, Huffington, and Armstrong, Black has resisted the trend to be courted by traditional players. He is based in Philadelphia, not Washington, and he has sought to remain in the background personally while his blog has become increasingly well known. The distance is intentional because, according to Black, "it's a lot easier to be critical when you don't know the people you're critiquing."[80]

Crooks and Liars   A less widely discussed but highly popular blog is Crooks and Liars. Created by John Amato in 2004, Crooks and Liars (also known as C & L) quickly became a well-trafficked blog. In 2006 it was considered among the top ten most trafficked political blogs, and, that same year it had the second most-linked-to blog post in the blogosphere and was awarded the best videoblog award.[81] Unlike the bloggers Michelle Malkin and Glenn Reynolds, Amato is not the sole voice on the blog. Others write frequently, although the blog is advertised as Amato's and he is the most prominent blogger. Unlike Moulitsas, Huffington, and Reynolds, Amato has not been a public voice for the blogosphere. However, more recently he has become an occasional news media source for journalists, appearing on MSNBC and talk radio. He even blogged the 2006 midterm elections for CNN.[82]

Talking Points Memo   Blog names may seem strange, particularly compared to newspapers that tend to focus on the words "news," "post," "press," and "times." The title of Talking Points Memo is one example. According to the blog's founder, Joshua Micah Marshall, the name stems from a memo of talking points that Monica Lewinsky prepared for her friend Linda Tripp when she was answering questions from Paula Jones's lawyers.[83] The Lewinsky scandal was still fresh when Marshall started blogging in November 2000. Even more recent was the 2000 presidential election, which finally prompted Marshall to create his blog. At first the blog served as an outlet for his political differences with the magazine he wrote for.[84] Marshall is among those bloggers who come from the ranks of journalism. Before becoming a blogger, Marshall worked as a professional journalist with the *Washington Monthly* and the *American Prospect*. At first he blogged on the side and then eventually made blogging his full-time job.[85] However, Marshall is not completely separated from traditional journalism. He still does a column for *The Hill*, a Capitol Hill publication, which makes him a model for the melding of working journalism and political blogging.[86]

Marshall did not intend to become a daily blogger. Over time, however, he felt pressure from readers to write more often than he originally had intended. Along with Eschaton, Marshall's blog gained notoriety as the first to write about Trent Lott's statements at Strom Thurmond's birthday party. Subsequently, Marshall has gained a reputation as an investigative blogger rather than just a commentator on events.

Wonkette   Wonkette is a breezy, gossipy Washington insider blog that gained popularity quickly as a place for irreverence and salacious rumor. One journalist summed up Wonkette's philosophy as "Try to be accurate, but more importantly, be funny."[87] The original Wonkette blogger was a former journalist named Ana Marie Cox. A native of Lincoln, Nebraska, Cox had jobs at the *Washington Post*, the *Chronicle of Higher Education*, and the *American Prospect* magazine before she became Wonkette in January 2004.[88] The blog was the idea of Nick Denton, a blogging entrepreneur who offered Cox a salary of $18,000 a year to become the first Wonkette.[89] Cox was not new to blogging; she had created a blog that caught the attention of Denton.[90] Wonkette was patterned after Gawker, a celebrity gossip site owned by the same blog network that created Wonkette.[91] The site, like other blogs, became highly dependent on information submitted by readers. Cox said she had "a network of a thousand tipsters" who "started sending [her] stuff right away."[92]

But the appeal of a gossip blog in Washington was not guaranteed. Cox might become a Washington insider and pull her punches. Cox wondered whether she would meet her targets at a social event. "The rule is that the more cutting the remark, the more likely that you'll meet the person at a party."[93]

Yet Wonkette quickly became a success. The blog's launch in April 2004 suggested that the Washington establishment would not shun it. The launch party included media celebrities from CNN and *Newsweek* and former White House and presidential campaign spokespersons.[94] On its first day in business, Wonkette had 55,000 visitors; within two months it had over a million monthly visitors.[95] The blog became known for puncturing images and posting humorously derisive headlines, such as "Breaking: CBS News Staff Uses 'Too Much Hair Product'" and "Study: Dems Slightly Less Gullible & Misinformed than GOP Voters." However, not long after its debut Wonkette went through a period of instability in editorial direction and even ownership. Cox left in January 2006, and Gawker Media hired David Lat and Alex Pareene to carry on the blog. Lat, a federal prosecutor, blogged anonymously for the blog Underneath Their

Robes, which uncovered gossip about the judicial branch that made it popular with many in the legal profession. But Lat outed himself in a *New Yorker* magazine article and, at the suggestion of his boss, closed the blog.[96] After writing about the "Bodacious Babes of the Bench," Harriet Miers's makeup, and Justice Souter's "hot, lean body," Lat seemed ideal as a blogger for Wonkette.[97] Later in 2006 he left the blog, as did Pareene in 2007. Wonkette went through a period of editorial transition before Gawker Media sold it in 2008 to Ken Layne, who had previously served on the Wonkette staff.

The Conservative Blogosphere

The other side of the blogosphere clearly leans to the right on the political spectrum. However, as in the liberal blogosphere, the A-list bloggers among the conservatives are hardly uniform in their ideological approaches. Some are libertarian; others break from mainstream conservatives on various issues. For example, many heavily criticized the Bush administration, particularly on its handling of the war in Iraq. But these bloggers share common traits: they are far more likely to attack Democrats than Republicans; they were fairly united in their early support for the Bush presidency; and their blog rolls are populated by fellow conservative bloggers.

Instapundit   One of the longest lasting conservative blogs and among the most popular of the political blogs is Instapundit. Started in August 2001 by Glenn Reynolds, a University of Tennessee law professor, Instapundit acquired a daily audience of 20,000 within a year.[98] Much of his audience came in the wake of the 9/11 attacks, when his blog became a common discussion forum for a nation coping with the tragedy. Reynolds's site traffic tripled as he posted thirty-four times in one day and offered fast-breaking news to his new audience.[99] Now it has over 200,000 visits daily. Reynolds eschews the term "conservative." He is pro-choice on abortion and is an advocate of embryonic stem cell research. He calls himself a "disenchanted libertarian Democrat." Like Armstrong, he is sometimes called the "blogfather" because of his seniority in the blog community.[100]

Within a short time, Reynolds became famous. Instapundit has been praised by the *Wall Street Journal*, and MSNBC asked Reynolds to blog for them, which he did for several years.[101] *U.S. News and World Report* columnist John Leo termed Instapundit "the 800-pound gorilla of blogging culture."[102] Reynolds sells his own merchandise on his blog. He also has used his new fame to push his own agenda. Like other bloggers, Reynolds has predicted a revolution through blogging in his book *Army of Davids*.[103]

Andrew Sullivan   Andrew Sullivan, an Oxford-educated native of the United Kingdom, came to the United States in 1984 to pursue a graduate education. After earning a Ph.D. in political philosophy, he began writing for the *New Republic* and started a career in traditional journalism. He was a columnist for the Sunday magazine of the *New York Times* and an editor and then a columnist at the *New Republic* when he decided to join the new blogosphere.[104]

After launching his blog in January 2001, Sullivan quickly became one of the first high-profile political bloggers. His blog, Daily Dish, attracted a conservative readership that enjoyed his critiques of liberals and the media. Within seven months of starting his blog, Sullivan was getting over 100,000 visits per month.[105] His attacks on the media, particularly the *New York Times*, led to the newspaper's eliminating his column. Sullivan used his blog to fight back, writing, "Most of the time, people in big media, being journalists, don't mind criticism, especially from a piddling one-man blog. But others take offense, and you get canned."[106] Sullivan is perched uneasily between conservatives and liberals. He is passionately conservative, but also openly gay and favors same-sex marriage. His approach to politics is eclectic: he endorsed George W. Bush in 2000 and then John Kerry in 2004.[107] In 2008, he supported Representative Ron Paul of Texas for the Republican nomination and Senator Barack Obama of Illinois on the Democratic side.[108]

To support his blog, Sullivan solicited donations from his readers. The tactic helped him raised hundreds of thousands of dollars. But eventually he accepted the offer of the *Atlantic* to blog for the magazine's Web site and transferred his blog there.

Michelle Malkin   A rising star in the conservative blogosphere and one of a small circle of prominent women bloggers, Michelle Malkin has attracted a passionate readership. The daughter of Filipino immigrants who moved to southern New Jersey, Malkin attended Oberlin College and then worked in journalism as a reporter for the *Los Angeles Daily News* and the *Seattle Times*. She moved to Washington, D.C., in 1999, started her blog five years later, and quickly became a lightning rod. She quickly acquired a reputation as a blogger who would write about things even other conservative bloggers shied away from. She has attacked Cindy Sheehan, the Iraq war protester whose son died in Iraq. She also has voiced support for interning Japanese in relocation camps during World War II and using racial profiling to fight terrorists.[109] Malkin was a strong voice in the campaign to embarrass John Edwards over his hiring of two bloggers who were accused of making anti-Christian statements.[110]

Malkin once admitted that she enjoys blogging because "you can respond, you can reveal people to be the liars and slanderers they are."[111] Malkin has a take-no-prisoners approach that distinguishes her blog. For instance, in 2006 she wrote, "The donkey party is led by thumb-sucking demagogues in prominent positions who equate Bush with Hitler and Jim Crow, call him a liar in front of high school students and the world, fantasize about impeachment and fetishize the human rights of terrorists who want to kill me. Put simply: There are no grown-ups in the Democrat Party."[112]

Some conservative bloggers criticize her shrillness. Andrew Sullivan concluded, "Sometimes you just can't believe what she writes—it's so out there, and in certain respects quite disgraceful."[113] But her most frequent critics are liberal bloggers. Duncan Black called her a racist. Some of her critics have gone beyond writing, including making personal threats. When critics posted her home address on the Internet, along with photos of her house, Malkin quickly moved.[114]

Rather than repel visitors, her controversial blog has become one of the most viewed political blogs. By 2007 her site had nearly 400, 000 visitors. Like several other bloggers, she has been able to move beyond the blogosphere into mainstream media, where she has become a syndicated columnist appearing in 150 newspapers. And she has become an author; her book, *In Defense of Internment*, reached the *New York Times* best-seller list.

Little Green Footballs Dan Rather and Reuters wire service have become familiar with Charles Johnson in a way that they would probably just as well forget. It was Johnson, a former Web designer, who was among the first to blog on his site, Little Green Footballs, that the Bush National Guard documents touted by CBS News anchor Dan Rather could have been made by a modern computer and not the manual typewriter claimed by Rather. The embarrassed network anchor soon took early retirement, and Johnson's blog moved on to other scandals. Johnson pointed out a problem with a Reuters news photograph of an Israeli airstrike on Beirut, questioning whether the photo had been doctored. The accusation prompted the chagrined news service to investigate and ultimately withdraw the photo as well as another one produced by a freelance photographer.[115]

Johnson did Web design until September 11, 2001, when he decided to start a conservative political blog. Since then, his main interest has been the Middle East and the war on terror. His comments about Islam have been condemned as anti-Muslim by the Council on American-Islamic Relations.[116] He refers sarcastically to Islam as a "religion of peace" and accuses Islamic groups of being too influential in American society. Many posts are condemnations of

Islamic violence and groups who support Muslim organizations that Johnson claims are fronts for terrorism. Unlike those of many other political bloggers, Johnson's own editorial comments are sparse. The blog primarily is an aggregation of writings from other places on the Internet. In the vast majority of posts, Johnson may write no comment or only a short introduction to the piece. Yet his blog has become so controversial it has created a cottage industry. One set of counterblogs is devoted to critiquing Little Green Footballs, while another defends *Little Green Footballs* and critiques Johnson's critics.[117]

Hugh Hewitt   Another law professor blogger is Hugh Hewitt. A constitutional law professor at Chapman University School of Law and a practicing attorney, Hewitt also is a nationally syndicated radio talk show host with Salem Radio Network and a columnist for the online edition of the *Weekly Standard.* He formerly hosted a PBS series and served in the White House Counsel's Office during the Reagan administration. In addition, Hewitt is the author of several books on politics, religion, and blogs.[118]

Hewitt once described his blog, which is hosted by the conservative Web site Townhall.com, as "primarily about politics and breaking news," but he also uses it to discuss "anything that interests [him]."[119] Along with Armstrong and Moulitsas, Hewitt has gone beyond the blogosphere to promote blogs. His book *Blog: Understanding the Information Reformation That's Changing Your World— Why You Must Know How the Blogosphere Is Smashing the Old Media Monopoly and Giving Individuals Power in the Marketplace of Ideas* argues what its title proclaims. Hewitt has become a highly vocal advocate of the role of the blogging movement and an advocate of universal blogging.

Power Line   Another popular conservative blog, Power Line, is run by three lawyers: John Hinderaker, Scott Johnson, and Paul Mirengoff.[120] Hinderaker created the blog in May 2002 and invited Johnson and Mirengoff to join him. The blog gained a reputation in the conservative community after talk show host Hugh Hewitt mentioned it on his radio show and then invited the blog creators to be guests on his show.[121] The blog became especially popular with conservatives when it was instrumental in showing that documents purporting to show George W. Bush's Vietnam-era National Guard service were fake. *Time* magazine declared Power Line "Blog of the Year" in 2004 after the Rather scandal.[122]

Power Line is known as a reliably conservative blog where readers will see well-articulated partisan views. One reader called it "a place where like-minded souls get together and get to vent."[123] It is also popular with reporters from conservative media organizations such as Fox News and the *Washington Times.*

Real Clear Politics   A different blog in the conservative pantheon is Real Clear Politics. Founded by John McIntyre and Tom Bevan in August 2000, Real Clear Politics is a portal for commentary and analysis on politics.[124] The site does include its own blog posts, but the emphasis is on the writings of others from a variety of sources. McIntyre and Bevan cull more than fifty publications daily and place about two dozen of them on the top of their home page.[125] News media such as the *New York Times*, CBS News, and the *Wall Street Journal* are frequently cited, but so are other blogs, including blogs from the left such as The Huffington Post. However, Real Clear Politics' own blog commentary tends to the right.

The purpose of the site is to offer a one-stop shop for people who don't want to surf through the Web to find timely articles.[126] The top of the main page, unlike nearly all other blogs, features the writing of others and not the blog writers. Posts original to the blog itself can be missed by a casual reader of Real Clear Politics.

Captain's Quarters   This conservative blog acquired a national reputation by breaking the law, at least in Canada. Ed Morrissey, the founder of and writer for Captain's Quarters, covered the proceedings of a trial in Canada involving corruption by the governing Liberal Party. The problem was that the Canadian media were banned from reporting on the trial. The blog suddenly became popular with Canadians who wanted news about the trial but weren't getting it from their own media.[127]

Morrissey, who launched his blog in October 2003, also helped spur CNN executive Eason Jordan to resign after Jordan was reported to have claimed the U.S. military targeted journalists in Iraq. Morrissey wrote about the incident extensively and even urged Congress to investigate Jordan's allegations. After the incident, Morrissey claimed victory over the media. He wrote on his blog, "The media can't just cover up the truth and expect to get away with it."[128] In addition, Morrissey has been an activist for the blogger community. He was one of the advocates of the new searchable government database of federal spending. Morrissey's efforts were designed not just to further more government transparency but also to promote the blogosphere. He contended that the new law would create 10,000 new blogs as people became "citizen auditors" of federal spending.[129]

Summary

The blogosphere is not the monolithic entity it may appear to be from a distance. Talk about the blogosphere needs to specify which blogosphere (left or right) and which level of the blogosphere (influential or common). To the non–blog reader the blogosphere is only the most visible blogs, the A-list. But Daily Kos, The Huffington Post, or Instapundit—those that get covered in news stories or occasionally serve as news sources—are, in comparison to the total number of political blogs, only a minuscule part of the blogosphere. The political blogosphere also includes hundreds of thousands of other bloggers who discuss politics, at least occasionally, on their personal and largely obscure blogs. But that other blogosphere remains hidden because the influentials dominate the blogosphere—blog traffic, blog rolls, blog readership—and the attention of those beyond the blogosphere as well.

Nor is the blogosphere only the netroots praised by Armstrong, Moulitsas, and other liberal bloggers. It also includes a large and active conservative political blogosphere. Some of those blogs—such as Instapundit, Power Line, and Michelle Malkin—have acquired large readerships and significant influence among conservatives.

Nor does the blogosphere consist only of the individuals who blog. It is also the content of the blogs. In fact, given anonymity and multiple author blogs, the individuals seem closeted compared to the content they produce on a daily, even hourly basis. To understand the blogosphere, it is essential to examine what bloggers are saying on their blogs: What do they talk about? And how does that content relate to traditional media? That is our next subject.

4

Inside the Blogs

My natural home is in the bipartisan center, arguing with center-right reality-based technocrats about whether it is center-left or center-right policies that have the best odds of moving us toward goals that we all share....The aim of governance, I think, is to achieve a rough consensus among the reality-based technocrats and then to frame the issues in a way that attracts the ideologues on one (or, ideally, both) wings in order to create an effective governing coalition.

—Daily Kos, September 3, 2006

I really hope Republicans just punt everything until after the election and get down to the important business of making nasty attacks on their political opponents. They're much better at that than governing anyway.

—Eschaton, September 21, 2006

The Democratic Party: A despicable, irresponsible fraud.
—Michelle Malkin, September 8, 2006

Tom Harkin isn't helping the Democrats....I blame Karl Rove's mind-control rays. Democrats: Protect yourselves before it's too late!

—Instapundit, September 23, 2006

From the thoughtful to the bombastic to the sarcastic, blog content, even within the political blogosphere, spans a wide range of approaches to political discussion. Some bloggers seem to be policy wonks offering up detailed policy treatises, while others are gossipmongers interested in passing on the latest salacious rumor. Yet despite the type of content, the mode of communication is surprisingly standard, even among the influentials. All center their writing on the post. The post, a discrete entry usually identified by date and time, is the basic contained unit of blogging. Like a diary entry, it is delineated by a historical point and space separating it from the next post. Bloggers uniformly use the post as the form of blogging.

Political communication scholars only recently have begun to analyze political blog content. Kaye Trammell examined a random sample of political posts of forty-six celebrity blogs over ten months. The focus of Michael Keren's research was one political blogger's posts over a five-year period.[1] Svetlana V. Kulikova and David D. Perlmutter analyzed blog posts of a samizdat blog in Kyrgyzstan during the "Tulip Revolution" that led to the overthrow of the government in 2005, and Antoinette Pole analyzed the role of blog content in mobilizing readers.[2] Susan C. Herring and others conducted a longitudinal analysis of blogs to determine change over time in such features as length of posts, number of links, and the type of sources linked to.[3] For this book, blog posts on seven national influential political blogs were examined over a one-month period to determine the nature of blog content. These blog posts were analyzed both quantitatively and qualitatively. (For a fuller description of methodology, see the appendix.)

Most bloggers follow conventional posting practices, but the definitions of set time, date, and space do not include length. Length of post varies considerably across bloggers and even within blogs. Some bloggers nearly always write short posts. Posts on Instapundit and Wonkette typically are no longer than a sentence or even a phrase; Michelle Malkin and Daily Kos feature lengthier posts. The length of the post also varies depending on the approach of the blogger to the inclusion of outside material. Whereas some bloggers merely link to material from external sources—news media articles, Web sites, other blogs—other bloggers include excerpts or even the full text.

It is rare for a blogger's own contribution—separate from inserted text—to go on for paragraphs or pages due to the blogosphere's emphasis on short bursts of writing as well as the inability to post as frequently (several times daily) when each post is essay length. Short posts allow bloggers to update frequently, sometimes even several times an hour. For example, on the fifth anniversary of 9/11, which fell during the month under study, Instapundit posted twenty-seven times.

Influential bloggers are not uniform in their approach to posting (see table 4.1). During the month of September 2006, the number of posts varied considerably across bloggers. Michelle Malkin's daily average was six posts and typically included more substantive offerings. Glenn Reynolds's Instapundit postings average nearly 20 per day.

Short, frequent blog posts draw readers back to the blog to make them feel they are getting the latest news and information. Such posts also highlight the advantage over most traditional media, which take longer to get a news story. In

Table 4.1   Frequency of Posting

Name of blog	Total number of posts	Average number of daily posts
Crooks and Liars	446	14.8
Daily Kos	429	14.3
Eschaton	529	17.6
Instapundit	585	19.5
Little Green Footballs	420	14
Michelle Malkin	161	5.4
Wonkette	381	12.7

addition, short posts take less time to read, thus encouraging readers to return frequently for brief updates. One blogger began writing lengthy posts, 800-word essays, but then shortened them into a staccato form that matches other A-list blogs.[4]

Unlike personal bloggers who originate nearly all of their content, political bloggers rely heavily on content they collect from other sources: wire service stories, news articles, video clips, and other blog posts. The material may be referenced in the form of a hyperlink, usually with a comment, or the text (or parts of it) may be inserted in the blog post. To differentiate the external material from their own, the inserted text is usually italicized, placed in a different font, accompanied by a contrasting color background, or indented.

When comments are added, perhaps no more than a recommendation to the reader to take a look at the original source, they are usually brief. Some blogs provide no comment at all, but just a quick description or title. At Instapundit the post may consist solely of a phrase, such as "recharging **the cars of the future**" or "Foleygate: '**The perfect blogstorm**,'" with the bold section constituting the hyperlink to the source.

Influential political bloggers rely heavily on other sources for blog content. One source is traditional media. The following is an example of a blogger, in this case Michelle Malkin, drawing from multiple media sources for one post. In this post, Malkin pulls text from an Associated Press story on Yahoo News, the *New York Sun*, the *New York Post*, and the *New York Daily News*. Each added number in brackets indicates a separate external source.

Showdown at Turtle Bay; "The world must stand up for peace"
By Michelle Malkin • September 19, 2006 09:05 AM

The **festivities**[1] begin at 11am. I'm lowering my expectations, actually. Ahmadinejad has **chickened out:**[2]

There won't be a confrontation on the General Assembly lunch menu today because the Iranian president has decided to skip it—passing up his best shot at ambushing President Bush with an impromptu debate.

Mahmoud Ahmadinejad has challenged Bush to a debate, and when the U.S. President turned him down, he suggested he would dog Bush at this week's General Assembly.

. . . It's not clear why Ahmadinejad is passing on the lunch, which Fidel Castro once successfully used to shake hands with former President Bill Clinton. Chances that the two men will bump into each other in the halls of the UN have been lessened by the fact that they are speaking nearly eight hours apart.

Bush is scheduled to speak at 11:30 a.m. discussing the war on terror, Iraq and Iran's nuclear ambitions. . . . Ahmadinejad will address the gathering between 6 p.m. and 7 p.m., according to the UN.

President Bush's prepared remarks will issue a **challenge**:[3] "The world must stand up for peace." Watch out for the **weasel Chirac**:[4]

Ahead of what is now certain to be a contentious meeting with President Bush today, President Chirac of France reneged on his previous support for a united international approach to halting Iran's nuclear program.

In two interviews on the eve of his trip to Turtle Bay to attend the U.N. General Assembly, Mr. Chirac threatened to restart negotiations with Iran. His comments called into question the united position of the five permanent members of the Security Council and Germany, whose foreign ministers had said that unless Iran suspended enrichment by the end of August, the council would consider punitive measures.

The **NY Daily News**[5] gives Ahmedinijad a Bronx cheer and rightfully calls out the CFR:

Dignitary that he is, Ahmadinejad is set to address the UN this evening. This would be the UN that appears to have no particularly large problem with President Mr. Ahmadinejad despite the fact that he: a) has openly defied every Security Council call for compliance with its peacemaking wishes, b) continues to assert that Iran is divinely entitled to secret nuclear programs that UN inspectors aren't permitted to inspect and c) just this week warned the UN that it had better not be "hostile" as he comes visiting.

Well, we don't imagine that the General Assembly will be too visibly hostile at that. We suppose that President Mr. Ahmadinejad will be giving all us infidels a good scold, and we suppose he might get a standing ovation from some quarters. What he won't get is any sense that he needs to fret too much about the possibility of sanctions. If he often looks to be enjoying himself, there's a reason.

Repellent as it is to have President Mr. Ahmadinejad among us, it's the price we pay for being the site city of the, you should pardon the expression, world peacemaking body. If the UN wants to give a speaking invite to a man who regularly spits in its face, well, there's not much to be done about diplomatic courtesies. Far less comprehensible is the Council on Foreign Relations' willingness to give him a platform and the credibility that the organization bestows.

The thing is, we're stuck with President Mr. Ahmadinejad. We try to be polite. Welcome to New York, you medieval goon.

The NYSun says **arrest Ahmadnijehad**.[6]

The **NYPost**[7] puts the heat on Sudan:

As President Bush addresses the United Nations today, the focus, rightly, will be on Iran's nukes and the War on Terror.

The president will reiterate the need for the world body to act on, rather than just talk about, these critical issues.

But there's another issue, too, on which the United Nations must act: genocide in Sudan. If it doesn't, the toll could be worse than in Rwanda a decade ago—a point made by the 30,000 people who rallied in Central Park last weekend (and thousands more in 30 other cities).

The mandate expires this month for the African Union peacekeeping troops now in Sudan.

The risk is that they'll leave with no U.N. forces to replace them—even as a cease-fire between government and rebel forces teeters on collapse.

When using sources, including news media, bloggers don't necessarily say where the text is coming from. In a post on September 25, Malkin's first excerpt was from a blog run by Mickey Kaus. However, for the second text she said only, "Here's an article that just amplifies my point about the need to put up or shut up." The article was from the *Houston Chronicle*. Similarly, a Daily Kos post from September 24 included links to *USA Today*, NPR's "All Things Considered," *Time*, and the Associated Press, but mentioned none of them by name in the post.

Multimedia have become common features for blog posts. Blog posts occasionally include video clips from YouTube or broadcast networks, interviews with political figures, advertisements, or news stories. Bloggers trumpet their broadcast of clips the traditional media ignore. For example, Little Green Footballs criticized broadcast media for censoring graphic images of the collapse of the World Trade Center: "The media has made a unilateral decision to be our collective nanny, and they've hidden all of their most disturbing footage away in archives."

The use of other material does not mean bloggers do not fill blog posts with original content, sometimes including personal content. The amount of personal content on A-list political blogs has been found to be quite small.[5] But there are times when political bloggers talk about their personal lives outside of politics. Charles Johnson on Little Green Footballs wrote about a fifty-mile bicycle ride he took on Labor Day. Michelle Malkin related her travel woes on September 22: "Been hustling back and forth across the Chicago airport for the last three and a half hours waiting for 'tornado' conditions to pass." Later, she wrote again: "**Update**: Another hour later and I am still not on the plane. The good news is I found an electrical outlet to charge my dead laptop. Question: Is there some section of the Chicago building code that bars O'Hare from having more than, like, five outlets per terminal?"

Because their blogging appears to be constant, bloggers even feel the need to explain to their readers why they are silent for a while. The explanation, if personal, suggests how dominant blogging is in their own lives. For example, Glenn Reynolds confessed he hadn't blogged much because a friend was "passing through town, and we hung out, had dinner, visited a brewpub, and recorded a podcast interview that will be up later. It was nice to see him."

Even when content is not personal, it may still not be political. Wonkette devoted space to gossip about entertainment personalities as well as political figures. Little Green Footballs mourned the passing of Crocodile Hunter Steve Irwin that month and also occasionally posted landscape photographs of a meadow, a country lane, or a beach. Similarly, Eschaton regularly displayed photographs of cats. John Amato of Crooks and Liars offered a regular feature titled "C&L Late Nite Music Club," where he posted videos of performers such as the Dave Matthews Band, Alice Cooper, and Marty Robbins.

But clearly political blogs are about politics: they cater to those who are interested in politics, and their topics are primarily political. Little Green Footballs concentrates on the Middle East, the war on terror, and Islam. Similarly, Daily Kos is election-related; posts are filled with information about the latest polls, the "inside baseball" of campaigns, calls for campaign donations, etc.

Blogs revel in the minutiae of political and policy topics that appeal to a small portion of Americans. For example, a Crooks and Liars post examined the FISA bill pushed by the White House and sponsored by Senator Arlen Specter. However, posts do not examine the fine points of legislation so much as they do the politics of it. This post said less about the specifics of the bill than a broad summary designed to interest readers. "It would, in sum, abolish all meaningful restrictions and oversight on the President's eavesdropping powers, formally adopt the administration's radical theories of limitless executive power, and destroy the ability to subject the President's eavesdropping conduct to meaningful judicial review."

Blog Topics

A-list bloggers are posting for hours each day. The range of topics, even within political blogs, must be vast to cover the amount of writing bloggers do on a daily basis. As table 4.2 shows, blog topics do cover a wide range of topics, from

Table 4.2 Topic Frequency by Blog, in Percentages

	Blog							
Topic	Crooks and Liars	Daily Kos	Eschaton	Instapundit	Little Green Footballs	Michelle Malkin	Wonkette	Total
Midterm elections	15%	44%	21%	11%	0%	4%	21%	18%
War on terror	17	13	19	11	19	32	8	16
Blog news	11	9	18	19	6	6	17	13
Iraq war	10	7	8	4	2	3	2	6
News media–related	7	2	8	5	4	5	5	5
General domestic policy	3	4	4	11	4	2	5	5
White House/Congress	7	5	5	4	<1	1	6	4
International relations/foreign policy	<1	<1	1	6	12	10	2	4
Other scandals	1	1	1	3	11	9	3	4
Middle East	1	0	0	1	13	2	0	3
Celebrity news	2	<1	2	3	2	2	6	2
Iran	1	0	1	2	8	4	1	2
Republican House scandals	2	3	2	<1	0	1	4	2
Economic	<1	0	1	3	<1	4	1	1
Defense Department	2	<1	1	1	0	1	2	1
CIA leak	1	<1	1	2	<1	2	0	1
Immigration	<1	0	0	1	<1	1	0	<1
Miscellaneous	19	9	9	13	16	10	17	13
Total	100%	100%	100%	100%	100%	100%	100%	100%
Total number of articles	446	422	494	558	420	161	327	2,828

the midterm elections to the Iraq war to the Republican House scandals. As anticipated, the most frequent blog topic was the midterm elections. This was September 2006, a period at the peak of the elections. Moreover, for liberal blogs it was an important moment because the prospect of taking over the House of Representatives and the Senate was tantalizing to them. Indeed, three of the liberal blogs—Daily Kos, Eschaton, and Wonkette—were the leaders in discussion of the midterm elections. The upcoming elections dominated Daily Kos discussion; over two of five posts there were related to the midterm elections. The exception was Crooks and Liars, which placed midterm election discussion second to the war on terror. In contrast, the conservative blogosphere was more interested in the war on terror. It was the leading topic for Michelle Malkin (one in three of her posts were on the subject) and Little Green Footballs. It tied for second place on Instapundit.

Interestingly, neither liberals nor conservatives spent as much time discussing the Iraq war as they did the elections or the war on terror. Only Crooks and Liars devoted a significant amount of time to the war (10 percent of posts and fourth place among its topics). Even though Little Green Footballs focused on the Middle East, it was the war on terror and not the Iraq war that commanded its attention. Little Green Footballs, Wonkette, and Michelle Malkin dedicated only 2 to 3 percent of their posts to Iraq. (To explain the difference between the two, any post that discussed any facet of the Iraq war, including Al-Qaeda in Iraq, was labeled an Iraq war story. Any story that discussed terrorism outside Iraq, including U.S. domestic security efforts, was coded a war on terror story.)

The conservative blogosphere's lack of attention to Iraq is understandable. The war was going badly in September 2006, and the Bush administration was struggling to determine how to save its Iraq policy. But the liberal blogosphere also seemed to downplay the issue. Perhaps liberal bloggers were preoccupied with the midterm elections and considered the Iraq war old news at that point.

A popular topic across the blogosphere was the blogosphere itself. It was the third most popular topic, and that emphasis was shared by most bloggers. Instapundit devoted nearly one in five blog posts to discussing the happenings in the blogosphere, and Eschaton and Wonkette were only slightly behind. Blog news included posts about the creation of new blogs, what other blogs were talking about, bloggers' personal and political activities, examples of the influence blogs were having on politics, prominent politicians' blogging, and bloggers' joint campaigns.

Bloggers were less interested in a wide range of traditional topics. For example, little time was spent on domestic policy issues such as health care, education, the environment, housing, and welfare. Instapundit was the only blog where more than 5 percent of posts addressed these topics. Most also did not discuss other foreign policy areas besides the war on terror or Iraq. The exceptions were Little Green Footballs and Michelle Malkin, who stood out among the others in discussing these topics.

In general the bloggers in this study preferred politics over policy. The midterm elections were attractive to liberal bloggers because of the prospect of victory in November. Similarly, the conservative bloggers likely discussed the war on terror because it was a perceived political weakness of Democrats. Blogosphere news was a universal topic, likely because it appealed to audiences who would be interested in the happenings of their newfound medium.

Editorial Categories of Posts

The majority of the content of blog posts falls into three broad categories. One is news and information, which includes breaking news that the blogosphere attempts to get out first, but primarily consists of information that the blogosphere has gleaned from other sources such as the news media. The second is commentary by others; these include text or links to commentary by other blog posts, news media editorials, and opinion pieces from various sources such as the e-magazines *Slate* and *Salon* or online versions of traditional print opinion magazines such as the *New Republic*, the *National Review*, the *Weekly Standard*, or the *Nation*. The third category is bloggers' own commentary.

News and Information

One reason an influential political blogger may be mistaken for a journalist is the amount of news provided for readers. The volume of information posted on a particular day by a blogger, especially where the blog has multiple authors, might equal what is available on a transcript of an evening news broadcast. The Huffington Post and Daily Kos would be even more extensive, particularly when including the Kos host bloggers. Nevertheless, bloggers are rarely news gatherers; they are aggregators and disseminators of information. They collect information (most of it funneled to them by others) and then pass it on to their readers. The route to the blog may be circuitous. For example, Little Green Footballs included a link to another conservative blog called Sticky Notes that, in turn, had a link to a YouTube video of President Bush being interviewed by *Today* host Matt Lauer. In another story, Little Green Footballs obtained news about a missile fired at Senator John McCain's helicopter while he was on a visit to the Republic of Georgia. The story was from an Arizona television station Web site that Little Green Footballs learned about from another blogger.

The rapid transmission capability of the blogosphere means that fast-breaking news can be disseminated more rapidly than in a hierarchical, structured news media organization. The nearly instantaneous nature of blog transmission—a turn-around of information within seconds, compared to the minutes required for wire services or hours or days for daily or weekly news media outlets—advantages the blogs over news media in terms of disseminating the latest news. For example, during the month of September 2006, blogs quickly posted late-breaking news such as the death of Steve Irwin and the Mark Foley scandal. On September 11, 2006, at 3:51 p.m. Little Green Footballs wrote a post about clips on CNN replaying its original 9/11 coverage. Then it updated the post twice, once at 4:04 p.m. and again at 5:34 p.m. The ability to update adds a "latest information" tone to blog content.

Blogs also are advantaged because they do not have to appeal to a general audience, as traditional media outlets do. The specialty nature of their audience—politically interested blog readers—allows them to concentrate on only a few stories that can be repeated regularly. In contrast, traditional media are expected to offer a broad smattering of news topics designed to cater to an array of interests.

However, the ability to break the latest news comes with the potential danger of getting it wrong. Like journalists, influential political bloggers face criticism when they err in reporting, particularly as their audience size grows and they occasionally move items onto the news media's agenda. Bloggers also face the dilemma of whether to put out information without checking. Michelle Malkin expressed this concern when she posted that there was "significant news" in a speech President Bush would give that day. Malkin wrote, "We actually got an inside tip about this earlier, but I sat on it because it wasn't confirmed." She released the information at that point because the White House press office was announcing it.

Others' Commentary

The more common type of content is commentary. The use of commentary for content over news may seem odd given the blogosphere's capacity to disseminate news faster than traditional media. But because bloggers do not possess surveillance capabilities as news media do, they are limited at the task of news generation. Commentary is a different story.[6] Commentary requires no real legwork by the blogger, nor even a staff. Commentary by others is readily available online; bloggers can access opinions from one another's blogs as well as from a host of online opinion sources. Rather than one piece of information, the news may be how other blogs are handling pieces of news. For example, the following is a September 30 blog post on Instapundit:

> **CAPTAIN ED:**[1] "I cannot tell CQ readers how disgusted I am with Speaker Hastert." He's referring to reports that Hastert knew of Rep. Foley's behavior but did nothing.
>
> I have been no fan of Hastert all along, of course. I wonder if this story ties in somehow with his over-the-top **outrage**[2] regarding searches of Congressional offices in the William Jefferson case.
>
> UPDATE: One of Capt. Ed's commenters is citing TV reports that Hastert asked Foley to resign as soon as he saw the IMs. I haven't seen those, but stay tuned. Lots of discussion, some of it informed, **here.**[3]
>
> ANOTHER UPDATE: John Hinderaker **weighs in.**[4]
>
> YET ANOTHER UPDATE: TigerHawk is **absolutely right,**[5] which means that—in a phenomenon as regular as the sunrise but more frequent—Glenn Greenwald is wrong again.

Bloggers' Commentary

Bloggers are accused of ranting on their blogs. But for the vast majority of posts, bloggers provide very little of their own commentary. When they pass on news or commentary from another source, often there is little or nothing added by the blogger. For example, Little Green Footballs included a blog post reporting that a flight from Qatar Airways had landed in Beirut and broken through a blockade set up by Israel. The blogger noted that, "like so many others, this great Arab victory is a sham. The flight was quietly cleared with Israel." The text of the news story in the post said the same thing. Here is an example of a full post on Crooks and Liars:

> September 5th, 2006
> **Nothing like the rich taking a year off to mess with those poverty figures**
> By: John Amato @ 5:45 AM—PDT 🗒 Digg This Story
>
> Kevin Drum **explains . . .** [1]

In another example, the only original contribution by Little Green Footballs was a title. "US Embassy in Syria Attacked" or "Air Defense Systems Seized in Cyprus" is followed, without comment, by the text of a news story from a traditional news media source. In a Crooks and Liars post on September 14, bloggers' addition to excerpts from a story in the *New York Times* was a one-word title: "Iraq." The sum total of an Eschaton post was the word "funny"; the word was hyperlinked to a post on another blog.

In most cases, however, bloggers add some comment and go beyond the mere transmission function. One approach is to comment prior to the post. The pre-link comment explains why the blogger is relaying the information and helps cue the reader what to look for in the text. For example, a Daily Kos post began with the following: "If you are voting Republican because you think it's the more fiscally responsible party, you might want to **rethink that position**." The hyperlink led to a *USA Today* story about huge federal budget deficits.

Another approach is a pre- and post-link explanation, or even one in the middle as well. In the post below from September 14, 2006, Little Green Footballs at first summarized the article, then posted the text of the article, and then added his own reaction.

Al Qaeda Declares War on France

Al Qaeda has announced an alliance with the Algerian terror gang known as the Salafist Group for Preaching and Combat, to take revenge against the imperialist crusading . . . French? **Al-Qaida joins with group against France.** [1]

PARIS—Al-Qaida has for the first time announced a union with an Algerian insurgent group that has designated France as an enemy, saying they will act together against French and American interests.

Current and former French officials specializing in terrorism said Thursday that an al-Qaida alliance with the Salafist Group for Call and Combat, known by its French initials GSPC, was cause for concern.

Al-Qaida's No. 2, Ayman al-Zawahri, announced the "blessed union" in a video posted this week on the Internet to mark the fifth anniversary of the Sept. 11 attacks in the United States.

France's leader have repeatedly warned that the decision not to join the U.S.-led war in Iraq would not shield the country from Islamic terrorism. French participation in the U.N. peacekeeping mission in Lebanon could give extremists another reason to strike.

That last paragraph is a hoot. The first sentence states that France is a target no matter how they try to appease Islam. Then the second sentence states that France is a target because of their participation in the UN Lebanon force.

Poor France. They just can't win for surrendering.

One exception to the above was Daily Kos. The Kos posts tended to be lengthier and less reliant on external texts than were the other blogs. One explanation may be the blog's use of multiple authors, which allows each individual blogger to develop the post to a greater extent than an individual blogger can do without reducing the pace of the blog. Another may be the scope of the blog, which tends to be narrow and concentrated on an area on which the blog's author and other writers have well-developed opinions.

The Functions of Posts

Studies of why common bloggers blog have found that they do so primarily for personal expression and to share experiences with others; other reasons include sharing practical knowledge with others, seeking to affect public opinion, entertaining their audience, and motivating readers to action.[7] Are influential bloggers different? Do their posts serve the same role or other roles?

One method of answering that question is to analyze the content of blog posts to see what functions they serve. On examination, five blog functions emerge from the post content. These functions are not meant to be exhaustive, but they do cover most of these influential bloggers' writings.

Advertising

One function of blog posts is advertising the blog. These posts are used to tout the blog to the readers. Advertising includes recounting the blog's successes in areas such as increasing audience size, the placement of the blog in blog rankings for numbers of readers and number of links from other blogs, and examples of the blog's role in affecting others.

Why do bloggers feel the need to advertise? One reason is to maintain the attachment to blog reading on the part of the audience. Readers may wonder whether this new phenomenon matters. Demonstrating that the blogger has had some proximity to public officials or that the blog broke some scandal suggests that blogs matter in the larger political environment. That reassurance helps readers justify the time necessary to maintain a blog reading habit or the choice to read that particular political blog.

Self-advertising is necessary because blogging is becoming a competitive business. The greater the audience, the higher the advertising rates and the larger the potential influence among the blogosphere. Bragging rights for audience size and actual advertising dollars earned make the difference as to whether blogging is a full-time activity accompanied by offers for consulting work, media attention, and invitations to star at blogging conventions or a part-time hobby in the basement.

Audiences do shift from blogger to blogger. Assuming a fixed amount of time available for blog reading, the audience member must choose where to devote his or her time during regular blog-reading moments. Will it be Michelle Malkin or Little Green Footballs or Daily Kos or Eschaton? The rise of The Huffington Post is an example of the fluidity of the blogging community.

Blogs, then, make a point of advertising themselves. This includes increasing audience size. For example, during the period of analysis, Crooks and Liars noted that the blog had passed the 50 million mark in number of hits to the site since its inception. Some blogs announce their charitable work. Michelle Malkin advertised T-shirts with "I will not submit" written in Arabic. She said the proceeds would go to a scholarship fund for children of those killed on 9/11.

And then there is the blog's success at influencing others. For example, Crooks and Liars publicized a book by CNN host Keith Olbermann and then tracked the results:

> Jane posted about it at **1:pm yesterday.** It was at # 19,000 at the time and then started to move onward and upward. At 2:25PM **I posted it** as well. Keith's was listed # 38 at 10:00PM PST on Thursday. He deserves it. I just checked and it's up to # 18. Let's keep it moving!

> Pre-order it here . . .

Bloggers even advertise their other ventures in and out of the blogosphere. Markos Moulitsas used his blog to publicize his own book-signing appearances in Austin, Texas—in fact, twice in one day. As bloggers have branched out into other blogs, they use one blog to advertise the other blogs they sponsor or affiliate with. Michelle Malkin wrote on September 22, "There's lots of good stuff over at Hot Air." Hot Air is another blog cofounded by Malkin. Similarly, Glenn Reynolds (Instapundit) often referred to Pajamas Media, another blog he is affiliated with.

They also advertise the blogs of like-minded bloggers. For example, Michelle Malkin listed various bloggers such as Charles Johnson, Paul Belien, and Laura Mansfield. She explained her reference to them by saying, "These men and women are inspirations who share a common intellectual defiance against submission to jihad."

A-list bloggers provide publicity to lesser known bloggers, as well. One method is passing on specific posts, such as Little Green Footballs' tip: "Here's an interesting post at Say Anything . . . " On September 10 Michelle Malkin urged readers to visit two other blogs that were discussing an upcoming ABC docudrama called *The Path to 9/11* and featured material she thought would be of interest to her readers: "Johnny Dollar's got **video of Michael Scheuer** on Heartland with John Kasich tonight. After you're done at RS, head on over and see what he has to say about culpability for 9/11." Crooks and Liars offered a regular blog roundup with summaries of posts from lesser known blogs. A-list blogs also advertise another blog generally rather than any specific post. Malkin called another blog "the single best clearinghouse on the 'net for fighting the tinfoil hat brigade." They advertise events occurring on other blogs. For example, on the morning of September 2, Crooks and Liars alerted readers to a live blogging session that afternoon at the blog Firedoglake. The next day the blog advertised a chat with John Dean about his latest book that was being hosted by another blog.

Bloggers also promote the blogosphere generally. They announce joint campaigns the blogosphere is conducting. One example is the effort discussed earlier to pass legislation establishing a database of federal grants and contracts. When the bill passed and the president signed it into law on September 26, 2006, Malkin praised bloggers who orchestrated the "porkbusters" campaign. Another effort discussed on the blogs during the month under study was a joint effort across the blogosphere to remember the victims of 9/11 on the fifth anniversary of the terrorist attacks. The blogs reported that over 3,000 bloggers had joined the remembrance campaign and used their blogs to promote it.

An important part of advertising the blogosphere is a comparison with the traditional media. Blogs often paint the media as corrupt and flawed. Although news media stories are used again and again, many without comment, traditional news organizations often become the targets of bloggers' criticisms. Little Green Footballs reported on a demonstration against the visit to Harvard University of Mohammad Khatami, "The blogosphere is way ahead of mainstream media again. We'll see if this demonstration even makes the news."

One of the common themes of the failings of the news media is bias. One Little Green Footballs post called a traditional media news story "possibly the most biased article masquerading as a news report by Reuters so far today." Then followed the story text with the comment "Agencies like Reuters don't even bother to hide their blatant, in-your-face bias any more; their writers take the viewpoint that their outrageously slanted opinions are simple facts." In another post, Little Green Footballs termed a *Chicago Sun-Times* piece an "unfortunately one-sided article on Monday, another dishonest smear job from the Council on American Islamic Relations."

According to some bloggers, news organizations employ their bias by omitting parts of stories that bloggers are aware of (as competitors of journalists with their own sources) but readers miss out on. An example from Little Green Footballs: "Today the Washington Post has a whiny article about the Muslim Students Association (and other radical front groups) that goes into great depth about the humiliation and discrimination they face on U.S. campuses—but not a single word about the MSA's well-documented history of radicalism, Jew-hatred, and connections to terrorism."

Crooks and Liars directed readers' attention to a new book about the news media titled *Censored 2007: The Top 25 Censored Stories*. On September 26 Michelle Malkin discussed the newly released National Intelligence Estimate. She quoted two paragraphs from the report with the preface, "Some of what you didn't read in the NYTimes."

According to bloggers, bias is not an occasional occurrence, but a repeated sin that news media engage in. Michelle Malkin termed the Associated Press "the Associated (With Terrorists) Press." Charles Johnson at Little Green Footballs criticized an AP story on a Palestinian teachers' strike: "This is a great example of how appallingly corrupt the wire services have become in their reporting from Palestinian areas, relying on Palestinian journalists and editors who are doing the bidding of terrorist groups and covering up atrocities."

The criticism isn't only from the conservative blogosphere. Liberal bloggers also chastise the press. Crooks and Liars called the media "a press corps that's never willing to do its research and always willing to spin for the GOP." Daily Kos described a *New York Times* story as "one of the shoddiest pieces of reporting you'll ever see." During the month under study, liberals were particularly incensed at ABC for airing the docudrama *Path to 9/11*, which blamed both the Bush and Clinton administrations for failure in the war on terrorism and manufactured quotes and scenes of real events. Daily Kos termed it "ABC's work of fiction."

However, each side usually attacks traditional news organizations they accuse of being allied with the other side. Liberal bloggers direct their criticism at, for example, the *Wall Street Journal* and Fox News, while conservatives do the same for CNN, the *Washington Post*, and the *New York Times*. Michelle Malkin blogged about a news story that liberal radio network Air America was experiencing financial difficulties. She asked her readers rhetorically, "Will the New York Times fiiinally get around to covering this story? Hmmm?" When the *New York Times* did cover the story, Malkin wrote, "You won't believe who finally covered the story. Yup, the 'paper of record' that has ignored the story for more than a year."

Agenda Setting

As discussed earlier, blogs have the potential to be new agenda setters, and agenda setting is an intended function of blog content. How do bloggers attempt to shape agendas? One way to answer that question is to examine blog content.

The blog agenda is hardly monolithic. Even an individual blog can be scattershot. Individual blogs raise many topics daily. For example, on one day in September, Daily Kos raised fifteen different topics in twenty-one posts. A few of the topics, suggesting the range represented, were the Democratic National Committee's fifty-state strategy, a set of new polls on the status of highly contested midterm races, a new campaign ad released in Pennsylvania, and a scandal involving U.S. Senate candidate Bob Corker from Tennessee.

Because bloggers lack their own investigative reporting staff they do not have the ability to find stories on their own. These bloggers took stories that received brief mention in the news media and magnified them in order to call greater attention to them. A September 17 story about a Catholic nun killed by Somali gunmen was covered by both traditional media and the blogs. However, traditional media did not continue the story. Michelle Malkin returned to it a week later: "To borrow a phrase from Rush Limbaugh, the 'drive-by media' gave a few hours' attention to the victims of jihadists' Pope Rage last weekend and then quickly moved on to the next headline. I think the murder of Sister Leonellas deserves a few more seconds of your time."

One facet of agenda setting is explicitly telling policy makers what to do. Bloggers did that on occasion. One post on September 13 on Crooks and Liars opined, "Democrats should have no fear of filibustering this bill. To the contrary, they should be eager to do so." The Daily Kos posted on the controversial ABC/Disney *Path to 9/11* docudrama scheduled to air that month, "Disney Chairman George Mitchell needs to pick up the white courtesy phone. If anyone associated with Mitchell is reading this, you need to get your man out there." In another Daily Kos post, party leaders were told not to hold the next Democratic National Convention in New York City: "So go somewhere where the local coverage will actually, you know, help. Colorado is a purple state moving our direction."

A related approach is to direct the news media specifically to follow the lead of the blogs in covering stories. For example, a post on Daily Kos included a statement by a *Washington Post* reporter in a chat room that the paper was following an issue regarding Senator George Allen's connections with a pro-segregationist group. The blogger posted a photograph of Allen, while governor, posing with leaders of the group and added, "Let me help The Washington Post out here."

As mentioned earlier, agenda seekers have discovered that blogs may become agenda setters. However, as is true with traditional media content, sometimes it is difficult to discern the origins of story ideas in blog posts. For example, a post on Daily Kos on September 9 publicized a new ad by the Democratic National Committee with a link to a video clip of the ad. Did the blog look for the ad, or did the DNC alert the blog to the existence of the ad? In another case, Instapundit on September 1 discussed reaction to a speech by Secretary of Defense Donald Rumsfeld and posted, "I just got copies of letters that Rumsfeld sent to Nancy Pelosi and Harry Reid. Click 'read more' to read them." Reynolds does not mention the source of the letters. Was it Rumsfeld's staff? It is highly unlikely that these bloggers found this material all by themselves. The material had to come from a source, and that source likely was the agenda seeker who sought attention for his or her perspective on current events via a sympathetic blog. It is no coincidence that the DNC or its supporters would have worked through Daily Kos, while the Defense Department or other insiders did the same via Instapundit.

But the agenda-setting efforts of agenda seekers occasionally peeked through even more explicitly when a blogger admitted that he or she was the target of a publicity campaign. For example, in a blog post titled "Bill Clinton Accepts Blame" Michelle Malkin wrote, "That's according to a *New Yorker* article by David Remnick just e-mailed to me by the magazine's P.R. people."

Even when the source is identified, and it is a reader, it is possible there is an organizational agenda seeker—an interest group, a bureaucratic agency, a member of Congress—who is involved indirectly through the reader. These sock puppets use their anonymous, seemingly ordinary positions to push agendas on the blogs. Even if the beneficiary of the reader's efforts is not involved and is even unaware of a reader's actions, the reader still may be attempting to set the agenda on behalf of the agenda seeker, although not necessarily in a coordinated fashion. The efforts of these agenda seekers will be discussed at greater length in a later chapter.

Framing

Another function is bloggers' ability to frame stories, as mentioned in chapter 1. The content analysis found cases of specific framing attempts by these bloggers. As mentioned earlier, Michelle Malkin posted a story about the nun killed by Somali gunmen. Malkin's framing came in the form of a preface to the story post, which offered context she wanted the reader to place on the event:

> Shot in the back three times. Fox News says four times in the back by two "armed gunmen" with pistols. The elderly victim worked at a hospital for mothers and children. Her bodyguard and another hospital worker were also murdered.
>
> Animals. Cowards. Barbarians.
>
> Watch as everyone strains to say this hate slaying has nothing to do with jihad and it was "not clear it had anything to do" with Muslim rage over the Pope (hat tip: SOS).

Malkin began with a summary of the story, then added epithets for the perpetrators of the attack. Then she framed by linking the incident to a statement by Pope Benedict about Islamic jihad against the West. She alerted readers to put this story in context with those events, particularly as she warned her readers that others (unnamed) would be offering a counter-frame of the event as isolated in nature.

The frame typically is a common theme for bloggers. Little Green Footballs framed by interpreting news items as further indications of the West's submission to Islam. For instance, on September 5 Little Green Footballs posted a news story about British hospitals adopting a surgical gown that looked like the burka worn by Muslim women. The excerpted text quoted the hospital administration as explaining that the robe "provides extra comfort and cover for patients undergoing medical procedures and whose culture or religion requires more modest attire." It added that patients have expressed appreciation for the new gown. However, the frame for Little Green Footballs was that the decision was another example of the West's capitulating to the demands of Islam. Little Green Footballs introduced the article with the title "Radical Islamic Misogyny Is Now Endorsed by British Hospitals."

Reinforcing

Framing is a way of providing news to partisans, but offering that news in a palatable way. Bloggers don't just frame events, particularly events that may undermine their views without the proper view. They also reinforce readers' views by offering them information that supports a particular worldview and spinning negatively any news that does not do so.

Bloggers are clearly partisan. They celebrate their own positions and attack the opposition. The information they provide is designed to show the intellectual superiority of their own worldview. Op-eds, blog posts, interviews, and news stories that support their position are repeated. For example, Crooks and Liars posted an excerpt from a transcript of a statement by Keith Olbermann criticizing President Bush for "accomplishing in part what Osama Bin Laden and others seek." The post added, "Nothing could be truer than that right there."

Successes on their side are trumpeted. These include electoral victories such as the Crooks and Liars post announcing that a Democratic challenger was well ahead of the Republican incumbent in a Pennsylvania district, and Daily Kos's celebration of early election-night predictions of a victory by a Maryland Democratic primary candidate he supported. (The candidate actually lost.) They also illuminate the failures of the opposition, such as the Crooks and

Liars post that related a new poll showing that the number of Americans calling themselves Republicans had fallen over 5 percent in two years. Crooks
and Liars added, "If I were a Republican, I wouldn't want to admit it either."
Problems for the opposition, particularly scandals involving opposition political
figures, are particularly blogworthy.

The largest scandal to break during this period was the one involving Florida
representative Mark Foley, who resigned after news reports of salacious e-mails
he had sent to pages. The story hit blogs on both sides of the blogosphere,
although the response was different. Conservatives condemned Foley's actions
but considered them an aberration. Michelle Malkin wrote, "If it is all true, and
it seems very likely that it is, Rep. Foley has shamed himself, his office, his district, and his party." Liberals, however, focused on the role of the leadership and
viewed the scandal as part of a corrupt environment among Republicans.

There were other scandals as well. Crooks and Liars posted on Ohio
Republican congressman Bob Ney pleading guilty to bribery. Senator George
Allen of Virginia was a frequent target of liberal bloggers that month. Daily
Kos reported on a claim that, as a young man, Allen had stuffed a deer head in
the mailbox of an African American family; Allen's statements about Jews and
alleged links to a white supremacist group were also described.

Political bloggers have no qualms about covering personal foibles of politicians they oppose. Crooks and Liars posted a story in the *Sunday Times*
(London) about the sons of Senator Bill Frist. According to the blog, one
"recently appeared on the internet wearing six cans of beer strapped to his
belt," while the other wrote online, "Let's bomb some people." Another focused
on House Speaker Dennis Hastert's tortured singing of the national anthem.
Titled "Dennis Hastert, Please Don't Sing," the post said Hastert mangled the
words and sang out of key.

Particular noteworthy for blogs are unexpected statements or actions by an
opposing figure that actually support the blogger's own position. An example
is a Crooks and Liars post about unexpected criticism of the *Path to 9/11* program that Democrats opposed coming from two surprise sources: conservative
commentator Bill Bennett and Fox News anchor Chris Wallace. Also newsworthy are those who would be expected to support bloggers' positions but who
had become traitorous in the eyes of bloggers because they did not do so. The
main case involved Senator Joseph Lieberman, who continued to support the
Iraq war and the Bush administration while other prominent Democrats turned
against it. Lieberman received continual criticism from the liberal blogosphere
during this period because he had just become an Independent after losing to
Ned Lamont, a favorite of liberal bloggers.

Reinforcement also occurs through debates with opposition bloggers. Each side was quick to lambaste the other's posts. Michelle Malkin noted a response to one of her blog posts: "**My initial post** prompted much caterwauling from tone-deaf moonbat bloggers who accused me of hypocrisy for simply noting that the defendants' supporters had raised concerns about the fairness of the trial. Profanity-laced messages poured in: 'You *&^%$. How can you object to the Indonesians' case while supporting the indefinite detention of AP photographer Bilal Hussein in Iraq?'" The criticism goes beyond individual posts to whole blogs and even includes the other ideological blogosphere generally. For instance, Little Green Footballs reported a meeting between former president Clinton and liberal bloggers: "The most hateful, deranged creeps of the loony left blogosphere meet with President Bill Clinton in New York."

Although hyperlinks to other blogs are abundant in the blogosphere, some are reluctant to provide any connection to bloggers they disagree with. Michelle Malkin discussed a liberal blogger's post, but wouldn't help readers get there: "You'll have to find his site for yourself, alas. No link to it will ever stain this blog while I'm a part of it." Reinforcement also meant that those in support of bloggers' positions received gentle treatment. For example, Crooks and Liars described a Fox News television interview of Howard Dean: "He breezed through Chris Wallace's interview with clear, honest and realistic answers."

But sometimes even those ostensibly on the same side came in for criticism. Conservative bloggers were particularly distressed by actions of the Bush administration and the Republican Congress. Michelle Malkin criticized the Bush administration on immigration, saying that the administration opened the door to "tens of thousands of new Saudi student visa holders" and had virtually no enforcement of visa overstayers in the United States. She also criticized Senate Majority Leader Bill Frist for failing to attack the Democrats on the Mexican fence bill, calling his actions a "Frist fence flake-out." On the other side, Daily Kos was a frequent critic of his own party's members: "Democrats would rather talk about how they need to be strong, than actually be strong. They would rather talk about 'moral standing,' than actually, you know, stand for what's right." He also criticized New York Democrats for wanting the Democratic National Convention to be held in New York City despite the need for the party to reach out beyond the coasts.

Reinforcement also comes in the form of rhetoric used to label opponents derisively. Conservative bloggers use a variety of terms for their opponents. The netroots, the liberal bloggers' term for the progressive grassroots, becomes the "nutroots." Opponents of President George W. Bush suffer from "Bush Derangement Syndrome." Liberals are "moonbats" or "the unhinged left," and liberal bloggers are "left-wing blog dupes." Those who believe that 9/11 was a U.S. government conspiracy are termed "the Tinfoil Hat Brigade," "truthers," or "conspiracy monkeys." More specifically, bloggers on Daily Kos are called "the Kos Kidz." The labels are not always directed at the other side: Malkin termed some conservatives "the obsequious Right."

Individuals come in for specific derogatory handles. One liberal blogger from the Progressive Jewish Alliance was called a "useful idiot." Senator Edward Kennedy was titled "the Windbag from Massachusetts." The handles are equally colorful—and harsh—on the left. Conservatives are "wingers" or "wingnuts." Bush supporters are part of "the Cult of Bush." Eschaton called Senator Rick Santorum a "lying freak," and Representative Tom DeLay became, in Daily Kos's words, "the prince of darkness."

Interestingly, the overheated rhetoric quickly can be discarded when attention turns to actual policy action. In September 2006 Senator Trent Lott was a key decision maker on whether a bill Daily Kos supported would come to a vote on the floor of the Senate. Daily Kos urged readers to contact Lott and urge him to support a vote on the bill. But this caveat was added: "If you can help us bring polite pressure to bear on Sen. Lott's office, we can get something good done today. (But seriously? It has to be polite and respectful—if you cannot be professional in doing this, don't. It may backfire.)"

Another method of reinforcement is employing sources that bolster bloggers' positions and undermine those of the opposition. Linking to another source—a blog, a Web site, or a news media outlet—is routine among political bloggers. In fact, it is the atypical post that lacks a link. Ninety-one percent of posts included a link to some other source. That is a significant difference between influentials, who heavily link, and common bloggers, who usually do not.[8]

The most common type of link, at 51 percent, was to another blog. Twenty-nine percent were to a media source such as the *New York Times,* the *Washington Times,* or Yahoo News. Another 20 percent were to other Web sites such as those for government or interest groups or Wikipedia. Most of the sources in the blogosphere are other blogs, that is, bloggers linking to and repeating each other.

One link per post is most common among these influential blogs. Nearly half of those with a link (48 percent) had only one. The mean number of links per post was 2.5. The explanation for the higher mean is that some posts, particularly on blogs such as Wonkette and Daily Kos, were roundups of what other blogs were saying on various topics. In those cases a blog post could include half a dozen links. As indicated in the blog post described above, Michelle Malkin favored longer posts with multiple links.

Bloggers varied in their approach to links. For some, such as Little Green Footballs and Instapundit, a post was merely a reference to some other source, perhaps with a short comment. Each reference warranted a separate post. For example, 71 percent of Eschaton's posts and 64 percent of Instapundit's had only one link, while 58 percent of Wonkette's posts and 73 percent of Michelle Malkin's had three or more links in the post.

Links don't just provide news and commentary to the reader; they often do so in a manner designed to reinforce. That's why nearly all these blogs linked extensively to themselves. Table 4.3 shows how often bloggers linked to themselves. All but one of the blogs linked to itself far more than to any other blog. Only Eschaton never linked to his own blog. Leading the reader back to bloggers' own previous posts not only reinforced bloggers' views, but also advertised the blog itself.

Blog linking to reinforcing sources, however, differed across the two camps of the blogosphere. Not surprisingly, liberal blogs linked to other liberal blogs. For example, Crooks and Liars linked to Daily Kos, Eschaton, and Wonkette but had no links to Little Green Footballs, Michelle Malkin, or Instapundit. Eschaton similarly never linked to the conservatives. Daily Kos linked to one conservative blogger, Instapundit, and then only once. However, it linked to liberal blogs, including itself, 282 times.

Interestingly, the conservative bloggers linked to both liberal and conservative blogs, although the latter were preferred. Michelle Malkin still linked to fellow conservative blogger Little Green Footballs more than she did to any other blog, but she did link to Wonkette more than to Instapundit. Little Green Footballs linked to Daily Kos more than to Michelle Malkin.

Table 4.3   Blog Cross-Linking

	Crooks and Liars	Daily Kos	Eschaton	Instapundit	Little Green Footballs	Michelle Malkin	Wonkette
Crooks and Liars	188	14	32	0	0	0	3
Daily Kos	5	265	11	1	0	0	1
Eschaton	11	6	0	0	0	0	0
Instapundit	0	1	3	42	0	4	0
Little Green Footballs	0	11	0	0	116	7	0
Michelle Malkin	0	1	0	3	12	131	4
Wonkette	3	0	0	0	3	2	225

Note: "Cross-linking" refers to the number of links from a blog to itself or one of the other six blogs.

Selective use of sources was true in relation to linking to media sources, as well, particularly for the liberal blogosphere. Conservative bloggers relied more on the *National Review*, Fox News, or the *Washington Times* for source material. Liberals have their preferred sources: the *New York Times*, the *Washington Post*, the *International Herald Tribune*, BBC, CNN (particularly "The Situation Room"), and MSNBC (particularly talk show host Keith Olbermann). Olbermann had become so popular as a source for liberal bloggers that a Daily Kos blogger stated that he was not one who belonged to the "Olbermann is great" camp but then proceeded to share a clip of something Olbermann had said.

Looking at just the four major newspapers examined for this study, how did the two sets of ideological bloggers treat media sources as links in their posts? Not surprisingly, the liberal blogs, Crooks and Liars, Wonkette, Eschaton, and Daily Kos, cited the more liberal papers—the *New York Times* and the *Washington Post*—far more than the conservative papers. Out of 358 links to newspapers, only 8 percent were to the more conservative *Washington Times* or *Wall Street Journal*. But the conservative bloggers also cited the liberal papers far more than the conservative ones, although not to the extreme of the liberal blogs: 70 percent of their links were to the *New York Times* or the *Washington Post*. Even within the conservative blogosphere, the more liberal papers are favored elite media sources.

Some of the links were accompanied by criticism of the source. For example, Michelle Malkin provided a link to the *New York Times* but added that the paper "relied on anonymous, unnamed leaders to spin its contents and embarrass the White House." Little Green Footballs inserted a link to a *Washington Post* story but titled the post "Washington Post Daily 9/11 Whitewash Continues." Sometimes the blogger agrees with the other side's favored sources. For example, Michelle Malkin cited a *Washington Post* article by David Broder taking the press to task for inaccurately blaming Karl Rove for the Valerie Plame controversy. Most of the references were made without a negative comment. Even in the conservative blogosphere references appeared primarily as news. Bloggers typically just reported the story, perhaps commenting on the substance of it but not the source. On the left, however, the inclusion of links to the *Washington Times* or the *Wall Street Journal*—on the rare occasions they occurred—was designed to ridicule conservatives. For example, Daily Kos linked to the *Wall Street Journal* opinion page to highlight Senator Joe Lieberman's changing positions on Iraq policies. Similarly, Eschaton cited a story in the *Washington Times* about former House Speaker Newt Gingrich's shifting views on Iran.

Even though bloggers lean heavily on other blogs, they routinely fail to mention other blogs by name in their posts. Seventy percent failed to mention the name of any other blog. Michelle Malkin was a notable exception. A majority of her posts gave the name of the specific blog she was linking to, and she specifically promoted other bloggers' posts. The same was true of mention of specific traditional news media outlets. Even though nearly 40 percent of posts linked to a media source, bloggers were reluctant to use the name of the source or the media generally in the post. Seventy-nine percent failed to mention specific news media sites. Eschaton was the least likely to mention other media, with only 5 percent of the blog's posts doing so. Michelle Malkin, again, was the outlier on the other end; nearly half of her posts mentioned a specific reference to a traditional news media outlet. This tendency is curious. Perhaps mention would indicate how much bloggers were drawing on other sources, particularly the traditional news media. Perhaps the blogger feels specific mention is unnecessary because the reader who follows the link immediately will know the identity of the source.

Mobilizing

Often bloggers go beyond reinforcement and attempt to mobilize their readers to take action.[9] Antoinette Pole found that bloggers use posts to encourage readers to become politically engaged.[10] Bloggers studied here occasionally did the same. For example, on September 24, Michelle Malkin posted a story about the Arizona 9/11 memorial, which it called "the Arizona 9/11 memorial disgrace" and a "Blame America monument." The story included photographs of the memorial and then comments by Arizona governor Janet Napolitano praising the memorial. Also included were Napolitano's phone number, regular mail address, e-mail address, and fax number, as well as the e-mail address of the Arizona 9/11 memorial organization. Another petition drive was recommended by Crooks and Liars, which included a link to a Democratic National Committee's Web site, with a petition to call on ABC to drop the *Path to 9/11* program. The blog went a step further and suggested that readers contact the program's advertising sponsors: "As many commenters have pointed out, often the best way to get through to networks is through their sponsors. Do some research and post here some names for other C&Lers to contact. Let's let them hear from us."

Mobilization once even led to countermobilization. Liberal bloggers' potential action on the issue of the ABC program led to a countercampaign by the conservative bloggers. Little Green Footballs also mentioned the Democratic Party effort, but told readers they, too, should go to the Democratic Party Web site and use the form to "add comments supporting ABC's courage for tackling the issues head-on, and requesting that ABC ignore the complaints and run the movie unedited."

Mobilization goes beyond e-mailing or filling out Web forms. Michelle Malkin posted details of a "National Solidarity Rally" on September 20, including the time and the location, and urged readers, "Mark your calendars." Little Green Footballs posted a photograph of a man wanted by the FBI as a terrorism suspect. The blog told readers, "Be sure to contact [the FBI] if you think you've seen him."

The most avid mobilizer is Daily Kos. Moulitsas and his fellow bloggers continually urge readers to take various types of action, including raising money, contacting politicians, and tracking electoral races in the online diaries Kos publishes on its Web site. The blog seeks to motivate readers to take some kind of action to further the cause, typically through supporting Democratic candidates. For example, Moulitsas wrote that his readers could end the Iraq war by "honoring the personal sacrifices of our candidates and giving them all the help we can offer."

Summary

Blog content is not merely the stream-of-consciousness ramblings of basement denizens. Rather, blogs fall in different editorial categories. Bloggers' own commentary is one of those categories, but not necessarily the dominant one. Among the influentials, blog posts are purposeful in their roles. Blog posts serve several specific functions for bloggers and their audiences: they advertise, set the agenda, frame, reinforce, and mobilize.

But are bloggers the instigators of blog content, or are others—agenda seekers—discovering that blogs are another forum for influencing press, public, and policy maker agendas? Do they seek to shape the blog agenda? These questions are the topic of the next chapter.

5

Agenda Seekers

On April 6, 2008, Senator Barack Obama, Democratic presidential candidate, stood before an audience of potential donors in San Francisco and told the group that rural Pennsylvanians voting in a presidential primary later that month who had lost jobs in their small towns "get bitter, they cling to guns or religion or antipathy to people who aren't like them....as a way to explain their frustrations."[1] Because the fund-raiser was closed to the news media, Obama's statements did not appear in the press. But a blogger, who was an Obama supporter and had donated to him, was present and audio-recorded the candidate's speech. After four days of agonizing over whether to blog about the comments, she finally decided that her journalistic role trumped her supporter role. She posted the audio recording on The Huffington Post.[2] Immediately the comments became news. Senator Hillary Clinton used them to prove that her opponent was an elitist. Commentators and pundits weighed in to criticize or defend Obama. Even Republican nominee Senator John McCain, who had largely stayed out of the Democratic nomination battle, joined in the criticism of the Illinois senator by suggesting that Obama's remarks demonstrated he was out of touch with average Americans.[3]

But the McCain campaign quickly found itself in its own controversy thanks to another blogger on The Huffington Post. On April 14 the blogger revealed that a reader had been conducting Google searches for recipes and found that the McCain campaign had plagiarized recipes from the Food Network Web site. The campaign had placed seven recipes on the campaign Web site and billed them as "Cindy's Recipes," the favorites of Senator McCain's wife. However, the post showed that three of the recipes were from the Food Network and one was essentially a recipe by Rachael Ray. Embarrassed, the campaign quickly removed the recipes from the Web site and blamed an intern.[4]

In both cases, the press moved on. But for a brief moment, the campaign agenda had been temporarily changed, particularly in the case of the Obama statements. Whether the new agenda item would shift the electoral outcome was unknown. The odds were slim. But a highly noteworthy point was the fact that the instigator in both cases was a blogger, and other players had responded to that agenda shift.

These incidents show that, rather than operate as a separate entity distant from traditional agenda setters—various agenda seekers, the media, and the audience—bloggers have begun to intersect with them and become intertwined in other players' policy agendas. This chapter, and the two that follow, describe the interaction between blogs and each of these other players as all seek to set the agendas that govern campaigns, politics, and policy making in American politics.

Chapter 1 showed that other political players accept blogs' potential role in shaping agendas. The examples of blog influence discussed earlier have given new respect to bloggers. As a result, other players' agenda-shaping efforts have begun to include blogs as possible tools for setting the public agenda.

The interaction between agenda seekers and bloggers takes various forms. The crudest form is intimidation. Some politicians treat bloggers who offer critical content the same way they treat traditional media they do not like. And in the political blogosphere, no matter what side politicians are on, there are a lot of blogs not to like. This kind of interaction is rare. Two prominent cases involved governors. Governor Ernie Fletcher of Kentucky, infuriated by bloggers' criticisms of him, banned state employees' access to certain political blogs. The governor's office contended that employees were spending too much work time reading the blogs. However, access to blogs not critical of Fletcher remained available to state employees. Bloggers also pointed out that only blogs were singled out; newspapers and television stations also critical of Fletcher were still accessible.[5] Another incident was the reaction of Governor Matt Blunt of Missouri, who had Capitol police remove a blogger from a bill-signing ceremony after the blogger had broken news about scandals regarding the governor's brother and father.[6]

These incidents are uncommon and far overshadowed by efforts to woo and co-opt the blogosphere. Those efforts, along with many bloggers' willingness to engage other political players, have led to the interactive nature of the relationship between the political blogosphere and other agenda seekers. Rather than remain a separate fringe force, the political blogosphere has become integrated into political life. In fact, the blogosphere has moved so deeply into the mainstream that affecting blog content has become a component of public relations strategies. Internet consultants monitor blogs for businesses, and some public relations firms now advise clients on the most popular blogs and how to reach them.[7]

Co-opting bloggers is a process that occurs because agenda seekers view bloggers as playing one or both of two roles. One role is as a consultant to political players. The other is that of a journalist who is to be cultivated. Let's review both in turn.

The consultant job has transformed the financial status of bloggers. Blogging is not a lucrative occupation, and many bloggers are willing to sign on with politicians, particularly in electoral campaigns, to supplement their income as well as their status. Bloggers work as consultants for parties and candidates, blog for candidates, or advise the campaign on outreach to the online community.[8] During the 2006 Virginia U.S. Senate race, for example, bloggers were paid by both Senator George Allen and his Democratic challenger, Jim Webb. One blogger was paid $100,000 for three months of consulting work. In 2008 bloggers joined presidential campaigns for major presidential candidates such as Barack Obama, Hillary Clinton, John McCain, and Mitt Romney.[9]

Attracting bloggers to the campaign (and away from another's campaign) has become part of a campaign's staffing strategy. Like a campaign manager or a press secretary, a blogger has become an essential appointment for presidential campaigns. While organizing a staff for a potential presidential bid, former Virginia governor Mark Warner hired a well-known political blogger as one of his first staff appointments.[10] Like other staffers, bloggers themselves even seek positions with campaigns. At the beginning of the 2008 campaign, one blogger said she would be interested in job offers from presidential candidates.[11] That example speaks to another effect of the mainstreaming of bloggers. That is, bloggers' need to demonstrate proximity to politicians in order to increase legitimacy and blog audience appeal. For example, one blogger who was credentialed to cover the Democratic National Convention in 2004 said that, during his coverage, his page views jumped sixfold, to up to 40,000 per day.[12]

The consulting role moves beyond the campaign itself. As consultants, the most popular bloggers are now courted by national political leaders. Speaking of the political blogs, Senator Harry Reid admitted, "I pay as much attention as I can. I think it's a voice I need to listen to. I listen."[13] Politicians take bloggers to dinner and meet privately with them to talk about politics and the blogosphere. Senator Barack Obama said, "If you take these blogs seriously, they'll take you seriously."[14] Conversely, as two political scientists concluded, "The politician who takes them for granted will find himself standing alone."[15]

Aware of the audiences bloggers have, and the eagerness of bloggers to express their opinions, political leaders have viewed bloggers as a force to be reckoned with in communication strategies. Failure to engage bloggers may lead to blog rhetoric against the politician. That possibility could be harmful to a presidential candidate seeking a nomination in a process dominated in early stages by the kinds of activists who are likely to read political blogs.

The consultant role becomes particularly important when a new appointment or policy is announced or being defended. For example, the Republican National Committee held a series of meetings with bloggers to maintain blog support of the Samuel Alito nomination during contentious Senate confirmation hearings. The meetings featured White House officials, including Karl Rove, and senators courting bloggers in order to avoid the fiasco with Harriet Miers.[16]

The other role is blogger as journalist. Similar to efforts directed at traditional media and talk radio, various agenda seekers orchestrate outreach efforts specifically to bloggers as disseminators of information to niches of political activists and partisans. Like journalists, bloggers are given exclusive face time with politicians. The Heritage Foundation hosts a weekly briefing specifically for conservative bloggers, which has become an opportunity for Republican politicians and conservative journalists to interact with conservative bloggers.[17] Members of Congress have given interviews to bloggers, including granting them space on Capitol Hill to cover Congress.[18] The Democratic National Committee set up an Internet department to get the DNC's message out via the blogs.[19]

Bloggers also get press status at events normally reserved for journalists. In 2004 thirty-six bloggers were credentialed as press to cover the Democratic National Convention, and fifteen did so at the Republican National Convention.[20] Increasingly bloggers are being included in press conferences held by politicians. Like print and broadcast journalists, they receive press notices and invitations, and they attend briefings by official spokespersons along with traditional media. Some politicians even give bloggers special press status. The White House has convened exclusive conference calls for conservative bloggers, as have presidential candidates, political parties, and members of Congress. Even governors and mayors have joined in with conference calls and special press conferences.[21]

This attention to bloggers is not without certain expectations of reciprocity. One blogger who met in a blogger conference with a governor admitted that bloggers "will provide cover [for the governor] during the looming special legislative session."[22] This expectation has led to criticism that bloggers have become too cozy, too quick to become shills for politicians because they have received sudden attention. One liberal blogger who was invited to a two-hour session with former president Bill Clinton told his readers the experience was "heady" and "one I will always appreciate and remember."[23] Another, who joined in via phone, related, that "Clinton was very funny and insightful on a host of topics which made the call sail along. He said he understands blogging is important to the political process now and will continue a dialogue with us."[24]

Another indication of mainstreaming is the entrance of bloggers into the realm of lobbying. Bloggers formed a group called the Online Coalition, focused on legislation related to bloggers' role in campaign finance. The initial issue of the group was blog exemption from Federal Election Commission (FEC) regulations similar to the status given traditional media.[25] Several prominent bloggers representing both ideological blogospheres, such as Markos Moulitsas, Jerome Armstrong, Michelle Malkin, and Michael Krempasky (RedState.org) signed a letter to the Commission contending that bloggers, like media, should be exempt from campaign finance laws.[26] Bloggers lobbied on behalf of a bill to codify that exemption.[27] However, when the FEC granted the exemption in 2006, the need for legislation was moot. The exemption placed blogs firmly in the same category as traditional media in terms of campaign finance laws.[28]

Another lobbying group is the Media Press Association, which has lobbied to equate bloggers with journalists. The organization was formed in 2004 to help bloggers obtain the same political and legal status accorded journalists. The MPA has sought to include bloggers under the protections accorded journalists, such as shield laws.[29]

Becoming Bloggers

Another way for agenda seekers to interact with the blogosphere is to become an actual blogger. The possibilities seem promising. The entrance fee for blogging is minimal, and the audience is in flux and may be attracted to a new blog. Moreover, because both the traditional media and bloggers can be uncooperative in acting as a public relations medium for political players, one's own blog becomes attractive as a bypass mechanism to the filter of traditional media and the established political blogs. The political player, not journalists or other bloggers, controls the message without concern for media or blog neglect or distortion.

All of that sounds enticing. However, the reality is something less than the promise. Creating a blog is not the same as initiating communication. The difficulty for players in placing their own entrants in the blogosphere is attracting an audience. Other factors—name recognition of the blog author, media coverage of the blog author and the blog, the power held by that individual, the monopoly of information provided by the blog, and the demand for information from the blog's author—have far more impact on audience size than mere creation of a blog. That is why Barack Obama's blog gained an audience in 2008 while many other candidates' blogs did not.

Because the blogosphere is still new and growing, with allegiances potentially shifting, a new blog, even one operated by a politician or a journalist, may achieve a wide audience. There is precedent: the Dean for America blog, which began as a shoestring operation of an unknown governor from Vermont, became one of the best-known political blogs in 2004. Presidential nominee blogs do well. In 2004 the blogs of Senator Kerry and President Bush were ranked twenty-second and fiftieth, respectively, among the top one hundred political blogs.[30] Arianna Huffington, an erstwhile candidate for governor of California in 2003 and a political commentator, took her new blog from a readership of tens of thousands at its commencement in 2005 to one of the best-read political blogs only two years later.[31] These examples give hope that either existing blog audiences are not wedded to particular blogs or the growth in the overall blog audience provides opportunities for new bloggers to tap into a potentially large readership.

Public notice of the phenomenon, the importance of the niche political audience, and the ability to control content have combined to make blogging appealing to many political players who had not even heard of blogs a few years earlier. Traditional media organizations, groups, and even politicians have become bloggers on their own blogs in order to communicate directly to a blog audience. Let's take a look at who is blogging.

Journalist Blogs

One group that has rapidly embraced blogging is the journalistic community. This includes both individual journalists and media organizations. The first journalist to blog on his newspaper's Web site was Dan Gilmor, a reporter and columnist for the San Jose *Mercury News*.[32] Gilmor subsequently has been joined by more famous media personalities, such as Katie Couric, Brian Williams, and Anderson Cooper. Williams sometimes writes several times a day.[33] Talk show hosts such as Bill O'Reilly (Fox News), Bob Harris, (Air America), and Hugh Hewitt (Salem Radio Network) also host their own blogs.

In addition, media organizations—newspapers, television and radio stations, and newsmagazines—sponsor their own blogs. These include elite newspapers such as the *New York Times*, the *Washington Post*, the *Wall Street Journal*, and the *Christian Science Monitor*. The newsmagazines *Time*, *U.S. News*, and

Newsweek, as well as specialized publications such as *Business Week, Barrons,* and *PC World,* have incorporated blogs into their online editions. Quite naturally, opinion magazines have become forums for blogs as well; the *Atlantic,* the *New Republic,* and the *National Review* carry well-known bloggers such as Andrew Sullivan and David Frum. ABC, CBS, NBC, CNN, and Fox have joined the blogosphere with their organization blogs. Local broadcast stations also have created blogs. For example, KING-TV in Seattle runs a blog featuring news from the area.[34] News organizations see the possibility of blogs helping them expand their audience. Journalist blogs may be able to reach an audience of young people who have not become print readers. According to a *Los Angeles Times* executive, the blog can "engage a whole new set of readers out there."[35] This may help newspapers stanch the flow of readers to other media forms.

Despite the imagery of the blog as an independent entity, blogs increasingly have become arms of existing organizations. These include corporations, interest groups, candidates, and even government. In these cases, unlike independent blogs, "the 'cost' of expression is subsidized" by some other entity.[36]

The integration of blogs and journalism has created a revolving door, so that a blogger-journalist can move from one medium to another, or even do both simultaneously.[37] Popular bloggers have joined with existing traditional media sites to create new forums for their blogs. *Time* magazine hired bloggers Andrew Sullivan and Ana Marie Cox.[38] Cox went on to become the Washington editor for the magazine. Glenn Reynolds blogged for MSNBC for four years and then moved to *Popular Mechanics.*[39] Mickey Kaus, who wrote for *Newsweek* and the *New Republic,* formed his own blog; then he moved the blog, Kausfiles, to *Slate.*[40] In 2004 Kevin Drum, a political blogger with his own blog, Calpundit, started a new blog, Political Animal, for *Washington Monthly.*[41]

Interest Groups

Another emerging type of blogger is the interest group. Groups are not blogging as readily as journalists. The vast majority have adopted a wait-and-see approach to blogs. But blogs are on the radar of groups. The National Association of Manufacturers runs the blog Shopfloor, authored by a senior vice president at the trade association, and the association seeks to use the blog for policy activism.[42] Cisco Systems started its own blog in February 2005 in order to communicate its views to policy makers.[43] Other groups, such as the U.S. Chamber of Commerce and the National Federation of Independent Businesses, are working with conservative bloggers to figure out the best use of the blogosphere to further their agendas.[44]

Corporations are using blog strategies to deal with a new world where the blogosphere can challenge corporate images of products. Blogs about products or companies provide independent assessments that potential customers can use to determine whether to buy the company's products or services. Blogs also make it difficult for business because bloggers are sometimes anonymous individuals. They seem to come out of nowhere, yet they can do serious damage to a company. A classic example is the case of the easily picked bicycle lock. Someone posted on a blog for bicycle enthusiasts that a bicycle lock manufactured by Kryptonite could easily be picked with a ballpoint pen. Other blogs spread the word. At first the company responded that their lock still worked to deter theft, but when the *New York Times* and the Associated Press picked up the story, the company was deluged with complaints, particularly when one person posted a video showing the procedure on a blog.[45]

Corporate public relations staff now monitor blogs regularly to spot problems before they become widespread.[46] Public relations firms suggest that companies use these blogs rather than fight or ignore them. In a more positive vein, blogs offer companies insights on public reaction to them without the cost of a focus group.[47] In response, companies are beginning to use blogs as vehicles for promoting products. Wal-Mart, Sun Company, IBM, and Wells Fargo are a few of the well-known companies operating their own blogs.[48] According to Blogpulse, approximately 30 percent of blogs are spam blog sites that are created to get products listed as keywords in search engines.[49]

Political use of blogs is a different matter. Corporations typically pursue direct lobbying rather than grassroots strategies where blogs might be useful. Trade and professional associations, with their array of individual members, can use blogs to highlight news of interest to individuals or businesses who hold membership. For example, the National Association of Manufacturers uses the association's blog to inform members about manufacturing and business news.

Corporations and associations aren't the only blog users. Some labor union sites now feature blogs. The AFL-CIO, AFSCME, the American Federation of Government Employees, and the American Federation of Teachers all include blogs on their Web sites. Noneconomic groups such as the National Rifle Association, Common Cause, and the World Wildlife Fund also have become bloggers. Nor is lobbying the sole objective of interest group blogs. Some interest groups are using blogs to recruit new members. The Center for American

Progress, a liberal think tank, advertised on various blogs and ended up getting contact information from 10,000 activists who wanted to help the group on energy legislation.[50]

Whether blogs will become an important tool for groups is a still unanswered question. At this point in time, such uncertainty actually helps promote blogging. One corporate blogger admitted that blogging was not "game-changing....But you won't know what will be a game-changing event necessarily. That is why you just have to keep doing it."[51]

Candidates

Perhaps the most visible new bloggers are candidates for elective office. Campaigns ranging from president to city council have incorporated blogs into Web strategies. Blogs clearly have moved beyond the presidential level. Candidate blogs emerged in 2004, but they proliferated in the 2006 and 2008 campaigns across national, state, and local campaigns.

Candidates use blogs to humanize themselves and appear accessible to interaction with voters, and they attempt to convey the impression that blogging is a natural activity for them. Spouses have even joined in. In 2004, John Kerry noted that his wife "blogs passionately, and I follow blogs, too."[52] In both the 2004 and 2008 presidential campaigns, Elizabeth Edwards blogged on her husband's campaign blog, offering her perspective on the activities of the campaign. During the 2008 campaign, Michelle Obama contributed to a blog for women.[53]

Beyond the role of self-presentation, candidate blogs have other uses. One is to distinguish the candidates from their opponents. Since the political blogosphere often features attacks on various figures, from George W. Bush to Nancy Pelosi to Don Imus, it should be no surprise that candidate blogs become forums for attacking opponents. One study of 2004 presidential candidate blogs found that half of blog posts attacked the opponent.[54]

Like blogs generally, candidate blogs are a reinforcement mechanism. Perhaps even more than the rest of the Web content, blogs are havens for those who support the candidate and want to express that support and bolster others. Reading blogs becomes a mechanism for reinforcing and increasing commitment to the candidate.

Another function for these blogs is as a potential mobilizer of the politically interested. This role clearly separates campaign blogs from other blogs. Due to the partisan nature of candidate blogs, coupled with explicit appeals to action, blogs are designed to activate readers. Matthew Kerbel and Joel David Bloom concluded that political blogs act as a mobilization mechanism in a way that does not exist in traditional media.[55]

Even though blogs constitute a new and popular portion of an Internet strategy, it is not the most popular part of a candidate's Web site. The Kerry campaign recorded that only 10 percent of site visitors went to the blog. However, blog reading helps the campaign by keeping site visitors there longer.[56]

One deterrent to the expansion of blogs across campaigns below the national level, particularly at the local level, is the lack of resources. Blog maintenance requires time. That time must be taken by the candidate, the campaign staff, or both. Presidential and statewide campaigns usually possess the resources for staff to write on the candidate's behalf and provide a steady stream of content for the blog. Candidates at lower levels, however, lack those resources. Not surprisingly, campaigns typically rehash material that is used in other ways. For example, candidate blogs often are dominated by press releases or announcements of events.[57]

The best-known candidate blog was the Dean for America blog established by the Howard Dean campaign in the 2004 presidential election.[58] The blog was started by Matthew Gross, a writer for the liberal political blog MyDD, which became instrumental in the creation of the campaign blog. While reading MyDD, Joe Trippi, a political consultant, discovered that Howard Dean was considering running for president.[59] However, Trippi didn't create a Dean blog until Gross tried to get a job on the Dean campaign. While the campaign's security force was about to haul Gross away, he yelled in the direction of Trippi's office, "I write for MyDD." Trippi heard the cry and yelled back, "You're hired."[60]

The Dean campaign staff spent a lot of time writing on the blog. Nearly all of the posts were original contributions by the campaign's Internet team. By the Iowa caucus, the number of posts by staff per month was 450.[61]

Not only was the existence of the blog novel, but so was the campaign's claim that the blog was an integral part of the Dean candidacy. The Dean campaign announced that the Dean for America blog community was an extension of the campaign effort, particularly in terms of mobilization. Trippi, Dean's campaign manager, wrote on the blog that its purpose was to "let people know when, where, and how you can help."[62]

The Dean for America blog became the first candidate blog to attract widespread attention and a relatively large readership. As a vehicle for input from average supporters, it was viewed as a model for public participation in the operation of a presidential campaign. Trippi called the campaign's use of the blog for decision making "open-source campaigning."[63] However, as mentioned earlier, the emphasis was more on the illusion of interactivity rather than its reality. The blog became much less a forum for deliberative discourse than a means for facilitating grassroots activity in support of the campaign. Despite the image of the Dean campaign blog as an open forum, the campaign required user registration to post comments and then screened out those who expressed dissenting views.[64]

For the most part, though, the Dean campaign became an actual rather than a rhetorical model for future campaigns. Subsequent candidates clearly employed the rhetoric of public engagement. But, like the Dean campaign, the medium of the campaign blog became a vehicle for enacting the campaign's goals rather than a medium for the public to affect the campaign's direction.

The fact that a campaign, including a presidential campaign, uses blogs does not mean that candidates and campaign operatives view blogs as critical to the campaign outcome.[65] Blogs still occupy a small niche in campaign communication. Even that niche has not proven to be meaningful in furthering the goal of winning elections.

Officeholders

Another indication that the political blogosphere has moved from fringe activity to the political mainstream is the adoption of the medium by public officials. Cabinet officials, members of Congress, governors, mayors, and others have started their own blogs. Why? Blogging offers an opportunity to bypass traditional media and deliver an unfiltered message. Again, creating a blog is not really costly because communications staff can simply add blog maintenance to their list of tasks.

Still another reason public officials have begun blogging is the increased expectation that politicians will acknowledge, respect, and even join the blogosphere. By doing so, the public official shows he or she is responsive to the niche of politically interested individuals who blog or read political blogs. As more politicians blog, the pressure grows for others to participate as well. One incumbent admitted that he participated in a blog debate because he didn't want to be labeled "technologically backward, a Luddite, a Neanderthal."[66] Although readership likely is small for blogs started by public officials, particularly compared with the audiences for the most popular political blogs, the appearance of blogging satisfies this niche of constituents who judge politicians on their extent of connection to the voters' own interests.

The blogosphere now is populated by politicians who have established their own blogs and update them regularly. These include members of Congress;

in fact, some congressional leaders have even started blogs. While he was Speaker of the House, Dennis Hastert (R-Illinois) had a blog in 2006 and, within six months, was attracting 50,000 hits a month.[67] Senator Harry Reid (D-Nevada) also started a blog in 2006 and uses it to support Democratic Senate candidates.

Members who are not leaders also blog. For example, Senator Thomas Carper (D-Delaware) blogs about his life as a senator, as well as more personal aspects of his life. An example of one post:

> **January 28, 2007—Wilmington, DE:** It isn't every day that a guy turns 60, but that's exactly what happened to me last Tuesday. As I rode the train from Wilmington to Washington, D.C., on the Monday morning before my birthday, I perused my schedule for the week ahead and mused to myself that it had the makings to be one of my most interesting weeks in the Senate to date. Looking back, that's exactly what it turned out to be.

Other blogs are primarily business-oriented rather than personal. Members of Congress relate their legislative activities—meetings, conferences, meetings with constituents, speeches, and floor debates. A blog post by Representative Phil Gingrey (R-Georgia) on his previous evening's activities is an example:

> Last night, I conducted a telephone townhall meeting with citizens in Cobb County. It was a lively discussion that lasted about 90 minutes. Some of the topics raised were: the **economy**, the **war in Iraq** and our greater **War on Terror**, reimbursement rates for the disabled, **veteran** healthcare, **immigration** and border security, the **Fair Tax**, violence on TV and **traditional values**. I greatly enjoy these tele-townhall meetings, because they're a wonderful way for me to talk with the folks back home when I'm in Washington. So far this year, I've placed calls to citizens in Paulding, Gordon, Cobb, Haralson, Polk, Chattooga, Floyd, Bartow and Carroll counties.

David Mayhew has identified three primary functions of constituent communication: credit claiming, advertising, and position taking.[68] Members of Congress use various media forms to carry out these functions. Like speeches in morning business, press releases, and newspaper columns, blogs are another venue for carrying out these functions.[69]

One example is credit taking for legislative work. One study of congressional blogging found that nearly every member who blogged used posts to claim credit for legislative activity.[70] This includes touting sponsorship of bills, membership on certain committees, and specific issues they work on. Senator Charles Grassley (R-Iowa) told his constituents, "As a steward of taxpayer dollars in the U.S. Senate, I work to bring accountability, transparency and integrity to the process when government workers are carrying out the people's business."

His colleague, Senator Tom Harkin (D-Iowa), wrote on his blog that he had recently "introduced legislation to address one of the most important issues facing American workers today: the rapid erosion of the traditional pension plan." Representative Ileana Ros-Lehtinen (R-Florida) was even more specific about the bills she had cosponsored: "Breast Cancer is a disease that affects hundreds of thousands of families each year....I have worked with my colleagues in Congress and....[am] a cosponsor of several pieces of legislation such as the Breast Cancer Patient Protection Act, Breast Cancer and Environmental Research Act, Mammogram and MRI Availability Act, and several other bills that will further our ability to detect and defeat breast cancer."

Another is advertising the district and the accomplishments of particular constituents. Representative Lois Capps (D-California) wrote in one post, "Yesterday, Monday June 18, 2007, I had the distinct privilege of welcoming the University of California Santa Barbara's Men's Soccer Team to Washington, D.C., in **celebration** of its historic National Championship season. As most of you probably already know, last year UCSB's Men's Soccer Team had a phenomenal season, culminating in a win against rival UCLA in the championship game to claim only the second Division I Title in the school's history."

Another, and perhaps the most common, use of blogs is position taking.[71] Blog posts communicate to constituents that the member shares the constituents' positions on issues of importance. Senator John Kerry (D-Massachusetts) blogged about the lack of adequate care provided for veterans in rural communities: "The rural veterans' care system has not been going the extra mile to care for young veterans who return to the same communities the government once visited to recruit them. It's time we fund our veterans' care system so that it can reach out to soldiers living all over our country—a promise should be a promise no matter where a soldier calls home."

Some members also readily adopt the partisanship of the blogosphere by using the forum to attack opponents. Representative John Campbell (R-California) posted on a Saturday to complain about the Democratic leadership: "I won't bore you with the circumstances that led to this weekend's legislative endeavor, I am sure you have heard or read about the mess the Democratic leadership has created over the past two days, but know that even on a weekend your pocketbooks & wallets are not safe from the tax & spenders in Congress."

Members of Congress attempt to get influential blogs to pay attention to their own blog. For example, Little Green Footballs posted a notice of a blog established by Senator Bill Frist, the Senate majority leader, called Blogging for Bolton. The site was designed to enlist the efforts of bloggers to support the confirmation of John Bolton as United Nations ambassador.

Members of Congress also occasionally write for top political blogs, although such blogging likely is just the work of staff. For example, Senator John Kerry blogged on Daily Kos to drum up support for a filibuster of the Supreme Court nomination of Samuel Alito, House Speaker Nancy Pelosi and Representatives John Conyers and Jack Murtha have blogged on The Huffington Post, and Senator Russell Feingold (D-Wisconsin) blogged on Talking Points Memo.[72] Such blogging efforts likely come about because of encouragement by younger staff members who are regular blog readers, follow the blogs for their bosses, and encourage them to participate.[73]

The fact that more members of Congress aren't blogging suggests they see both pros and cons to this communication mode. One of the pros is the ability to project humanness and intimacy. Much like television in an earlier era, the first impression of blogging is that it strips away façades and allows the individual to communicate directly and personally with others. Blog readers can see members as human beings and move beyond structured communication. Blogging also is attractive due to the illusion of interactivity. Recipients of those communications—the member's constituents—can believe they are getting a closer view than that available in the formal press announcement. According to Michael Cornfield, "Constituents want to engage members in conversation. They don't want to read the latest press release, let alone download it on the iPod."[74]

But that "conversation" is precisely the problem. A blog by a controversial politician can become an open invitation for those on the other side to appropriate the forum for their own ends. According to John Hinderaker, cofounder of the blog Power Line, the online activists from one side will take advantage of the opportunity to comment: "What would happen is, Daily Kos will put up something saying, 'Denny Hastert has a blog. Let's go tell him what we think.' "[75] Another drawback is that the conversation takes time, and time is not a commodity members of Congress have. The expenditure of time must provide a significant payoff to the member. If members perceived that a significant minority of their constituents read the members' blogs, then the time spent would be highly worthwhile. Members could use the forum to bypass traditional media filters and directly communicate to constituents.

On the other hand, those who blog may simply view the audience, however small, as one worth communicating with (or even merely showing that the member is technologically savvy) providing there is a limited time investment. The member's time can be protected by relying on only occasional direct member posts or using staff to blog in the member's name.[76] One member of Congress admitted that he wrote less than 15 percent of the content on his blog. Another said he puts notes on his BlackBerry and his aides use those to write blog posts.[77]

The politician who is most closely associated with blogs is Howard Dean. Although his campaign became known as the pioneer of campaign blogging, as a presidential candidate it is likely he himself never blogged. In fact, in his last campaign for governor of Vermont in 2000, Dean was virtually alone as a gubernatorial candidate who did not even put up a Web site.[78]

Other bloggers decry blogging that is not personal. "Too often, what we see is, 'Oh, I'll just get one of my staffers to write something and send it to Huffington Post,'" writes Jerome Armstrong. "It's not like we can't see through that."[79] But members, and other politicians, can absorb that criticism and still convey the impression of interactivity and proximity to the constituent.

Another protection for members in navigating the blog world is the set of congressional rules on blogging. For example, congressional rules forbid instant comments, a policy which limits the kind of interaction blogging aficionados crave. The individual can write a comment, but it will not appear without action by a staff member. That rule allows the staff to decide whether to post the comment, reply privately, or ignore it.[80] Because it is a congressional rule and not one set specifically by the member, it allows the member's staff to maintain control over blog content without having to take the heat from the blogging community for doing so.

State and local officials also blog. An early blogger was state representative Ray Cox of Minnesota, who created a blog in December 2002 to help him communicate with constituents.[81] Some other state and local politicians have started their own blogs. Jerry Brown wrote a blog while he was mayor of Oakland, California.[82]

The reasons for blogging vary. One is to bypass the press. A San Francisco city supervisor admitted that he started a blog because he was getting negative press coverage and wanted to counter it: "The Internet is a way to get my message out to people who are wired."[83] Another used his blog to respond to a comment made by a fellow legislator on the floor of the state legislature.[84] Still another saw his blog as adherence to a democratic notion that the public official ought to be transparent in his or her own views. A Utah state legislator who started a blog in 2004 offered this reasoning: "[I want] to lay out my thinking in great detail and invite voters to inspect it and elect me if they like it or throw me to the curb if they don't." But the legislator represented a safe district and his blog writings were unlikely to affect his electoral standing.[85]

Other legislators may have a more difficult time. Blog content can be used against an officeholder in the next election. One British MP blogger has been criticized repeatedly for her blog comments.[86] It would seem that members of Congress with safe seats are more likely to blog than those in marginal districts.[87] This may be due to the relative safety members of Congress feel in making statements on blogs when there is little chance they will be used against them.

Overall, blogs by officeholders have not caught on as much as might be assumed. Nor is this reticence unique to the United States. Only 30 of 650 members of the British parliament have blogs.[88] Even though blogs are inexpensive to establish and apparently offer an unfiltered opportunity to speak to constituents, the potential drawbacks hold off many public officials who might otherwise blog.

Government Agencies

Even government agencies have created blogs. By December 2007 federal agencies ran sixteen blogs.[89] The State Department sponsors its own blog, which it advertises as "an alternative source to mainstream media."[90] The National Agricultural Library in the Agriculture Department has a blog about farm news, and the Peace Corps blog features blog posts by current volunteers.[91] State and local governments have joined in. For example, the Rhode Island State Council on the Arts Web site includes a blog, as do the Montgomery County Division of Solid Waste Service and the Agribusiness Collaborative of the Mid-Region Council of Governments of New Mexico.[92]

Agency blogs may ostensibly be the work of the agency head, but the actual writing may be the work of others. For example, the consumer blog of the Missouri attorney general's office has the attorney general's name at the top of the blog, but posts are submitted by staff.[93] The blogs are written in a conversational style designed to attract people who read blogs, but they still serve the purposes of providing citizen information, particularly consumer-related information, and promoting the agency's mission. Like other blogs, the dilemma is how to use the blog to serve the agency's purpose while conforming to the expectations of readers of blogs.[94]

Integrating Blogs and Politics

Mainstreaming of blogs into traditional politics is not a surprise to some bloggers. In fact, it may even be a goal. In 2006 Markos Moulitsas predicted, "By 2008, the blogs are going to be so institutionalized, it's not going to be funny."[95]

Moulitsas even argued that bloggers already were mainstream in a sense. He urged other bloggers not to use the term "mainstream media": "We are representatives of the mainstream, and the country is embracing what we're selling."[96]

The Daily Kos founder was predicting that bloggers would take their place as powerful players in their own right within the mix of existing political actors. The implication of blog mainstreaming was that existing political players would be adapting to the blog world—admittedly for their own purposes—but still with the result of significant changes to the world of politics. How much blogging itself would change, however, was left unsaid.

Indeed, mainstreaming has not been as simple as getting interest groups, politicians, and candidates to take blogs seriously. The integration of blogs into political life has carried its own set of problems for bloggers. Adjusting to mainstream status has not been easy for those who once saw themselves as inhabiting a new world unfettered by the traditional rules of politics or past expectations of behavior. Bloggers saw their world—the blogosphere—as an escape from social mores governing politics. They could be honest and open. They didn't have to curry favor or cater to certain constituencies. They believed they were the voice of common, ordinary people expressing their will about politics. One blogger suggested that blogging worked best as an independent endeavor: "The best political blogs thrive on a discourse built in opposition to the mainstream; people gather to commune in ways not permitted by media and political gatekeepers."[97]

Nor did they have to express that public will in politically correct terms. The form of expression was as important as its substance. In fact, if bloggers expressed themselves bluntly, even crudely sometimes, so much the better for facilitating free expression and puncturing the carefully crafted false images created by politicians. One scholar, noting that the Internet is in only in its second decade of existence (and blogs in their first), compared the medium to a teenager. He called the Internet, including blogs, "brash, uninhibited, unruly, fearless, experimental, and often not mindful of the consequences of its behavior."[98]

For traditional political players, that seeming abandonment of social rules was a serious deterrent. A sore point for those dealing with the blogosphere was its apparent lack of civility.[99] Whereas traditional politics and journalism seek to avoid offending voter and audience segments, blogs appear to thrive on it. Ad hominem attacks are common; the opposing viewpoint is not just wrong, it is bad or evil. One female blogger asked, "Is the price of expressing myself on Iraq [that I get] e-mails describing how I should be raped and burned?"[100]

Related to civility is the use of profanity. On broadcast media profanity is regulated by the Federal Communications Commission, and most daily general consumer newspapers avoid profanity to avoid offending readers, but such language is ubiquitous in the blogosphere. The blogosphere may encourage people to say things online they would not say face to face. Ana Marie Cox described Wonkette this way: "[It's] like me after a few margaritas."[101]

But acceptance of bloggers by the larger political world requires adherence to standards of civility. Bloggers face the choice of holding to the "anything goes" culture of the blogosphere or incorporating standards of civility in order to become accepted as a mainstream player. For many bloggers the choice is easy: they prefer to remain on the fringe. However, for those who receive a taste of social acceptance, such status will be alluring enough to affect how they conduct themselves online.

Mainstreaming has required bloggers to adapt to that same political process many bloggers promised to hold at bay. To gain legitimacy, bloggers have agreed to become consultants to politicians, hold campaign staff posts, and serve as information gatherers and disseminators for those who pay them. Gone by the wayside is the Wild West nature of the blogosphere.

Bloggers who have become more mainstream face criticism from those who hold the ideal of the blogosphere as something different, something revolutionary. One telling example is the case of a blogger who hired a press secretary. Other bloggers quickly criticized the move, arguing that a populist medium wouldn't use a press contact because ordinary people didn't have them.[102] Yet press secretaries are ubiquitous for political players who seek to get the press's attention. Press agents will be more common, not less, as bloggers realize that the rules of attention getting have not changed for them.

Another aspect of accommodation is the acceptance of business realities. In order for a blog to be sustained, it needs money. Because that revenue has not come in the form of a subscription charge, such as print media use (although that is not impossible), bloggers have relied on two sources of income: advertising and donations from readers. Of the two, donations are by far the less effective. Some bloggers have raised money via donations, but the vast majority of readers, like public television viewers, are reluctant to pay for what they can get for free. By contrast, advertising, or the commercialization of blogging, accelerates mainstreaming. Bloggers become dependent on the revenue source from candidates, groups, and corporations. They are aware of this prospect, and some seek to delay it. Joshua Marshall of Talking Points Memo has established new blogs by asking for small donations from readers. "I prefer that for a lot of reasons, not the least of which is I'm not beholden to really anybody."[103] Using advertising to support blogs follows the model of traditional broadcast media, but it also helps undermine the countercultural nature of blogging.[104] Bloggers may well become so dependent on advertising that it affects their content. That is what will happen to the A-list blogs as they face the dilemma between saying what they wish to say and acquiring or maintaining a lucrative revenue source.

The financial ties are steadily increasing. Candidates are gravitating toward blog advertising; major presidential candidates advertised in the 2008 campaign. Typically, Republicans were on conservative blogs such as Captain's Quarters and Townhall.com, while Democrats frequented liberal blogs such as Daily Kos. Hillary Clinton violated the separate spheres of the blogosphere and advertised on conservative blogs as well.[105] Political blogs receive advertising from candidates and groups that agree with the blog's tone, but controversial blogs may be detrimental for candidates who become associated with that blog in the eyes of the news media as well as potential supporters.

Another largely untapped source is corporate advertising. Corporations may be wary of the content of political blogs, but it will be difficult to match blogs' ready access to large numbers of specialized consumers. Daily Kos, for example, is a site where advertisers know they're reaching partisan Democrats.[106] Aside from being politically interested individuals, readers are probably middle- or upper-class consumers. And the cost of advertising on blogs is minuscule compared to other media. For example, in 2008 Wonkette charged $4 for every 1,000 impressions (or viewings) for a rectangular ad between the fourth and fifth posts on the blog.

Advertising is not an insignificant force affecting blogs. Reliance on advertising makes blogs less like free speech venues and more like corporations looking after the bottom line. One blogger called the advertising side of his site "strictly a business decision."[107] The nexus between corporate advertising departments and blogs will grow as well through the conglomeration of blogs. Much like print and broadcast media before them, blogs are becoming units of corporate networks. Markos Moulitsas runs several blogs, both political and sports-related. Blog entrepreneur Nick Denton has turned blogging into a profitable corporate enterprise by creating new niche blogs.[108]

Mainstreaming means bloggers increasingly are viewed as a force in American politics. That means bloggers are courted by existing players. As that happens, bloggers are likely to respond in kind. This is particularly true because many bloggers are experiencing fame for the first time. It is ego building to be taking phone calls from the White House, congressional leaders, and governors. And the attention may temper future content. After public criticism for a post, one national blogger admitted, "Maybe I need to be a little more careful about how I say it."[109]

The integration of blogs into the mainstream has impacts on politicians as well. The marriage of campaigns and blogs has been fraught with tension. Candidates have found that they are now allied with a group whose values and norms often conflict with their own. Stephen Coleman compared politicians attempting to adapt to the world of blogs to "those old Communist apparatchiks who had to sit in the front row at rock concerts and pretend to swing to the beat."[110]

While politicians seek coalition building, bloggers usually thrive on rhetoric. Politicians value well-honed statements avoiding offense, whereas traditionally bloggers prefer bluntness and often do not care about giving offense. This is exemplified in cases where bloggers have become embarrassments to candidates seeking to incorporate bloggers as representatives of a new community while still pacifying existing groups who could be offended by blog content. One such case occurred in early 2007, when two political bloggers joined the John Edwards presidential campaign. Prior to enlisting in the campaign, they had published anti-Christian statements. A Catholic interest group publicized the statements and called on Edwards to repudiate them and fire the bloggers. The candidate faced a dilemma: Repudiate the bloggers and their statements and risk criticism from the liberal blogging community (which he was explicitly attempting to court with the employment of bloggers), or defend the bloggers and offend an important religious group. Edwards split the difference. After chastising the bloggers and issuing public apologies from them, Edwards announced that the two would stay with the campaign. But the bloggers continued to write inflammatory statements and the criticism continued. Eventually, the Edwards campaign chose traditional political constituencies over the blogging community and announced that the two bloggers were leaving the campaign.[111] Edwards's was not an isolated case. Governor Tim Kaine of Virginia hired a blogger to interact with the Internet community, allowing the blogger to continue to blog on his own site. The site itself became controversial as the blogger labeled Republican opponents "rightwing crazies" and accused Senator George Allen of being a racist.[112] In another case, John McCain hired Patrick Hynes, a conservative blogger, who was criticized because, before joining McCain, he had contended that the United States was a "Christian nation."[113]

Even bloggers who are merely supporters rather than paid consultants or employees can cause candidates significant trouble. In 2006 a blogger who supported Ned Lamont in his bid for the U.S. Senate from Connecticut placed a fake photo of opponent Joe Lieberman in blackface. Lamont said he had no responsibility for the actions of his supporters, but the stunt still attracted negative publicity for Lamont's campaign.[114]

These examples demonstrate the dilemma for candidates as they integrate political bloggers into their campaigns. Criticizing bloggers suggests the candidate is unsupportive of the blogosphere's unrestricted personal expression. On the other hand, those outside of the blogosphere, particularly opponents, easily can tie the candidate to extremist or crude statements propagated by bloggers affiliated with the campaign or even merely supportive of the candidate.

Understandably, candidates fear association with a blogger who attracts controversy. An example is the 2004 furor over a statement mentioned earlier by Moulitsas that he felt no sorrow for four contractors who were killed in Iraq. The reaction to the statement led the Kerry campaign to drop the Daily Kos link from their Web site, and other candidates stopped advertising on Daily Kos.[115]

Some bloggers have suggested that the two worlds can be conjoined if traditional political players accept the blogosphere's eccentricities. Politicians and their constituents need to view bloggers as separate from those politicians they work for or support. In other words, the two can intersect, but that does not mean that bloggers' activities that are distinct from those of the candidate mirror the candidate's own views or behavior. The conservative blogger Patrick Hynes argued that people should not hold "candidates responsible for what their bloggers and blog consultants have said in the past."[116] However, bloggers are not like other staffers or paid consultants. They have extensive verbal trails (electronic, rather than paper) in a medium that sometimes encourages shrillness and crudity. And when the individual becomes an employee of the campaign, his or her previous writings become viewed as reflections of the candidate. At least that is how the situation will be portrayed by the opposition, and it would be unusual for the candidate's opponents not to use such an opportunity when it presents itself.

Another issue of adaptation of the blogosphere by political players is the extent of control over the message. Blogs are attractive precisely because a political player can control the message rather than depend on the often uncooperative media operating under their own imperatives. The blogosphere, like the early Internet, has been built on a horizontal structure that eschews control. In theory, no one controls what others say, and all can participate. The idea of the blogosphere is of an interactive medium where posting and commenting are intertwined. In other words, a discussion ensues. Importantly, that discussion may or may not go the way a single individual intended. The ideal is not necessarily reality. Some popular political blogs do not allow comments. As mentioned earlier, campaigns censor comments, and comments to blogs of members of Congress need to be approved. Corporate blogs also wrestle with whether to allow comments.[117]

For a political player, the potential of losing control is hardly attractive. Allowing comments, particularly those that are unfettered, runs the risk of sponsoring speech that runs contrary to the message of the player. A political player who initiates a blog does not do so as a medium for discussion and exchange. Rather, it is the means for some other goal, such as electoral victory, image making for the individual or group, or pursuance of specific policy objectives. Failing to control content creates the real possibility that the blog will become a forum for others to use for their own purposes. In politics, those who comment may demean the candidate or politician who hosts the blog, or they may use the blog for other candidates or causes at best irrelevant and at worst detrimental to the objectives of the blog owner.

The decision for candidates, elected officials, government agencies, etc., is whether to allow open commenting on blogs and risk reactions that undermine the host's message, or to ban such comments and incur the wrath of the blogosphere. Despite blog origins and culture, the decision is not a difficult one. Limitation, the absence of comments or the censorship of comments, clearly has become the rule, not the exception. One study of blogs written by members of Congress found that most did not even include a comment section.[118] One British politician turned off the comment capability on her blog, explaining that she was "horrified by some of the totally inappropriate comments that have been made about third parties."[119]

Still another mainstreaming issue is the factional nature of the blogosphere. As discussed earlier, the blogosphere is divided into two broad camps: liberals and conservatives. There are centrist blogs and blogs representing other points on the spectrum to the left and the right, but the fragmentation of the blogosphere means individuals remain in their relative corners. This limits the blogosphere's ability to serve as a deliberative forum.[120] Indeed, balkanization is revealed in the existence of separate communities establishing their own sub-blogospheres. For example, Hispanic bloggers speak primarily to Hispanic audiences by emphasizing Hispanic topics.[121] Evangelical groups use blogs to communicate, as do sports fans, students, and even white supremacists.[122]

Then there is the problem of anonymity. Anonymity has been a feature of the blogosphere since its inception. Bloggers and blog posters can and do operate anonymously. According to a survey by the Pew Internet and American Life Project, 54 percent of bloggers use pseudonyms when blogging.[123] Anonymity is not reserved just to bloggers, but also frequently occurs among those who comment on popular blogging sites. Advocates of anonymity argue that it gives bloggers the ability to speak the "truth" without fear of consequences. Bloggers are more candid, more willing to share genuine attitudes, because they can operate under the guise of anonymity. Without anonymity, individuals will self-censor to conform to social expectations. Some, such as whistleblowers or leakers inside government or business, may even face serious repercussions for the truths they state.

However, anonymity in online discussion has its drawbacks for traditional politics. It can encourage ad hominem attacks and an overall lack of civility due to the absence of accountability for expression. If people are not afraid of being caught, they may be less civil, more likely to make malicious statements about others. Anonymity can lead to cyberbullying. This refers to verbal pressure placed on others, usually coupled by outrageous accusations and even threats. The phenomenon has even led some bloggers to withdraw from the blogosphere altogether.[124]

Another problem with anonymity is deception. Bloggers can pretend to be people they are not.[125] A staff member for a Republican member of Congress running for reelection was caught posing as a Democrat criticizing the congressman's Democratic opponent on a blog.[126] In another case, a conservative site began to get anonymous postings praising John McCain that actually came from a political operative working for a McCain political action committee.[127] Blogs run under a pseudonym or a deceptive label may confuse voters. For example, political sites designed to embarrass Republican members of Congress were covertly run by Democrats.[128]

Related to anonymity is the ethical dilemma of a blogger who appears to be independent but actually is paid by someone else.[129] Some bloggers have worked for candidates but failed to disclose this. Markos Moulitsas has refused to disclose the names of candidates he has worked for, raising questions about whether he is helping them through his blog without informing his readers of those connections.[130] Patrick Hynes, founder of the blog Ankle Biting Pundits and a consultant for the McCain campaign, wrote posts supporting McCain and criticizing Mitt Romney without disclosing to his readers that he was being paid by the McCain campaign.[131] The potential of crossing the line between advocate and independent commentator or reporter becomes easier when the blogger remains anonymous.

The trends toward anonymity come at the same time as cross-pressures on government for greater transparency. This applies not only to elected and appointed policy makers, but also to candidates who frequently have their personal lives publicly exposed to the view of voters. The mixture of blog culture and politics will mean—indeed, already has meant—that anonymity must give way when bloggers become mainstream. Nevertheless, it may be a difficult abandonment of a cultural trait within blogging.

The integration of blogging into mainstream politics also is problematic due to the blogosphere's difficulty in defining its own ethical standards.[132] Part of that struggle over standards is the inability to determine whether blogging is journalism or merely commentary, or perhaps, with the growth of blogs by traditional political actors, merely a mouthpiece for existing players. The absence of a clear definition of blogging's role makes setting the rules of engagement even more difficult. But the challenge of integration also stems from the blogosphere's own unwillingness to rein in incivility, which is related to anonymity and an "anything goes" attitude among many bloggers. Some bloggers, insisting on the "free" nature of the blogosphere, have resisted any rules or expectations. They perceive blog posts and comments as part of a large public sphere that should not be censored.[133] Other bloggers, however, see the need for such standards to help govern behavior in the blogosphere.[134]

Some bloggers have pushed for a blogger code of ethics. One proposed code would prohibit anonymity and commit bloggers to refuse to post content that abuses others, is misrepresentative, or violates individual privacy.[135] No blogger would be forced to adhere to such a code, but its existence would differentiate in the public's mind those bloggers who adopt such a standard from those who refuse to agree to community standards of behavior. Typically it takes some time for a community engaged in a similar activity to establish set standards. Because there is no control mechanism over bloggers, standards may be difficult to impose on the blogosphere, particularly given widespread opposition to any rules.[136]

A set of ethics also could apply to bloggers' association with others who have a financial interest with the blogger. As mentioned earlier, some have been willing to use their blogs to advocate for candidates with whom they have a financial relationship. However, disclosing ties with those they write about is not a universal practice in the blogosphere. MyDD blogger Jerome Armstrong was fined nearly $30,000 by the Securities and Exchange Commission for promoting stock in a software company without disclosing that he received a payment from the company to do so.[137] A company in Vancouver paid bloggers to mention the company on their blogs.[138] And a staffer for the Howard Dean presidential campaign charged that bloggers were paid by the campaign to write positive things about the candidate. Even though another campaign staffer disputed the accusation, the controversy suggested the potential of bloggers selling their space to candidates without informing the public of the relationship.[139]

Some bloggers respond that they should not be bound by journalistic ethics because they are not journalists. Negative reaction to codes of ethics, particularly journalistic ethics, comes from some of the most prominent political bloggers. Markos Moulitsas, for example, states that he is not a journalist, but an activist. He admitted that if he were a journalist he would be "breaking half the canon of journalistic ethics."[140]

The debate over whether bloggers should disclose their connections with politicians suggests that the blogosphere's ethical norms are still in development.[141] However, as the blogosphere becomes more mainstream, it will face increasing pressure to define and adhere to a code of ethics. Political players will expect the blogosphere to act like other mainstream players and act in predictable and acceptable ways in order to participate in traditional political activities.

Interaction with Traditional Players

Blogs have become a part of the political landscape. They have caught the attention of political players from presidents to local officials and across interest groups, political parties, and the press. More than that, blogging has gone mainstream. A-list bloggers have acquired a place in the political communication strategies of other players. Political organizations—parties, groups, candidate campaigns—have become blog sponsors themselves. Even government agencies have created blogs. Yet the integration has not been an easy one. The blogosphere's Wild West culture has not been a neat fit with traditional American politics and media. The two sides would seem to be at cross-purposes, particularly when, as judged by its occasional rhetoric, one side possesses the explicit objective of overthrowing the other. Nevertheless, interaction is more the norm, and will continue to be so because both sides possess strong incentives to interact. For traditional players, blogs are a new medium for communication that offers them new access to important audiences. In turn, bloggers are benefited by the heightened status of association with key players and the ability to be heard beyond the confines of the blogosphere.

Rather than remaining two separate spheres (the original state of the blogosphere and probably the expectation and intent of early political bloggers), traditional political players and blogs have overlapped. That intertwining means both are affecting the nature of the other. The integration may well be at its height with the topic of the next chapter: journalists and bloggers.

6

Journalists

On March 22, 2007, the presidential campaign of John Edwards announced that the candidate and his wife would hold an important press conference that afternoon. Shortly before the press conference, CNN, Fox News, and other cable networks began broadcasting stories that Edwards's wife, Elizabeth, would announce that her breast cancer was no longer in remission and that her husband would suspend his presidential campaign. The story spread across the Internet as well. The campaign told journalists the rumor was not true, but the denial failed to halt the spread of the story. The problem was the story really was false. When the news conference occurred, the Edwardses announced that they would continue their campaign despite the cancer news. Journalists struggled to explain how and why they had given out false information. The source for the news media accounts turned out to be a recently created blog called Politico.com. In contravention of traditional journalistic standards, the blogger who broke the story, a former *Washington Post* reporter, had reported the rumor after hearing it from only one source. That source turned out to be mistaken. The journalist justified his use of only one source by saying that blogs "share information in real time."[1]

The Edwards campaign story highlights a problem for journalists "shar[ing] information in real time." When seeking confirmation, a reporter may find the initial source was wrong. Publicizing that information before it is checked can confuse the audience, who, assuming journalistic standards that apply to traditional news media also apply to blogs, will take the story as fact.

This incident has a larger significance as well. It demonstrates how blogs are affecting traditional journalism today. How is a community with long-held traditions and professional norms being affected by a community that seems to play by its own rules? What is the relationship between these journalists and bloggers, and how is that interaction shaping the way both approach what they do?

Battling the Media

Each new form of news dissemination has trumpeted itself as superior to the existing media. Radio brought listeners a human voice rather than the dry printed text. Television added visual images. Similarly, bloggers view themselves as part of a new medium that is superior to existing traditional media.

Blog boasting is at least partly driven by a strategy of self-protection. As each new medium arrives, it is required to elbow its way into the universe of media in order to survive. The strategy requires not only trumpeting one's own virtues but also disparaging the existing order, the competition. That means bloggers must engage in continual comparison with traditional media in order to acquire their own niche. Nor are bloggers alone in making that case. Others sometimes do it for them. One political scientist heralded blogs because they "provide a channel for authentic expression that is free from the repressive controls of traditional media."[2]

It is not surprising, then, that bloggers feed the perception of competition between blogs and traditional media. When traditional media critique bloggers, the perception is given further credence. For example, when a *New York Times* story reported that MyDD founder Jerome Armstrong had been involved in a stock-touting scheme, his former consulting partner, Markos Moulitsas, sent an e-mail to 300 liberal bloggers and activists urging them not to discuss the article. Marcos wanted to prevent the story from being picked up by other traditional media. Moulitsas's attempt to squelch the story was repeated by the *New Republic* and the *New York Times* columnist David Brooks, who accused Moulitsas of becoming what he claimed to be railing against.[3]

In that competitive environment, it should be no surprise that, despite their different ideologies, blogs almost uniformly criticize existing media. One survey of bloggers found that the vast majority used their blogs to criticize traditional media.[4] That criticism usually centers on media bias. Conservative bloggers fault journalists for catering to the left, and liberal bloggers often write that the news media are cowed into serving the interests of the right.

The criticism can become more personal. One example was the reaction of a blogger at the 2004 Democratic National Convention to the sight of ABC News reporter Sam Donaldson conducting an interview. The blogger wrote, "Without being too obvious, I tried to look at the marmoset that lives on his head."[5] Another was a post on Daily Kos calling *Washington Post* reporter Howard Fineman "wimpy" and "slime."[6] One blogger explained, "The only way you can really deal with the press corps is to beat up on them."[7] Yet while bloggers are "beat[ing] up on them," they also are relying on the news media as regular news sources. One survey of blog content found that 69 percent of blog posts included as a source a traditional media outlet such as the *New York Times*, the Associated Press, or the *Washington Post*. According to this survey, bloggers rely on the traditional media more than they do each other. Sixty-four percent of the sources identified in blog posts were from other bloggers.[8]

Competition between journalists and political bloggers is odd because the two groups have much in common. Many A-list bloggers come from traditional journalism. One survey of thirty political bloggers found that twelve had journalism experience. These included some of the best-known bloggers, such as Ana Marie Cox, Hugh Hewitt, and Andrew Sullivan.[9] Joshua Micah Marshall of Talking Points Memo has been described as "an old-fashioned political reporter who happens to be very open to the possibilities of the Web."[10]

Bloggers stress the accuracy of their reporting over that of traditional media. One blogger wrote, "So far, the blogosphere has a far better record of honesty and accuracy than mainstream organs like the *New York Times* and CBS."[11] Bloggers also point out that blogs can fix errors more easily because they don't have to wait for the next day's paper.[12] One blogger claimed that checks and balances in the blogosphere "are far stronger and more effective than the alleged 'checks and balances' of the mainstream media, which, in the absence of political and intellectual diversity, may not operate at all."[13]

Some bloggers tout their honesty as sources of information. They view journalists as fundamentally dishonest when the standard of objectivity is held up as distinguishing the traditional media from blogs or others who pretend to act as news reporters. Bloggers contend that the traditional media masquerade as objective purveyors of information. Joshua Micah Marshall asserted that his blog's reporting "is more honest, more straight than a lot of things you see even on the front pages of great papers like the *Times* and the *Post*."[14]

The difference, according to bloggers, is the straightforward nature of their partisanship. Traditional media, they contend, are biased but refuse to admit it; bloggers are biased but don't lie about it. According to Hugh Hewitt, journalists' failure to tell the audience their own views makes their news product fundamentally flawed: "I am unwilling to trust the conclusions of somebody who won't tell me their opinions and background."[15] The accusation implies that blogging is the true journalism while traditional journalism is false because it assumes that the news professional can be objective. According to Jay Rosen, the criticism is "really an attack not just on the liberal media or press bias, it's an attack on professionalism itself, on the idea that there could be disinterested reporters."[16]

Some bloggers see themselves as smarter than traditional media.[17] The A-list bloggers may have a point. As mentioned earlier, A-list bloggers tend to be highly educated individuals drawn, in many cases, from Ivy League universities, and they have more graduate degrees than even the elite of news media, the opinion columnists.

Bloggers see the dichotomy as one between the past and the present. They decry the media as outdated, relics of the past. One conservative blogger labeled news organizations "obstinate, lumbering, big-media dinosaurs."[18] Bloggers, on the other hand, are the future of information dissemination and gathering. According to one blogger, "Weblogging will drive a powerful new form of amateur journalism as millions of Net users—young people especially—take on the role of columnist, reporter, analyst, and publishers while fashioning their own personal broadcasting networks."[19]

The battle is not necessarily joined. Journalists still debate whether to respond to blogs' criticism of them. For the most part, they don't view the political blogs as media outlets worthy of response. They likely agree with one former CNN executive who argued that journalists shouldn't respond to bloggers "until they are held to the same standard that [journalists] are."[20] Even when journalists do respond, the reaction can be dismissive. One news story about blog theories of a jihadist suicide bomber at the University of Oklahoma pointed out that a host of blog "facts" about the student who committed suicide by blowing himself up were inaccuracies. The story quoted the student's father, who said that his son was depressed and that "this blog stuff is just smoke. It's bilge."[21] But others argue that blogs, particularly the A-list ones, should be responded to. They contend that these blogs should be held to a higher standard than common blogs.[22] The argument itself is underlined by an assumption that a medium attracting large audiences should adhere to journalistic standards in serving their readers. It is, in essence, an assumption of equivalency with traditional media.

Blogs: The New Journalism?

One of the problems with blogs' relations with journalism is that, as discussed earlier, bloggers are uncertain what they really are. Some view themselves as journalists, even the "new journalists." They disseminate news to an audience, particularly information their readers may not get elsewhere. Those bloggers seek to abide by standards of fairness in reporting. They do investigative research.[23] They have been called participatory journalists because theirs is a journalism featuring interactivity and participation over spectating. These reportorial blogs also have been termed "black market journalism" because their product is outside of the journalism system dominated by large media conglomerates.[24]

One critical difference from traditional journalists is that these bloggers would not argue that they are unbiased in their news presentation. Rather, the news presentation reflects their own perceptions of events and issues. After all, they argue, traditional journalists are biased as well and shape news gathering accordingly.

Other bloggers views themselves primarily as commentators, not journalists. John Hinderaker of Power Line said that he is not a journalist or even a part-time journalist.[25] Eugene Volokh (Volokh Conspiracy) admitted that he is "an amateur pundit, which is to say someone whose hobby it is to opine on various matters that are in the news."[26] Still others admit that they are no substitute for journalists and do not claim to be. Instapundit's Glenn Reynolds urged his readers not to rely solely or primarily on his blog for news. "What you get here—as with any blog—is my idiosyncratic selection of things that interest me, as I have time to note them, with my own idiosyncratic comments."[27]

Others see themselves as activists. For Moulitsas, a paramount goal of his blog is to help the Democratic Party win elections. He consults with candidates, raises money for them, and generally helps further the party.[28] Nor is activism true only on the left. The objective of the blog ConfirmThem was to help win confirmation of President George W. Bush's judicial appointments. Daily Kos is an activist blog where readers routinely are instructed to do something besides read the blog. Calling readers to action is common on some blogs. One study of four influential blogs found that 11 percent of the posts on Daily Kos called for readers to take some action. But such action is uncommon for the vast majority of blogs.[29]

Still others see themselves as journalists and commentators and even activists—all at the same time.[30] One scholar termed the blogosphere "activist media punditry."[31] According to Moulitsas, blogging has blended historical roles: "Traditionally it was easier for people to find the niche....you were either an activist or you were a writer or you were a pundit....We're all of the above."[32]

Bloggers do not see a fundamental conflict between reporting on the news and commenting on it at the same time and also attempting to change policy. In the same post a blogger can report news, add commentary, and urge action on the part of the audience and policy makers. One journalist has summed up blogging as having "all the liberties of a traditional journalist but few of the obligations."[33] Bloggers emphasize the differences in their approach to journalism. Whereas traditional journalists value detachment from the story, an emphasis on description, neutrality in presenting conflicts within the story, the unidirectional nature of the communication, and the importance of structure, bloggers' traits include the importance of personal subjectivity, the honesty of opinion expression, a role for the audience in the communication process, and the absence of cohesion and organization.[34]

The journalistic style proposed by bloggers is not new. Over time traditional media have experienced the same angst over the nature of journalism. During the colonial era, printers of broadsheets agonized over their preferred role as commercial printers and the expected role of patriot, either in defense of the Crown or in the service of the Revolution. The same debate erupted during the framing of the U.S. Constitution as newspaper publishers sought to return to their old commercial role but were pressed into service as advocates or opponents. Debate over journalism's role continued throughout the 19th century as some elements of the press sought more independence from the clutches of partisan organizations and leaders, while others saw the press as a mouthpiece for party principles. Still another conflict came at the end of the 19th century over whether journalists should manufacture news to boost circulation or merely report news as presented by sources.[35]

Only in the 20th century did the practice of interweaving opinion and news begin to give way to a new standard of professionalism and objectivity.[36] Yet even that change seemed artificial. While many of the newspapers of the 18th and 19th centuries in the United States were proudly partisan and erected no barriers between news and commentary, even those of the 20th and early 21st century have contained both editorial opinion and news reporting, although on separate pages. Separating the news from the op-ed pages gave readers the impression that news stories were not affected by the editorial position of the paper and vice versa. By the end of the 20th century, however, explicit news analysis and commentary began to creep out of the editorial pages and into the news sections. Journalists also appeared to have freer rein in expressing opinions in the body of a news story, particularly a feature story.

Hence the role of the traditional media is hardly settled in American life. Public opinion about journalists has shifted in recent years. News audiences today are less likely than they were ten years ago to view the news they acquire from news organizations as credible.[37] Journalists themselves still debate the role of journalism. The appearance of the blogs, with their new standards of reporting, has accentuated that debate. For example, the blogosphere has altered somewhat the role of the journalist as gatekeeper. Readers now have access to original documents and other sources that blogs link them to. They also have news that journalists do not include because news professionals consider that information as not meeting the definition of newsworthiness.

Yet journalists still see themselves as performing the function of helping the average reader make sense of the surfeit of information before him or her. That comes in the form of filtering out what may not be important for the reader, listener, or viewer, and also placing that news in context for the reader.[38] For the vast majority of readers who are not interested in searching the Internet for additional information, that journalistic function is critical. If traditional journalism, with its over 200-year history in the United States, is still deliberating its role, it should be no surprise that the political blogosphere, with a life span in the single digits, would still be doing so.

Moreover, the roots of the blogosphere suggest no such role for bloggers. Although the blogosphere may be viewed by many as an alternative political information source and therefore in competition with the traditional media in their coverage of public policy and politics, blogs certainly did not start that way. It is easy to forget that early blogs were personal journals featuring individual expression, primarily by teenagers. Any political role was tangential at best. In fact, that description is still true of a blogosphere that is populated primarily by personal journals unread by all but a handful of other people.

But as a few of those blogs turned to national politics and attracted media circulation–size audiences, they morphed from introspective diaries to political news sources. Still featuring personal expressions by their authors (in the tradition of early blogs and the blogosphere generally), these blogs also disseminated news stories about political events, many of which were not covered (or perhaps were under-covered) by the traditional media. As they went from personal diaries to political news and information gatherers and disseminators, some bloggers envisioned themselves not as anonymous writers to family and friends but as the future of journalism. A new generation of media consumers would eschew the traditional media forms and supposed objectivity and gravitate to the partisan but far more interesting blog sources.

Impact on Journalists

That eschewing of traditional media has not yet occurred. However, the presence of the blogosphere has had an impact on traditional journalists. Even though individual journalists may ignore the blogs or express disdain for them, the blogosphere has affected how most of them do their job. The style of reporting by blogs, as well as journalists' own use of the blogs, has magnified blog impact on journalism in several ways.

Defining Journalists

One effect is on the debate over the nature of a journalist. The appearance of bloggers has raised that question once again. Should bloggers be considered part of the journalistic community? Should only certain types of bloggers enter the ranks of journalism, such as those on the A-list or those who report more than they comment, or perhaps those who claim to be journalists?

Traditional news professionals have some ambivalence about whether to consider blogs part of the journalistic community. After all, paying attention to them means acknowledging a potential competitor and perhaps giving a measure of legitimacy to a perpetual critic. As one scholar put it, "If [journalists] adopt [blogs], it's like having a spastic arm—they can't control it."[39] On the other hand, how do you ignore blogs like Instapundit, The Huffington Post, and Daily Kos that have larger readerships than most daily newspapers? How do you ignore the work of people with whom national political leaders meet? How do you account for the millions of Americans, many very politically interested, who read political blogs? The issue is hardly abstract. It becomes concrete, for example, when journalists are required to carry credentials to gain special access to places such as the White House Press Room and the congressional press galleries. These credentials allow them into areas not available to non-journalists and grant them space within those areas, the warren of desks and cubicles where journalists write and submit stories.

Bloggers are being accorded treatment similar to that of journalists who cover government agencies and legislative bodies. Bloggers are now given press passes that grant access to the White House press conferences. They are moving into the congressional press galleries as well as into press galleries of state legislatures.[40] They also are receiving recognition from the judicial branch. The Supreme Court has not credentialed bloggers at this point, but the judicial system generally is acknowledging the role of bloggers. After two years of negotiating with the judiciary to obtain press credentials, bloggers are now beginning to get press credentials to cover trials. Two bloggers were credentialed to cover the trial of former vice presidential chief of staff Scooter Libby in 2007.[41]

Does this make bloggers journalists? Should they be accorded the same privileges as a reporter for the Associated Press or the *Los Angeles Times*? Do they qualify? Are they journalists if they approach their task significantly differently than news reporters? For example, a blogger who was credentialed to the Democratic National Convention decided to blog from his home in Boston after a couple of days, saying, "It was easier to just be able to walk around in my shorts and get something to eat when I wanted to."[42]

The question of whether the definition of a journalist should be stretched to include bloggers is one that news professionals are still wrestling with. The solution may well be a distinction between bloggers who look much like journalists—have large readerships, work for organizations rather than on their own, and are primarily in the business of news gathering and reporting—and those who write primarily for family and friends. But that solution would grant even some blogs a status that equates with traditional journalism.

Accelerating Reporting

Another effect on journalism is pressure to accelerate the speed of the news-gathering and—reporting process. The pressure to get news out fast has long characterized the news business. In the days before radio, newspapers printed several editions throughout the day in order to deliver the latest news.[43] The advent of twenty-four-hour television news channels in the 1980s challenged the major network news divisions to broadcast news more frequently. In the mid-1990s the Internet offered a new venue for constant news transmission, which required a steady dose of news content by media Web sites. Journalists now were driven by deadline pressure imposed on them by their own news organization's embrace of new technology.

The latest source of pressure is the blogosphere. As a medium that is defined by time—the inclusion of a date and time with nearly all posts—and is capable of instantaneous updating, the blogosphere offers a near constant content feed. In terms of news, blogs can broadcast a story far more rapidly than traditional journalists can. In the case of the Trent Lott story discussed in chapter 2, bloggers did not originate the story; ABC News and the *Washington Post*, traditional news media sources, disseminated the story first. But bloggers jumped on the story faster than most of the traditional media did.

One reason bloggers can act so quickly is that they need not take the time journalists do to produce a news media story. The news media decide whether to cover the event and then send a journalist out to report on it. The reporter takes the time to attend the event and then write the story, including collecting contextual information and material from sources. Then there is an editing process in which the story goes through layers of editors before being approved for publication. And time is needed to physically publish the newspaper. News for the Web site skips the production stage but still must go through the rest of the cycle. For television, the process usually is more complex due to the constraints of film crew allocation and placement, as well as production requirements.

By contrast, a blogger can post to his or her Web site in minutes. There is no prior assignment, no need to physically attend the event, no organizational layers, no production time. Blogging may have accelerated the process even more. In less time than a journalist can be assigned a story, go and cover it, come back and write it, and have it edited (even for the Web edition), a story can go through various iterations on a blog and become old news. This advantage can provide blogs with an important niche in delivering breaking news. In an era of twenty-four-hour news cycles and audience expectation of near instantaneous delivery of news of an event as it occurs, traditional news media organizations face enormous pressure to be fast and first in delivering the latest news. Blogs can match, and often exceed, the traditional media's ability to inform an audience quickly.

The speed of the blogosphere presents a challenge to media accustomed to being the first to report a story to the audience. Have the traditional media, then, lost their ability to be the first to publicize a story? If so, much like newspapers' adjustment to radio, will they have to find a niche of more in-depth reporting or more informed news reporting to replace their lost position of first out with the story?

The media's demise may be exaggerated, to paraphrase Mark Twain. The blogosphere's jump on news stories is likely to be rare because blogs lack the surveillance and news-gathering capabilities of traditional media. The kinds of stories that blogs can scoop most probably are those that news media don't pick up because they discount their newsworthiness, or those that emanate from a source in the blogosphere. This could be news held by an individual or a group with unique access to information, as well as a preference to pass it through the blogosphere rather than the media. Although either scenario is possible (and the former is discussed below), the odds of such scooping on a regular basis are low.

There is another impact on journalism related to speed beyond the opportunity to scoop others. It is the ability to frame a story in a certain way that constitutes the first impression for the news audience. Two scholars have called this a "first-mover advantage in socially constructing interpretive frames for understanding current events."[44] One could argue that the Harriet Miers case is an example of that "first-mover advantage." Blogs disseminated negative information about Miers faster than the White House could initiate its own image-making effort.

The blogosphere's ability to frame is contingent on one major condition, that is, the presence of a fairly universally accepted frame. Without it, there is no single frame but only conflicting frames. Because the blogosphere is divided, such a frame consensus is difficult to achieve. In the case of Miers, the frame of her shortcomings was accepted across both liberal and conservative blogs. That is an uncommon event.

Changing Professional Standards

Related to speed is the absence of professional standards by bloggers. Journalists are trained to follow certain norms and codes of professional ethics in the construction of a story, but bloggers have no such guidelines. For example, a blogger need not get confirmation of a tip or check the authority of the source. Some may choose to do so to maintain their own credibility, but blogger norms don't encourage them to do so. Andrew Sullivan said blogging is "a way you can throw ideas around without having to fully back them up, just to see what response you get."[45]

Bloggers even brag about their failure to check rumors they broadcast. The owner of a network of blogs explained, "It's implicit in the way that a Web site is produced that our standards of accuracy are lower. Besides, immediacy is more important than accuracy, and humor is more important than accuracy."[46] While blogging as "Wonkette," Ana Marie Cox saw herself as competing against gossip journalists in print media. But she said the best-known print gossip columnist in Washington could not compete with her because "he reports, that's the problem. He, like, checks facts."[47] Of course, such a norm has its downside. Blogs are susceptible to false information. The Edwards story above is one example. Another was election night of 2004. The broadcast networks were reporting election results from state to state, but the blogosphere was distributing exit poll results that supposedly showed John Kerry ahead in key swing states. Early exit poll numbers, which are incomplete, had been leaked and the blogs were reporting that Kerry would be president.[48] Bloggers admit that blogs can be "raw emotion and that there are times when blogging would be better if it were tempered with more deliberation." Moulitsas said, "I'll write something that later on I'm thinking, yeah, maybe I should have waited 10 minutes to post that."[49]

In 2004 the traditional media resisted the temptation to report information from blogs as fact, unlike in the Edwards suspended campaign story two and a half years later. However, that was 2004. By 2007, the pressure blogs placed on journalism was more intense.

Both stories—the 2004 election night and Edwards's non-suspension of his campaign—suggest that journalists see themselves as engaging in some form of competition with bloggers, and bloggers see things similarly. And that competition places new pressure on traditional journalists who are used to playing by a certain set of rules. While journalists operate according to rules of obtaining confirmation, which typically takes time, the blogosphere is able to ignore such norms. As a result, the blogosphere can lead journalists to cast aside their journalistic training in the rush to be first, or even merely to retain a measure of relevance in a fast-moving Internet environment. Bob Steele, a media ethicist, concluded, "The Edwards story speaks loudly to how fast those values can get lost in a hurry."[50]

The pressure becomes most acute when the story has the potential of turning history. Journalists remember the *National Enquirer*'s story and photograph of Gary Hart's dalliance with Donna Rice on the boat *Monkey Business* that helped doom the Democratic front-runner's presidential campaign.[51] Eleven years later, the Drudge Report Web site broke an even bigger story: the Monica Lewinsky scandal.[52] In 1987 and 1998 there was no blogosphere. By 2004 there was one, and the potential of the blogosphere affecting a presidential election outcome was tantalizing. This would be particularly true if traditional journalists followed the blogosphere's lead, which they did in February of that year. On February 6, 2004, a little-known blog, Watchblog, included a post about a rumor that John Kerry had been involved in a long-running affair with an intern, and that his affair would soon be exposed by *Time* magazine. The Drudge Report picked up the rumor on February 12. Other blogs immediately repeated the story.[53] It circulated widely and was reported in the press before it was dismissed when all the parties involved denied it and no evidence of the affair was produced.[54]

Bloggers claim that the blogosphere possesses an internal check. Glenn Reynolds of Instapundit contended that the online community is its own ombudsman: "The check on blogs is other blogs. . . . If you get a reputation for not being honest about your facts, people pay lots of attention to you."[55] Yet blogs remain popular even when they get stories wrong or merely spread rumors. The best example is Wonkette. There is strong pressure to repeat rumors heard elsewhere on the blogosphere or the Internet merely because they are in circulation rather than stopping the momentum to examine the authenticity of the rumors.

Usurping the Watchdog Role

Journalists have long viewed themselves as media watchdogs who reveal politicians' mistakes and government errors. The role became idealized particularly in the wake of the Watergate scandal and the role of Woodward and Bernstein in the fall of Richard Nixon. But bloggers challenge that watchdog role. They argue that traditional journalists have become too comfortable in their relationship with politicians and other elites. Bloggers claim they, not traditional journalists, are the real watchdogs today. They contend that the blogosphere can be more critical of political insiders than are journalists because, unlike journalists, they enjoy a healthy distance from politicians. Journalists are unable to engage in the kind of investigative journalism they used to do because of their proximity to politicians. One blogger argued that traditional reporters missed the significance of the Trent Lott story because of "journalistic clubbiness" with politicians.[56] Bloggers are the only ones left who can actually investigate stories without being influenced by politicians.

The bloggers' point speaks to the inherent ethical dilemma of a permanent press corps, that is, how to stay close enough to sources to get information but not so close as to become partial toward them.[57] The treatment of journalists by governmental bodies adds to the problem. In an earlier age, journalists who covered national politicians spent their day waiting outside buildings to catch a word from politicians as they walked by. Now those assigned to a beat are more likely to sit in government-provided press rooms at the White House, the Capitol building, the Supreme Court, and various bureaucratic agencies and be given regular briefings and access to policy makers. Moreover, some prominent journalists have become establishment figures in their own right. Nationally syndicated columnists, television news anchors, Washington bureau chiefs, political interview hosts—all have become fixtures in Washington and coveted guests at dinners, parties, and other social events. Bloggers, however, are still the upstarts. There is still an outsider quality to their content and their approach to politics. Some on the A-list, such as Markos Moulitsas and Jerome Armstrong, have acquired status among national political figures, but most have not.

That doesn't mean it will always be that way; this virtue likely will fade over time. Integration to Washington social circles is still in its early stages but will continue as bloggers carve a niche in journalism and commentary. The fact that many political bloggers today live away from Washington, D.C., and New York may make co-optation more difficult, but a centralization of political bloggers in the vicinity of Washington may occur over time and accelerate the process of going native.

Watching the Watchdog

Another effect of the blogosphere is the creation of a new force that is watching the watchdog. The news media, rather than those they report on, have become the object of scrutiny. Bloggers examine the news media's content thoroughly and publicize media mistakes. One blogger warned the press that he would scrutinize every aspect of media content: "The level of scrutiny will make your editors blush."[58]

Media watchdog groups are not new. Groups on the left (FAIR) and those on the right (AIM) have critiqued the media for years. But there is a difference with bloggers. To reach an audience beyond their own mailing lists, these groups are compelled to work through the very media they are criticizing. The influential political bloggers need not do that. An A-list blogger can avoid media to communicate with hundreds of thousands of readers on a daily basis. Moreover, as mentioned earlier, the tone of blog content typically is highly critical of media content, thus making the watchdog role a natural development for blogs. And the blog audience would seem to be a highly sympathetic one for media critique.

The new watchdog not only is a critic of existing political players, but also is a frequent critic of media bias. Conservative bloggers particularly charge media outlets with liberal bias and twisting events to conform to that bias. For example, some bloggers questioned the accuracy of an Associated Press story of a Bush campaign event in 2004 that stated the crowd had booed when Bush announced former president Bill Clinton would undergo heart surgery. Bloggers placed audio and video of the event on their sites as evidence of their assertion that the crowd didn't react that way. The AP issued a retraction.[59]

For conservatives the blogosphere is an alternative source of information but also a forum for uncovering liberal bias in what the media report. An example is the *New Republic's* publication of blog postings by a U.S. soldier in Iraq writing under a pseudonym. The soldier related atrocities against Iraqis by U.S. troops, including an incident in which troops cut out the tongue of an Iraqi boy who had befriended the troops and another in which a soldier mocked a disfigured Iraqi woman.[60] Conservative bloggers claimed the accounts were false and criticized the *New Republic* for publishing them without verification and under a pseudonym. A private claimed responsibility for the stories and the U.S. Army issued a report concluding that the stories were fake. The *New Republic* initially stood by the stories, but then disavowed them.[61] An array of conservative bloggers used the incident to repeat charges of bias in the media. One wrote that the entire incident was "another chapter in the sad history of 'fake, and not accurate, either' news stories."[62] Another pointed to "editorial failures and ethical breaches of the magazine's senior editors."[63]

Liberal bloggers have attacked conservative media as well. The blogosphere played a role in uncovering the identity of a man accredited to the White House press corps for a supposedly independent news service, but who actually was affiliated with a Republican Web site. Liberal bloggers also discovered that the would-be reporter had set up pornographic Web sites and even advertised himself, in the nude, as an escort.[64] In another case, a reporter at The Huffington Post investigated a blogger who regularly contributed stories on Lebanon to the online version of *National Review* and concluded that the blogger's postings were fabricated. The conservative opinion magazine admitted the postings were "misleading." Other liberal blog posts criticized *National Review* for not exercising better editorial judgment and using supposedly descriptive stories to further their own ideological agenda. Sometimes liberal and conservative bloggers join to criticize the traditional media. Both Michelle Malkin and Andrew Sullivan criticized the *National Review* postings; Little Green Footballs did the same to the *New Republic*.[65]

Left, right, or middle, bloggers enjoy pointing out traditional media mistakes and forcing corrections and apologies from what they call "big media." The previously discussed example of Dan Rather is the best known, but several others have occurred since the beginning of the blogosphere. For example, when the *Guardian* misquoted Deputy Secretary of Defense Paul Wolfowitz. bloggers pointed out the misquote. That led the paper to retract it and apologize to readers.[66] Another instance involved a blogger who accused a *New York Times* arts reporter of a conflict of interest because she served simultaneously as a member of the board of directors of an art institute. The blogger claimed the reporter was giving the art institute more press than it deserved. The reporter denied the accusations but also resigned from the board.[67]

Another element of the watchdog role is covering stories that traditional media do not. One blog even has as its slogan "All the News the MSM [mainstream media] Forgot to Print."[68] Blogs are most interested in missed stories about journalists themselves. Bloggers view themselves as checking journalists' tendency not to criticize their own profession. Indeed, journalists are reluctant to cover their own organizations critically. Nor are journalists quick to criticize one another. This includes critique of others' work, but also their non-journalistic activities.

This practice moves into shadowy areas when news professionals themselves become news sources, as when they give speeches or appear on panels. One example is the case of CNN executive Eason Jordan. At a panel of the World Economic Forum in Davos, Switzerland, in 2005, Jordan accused the U.S. military of purposely shooting at journalists. When challenged by others, Jordan backed away from the allegation. But a blogger at the summit decided to write about the incident on the meeting's own blog after he noticed that traditional

media were not doing so.[69] There was furor over the content of Jordan's assertion. But there was another furor over whether the news media had ignored
Jordan's comment because he was a fellow news professional. Bloggers accused
the media of ignoring the incident because it involved one of their own, and the
traditional media responded that the accounts of what Jordan had said varied
and no transcript offered a reliable arbiter because the event was officially off
the record.[70] The controversy eventually led to Jordan's resignation.[71] Bloggers
gloated over their victory. One characterized it as "Blogs 1 CNN 0." Another
claimed, "The Blog is turning into a great equalizer."[72]

Political bloggers also view themselves as watching the watchdog by including those elements of a story that traditional media ignore. Bloggers sometimes
see themselves as completing the story, offering perspectives that traditional
media do not. This is particularly true of conservative bloggers who view traditional media as slanted to the left. One example is media coverage of the Iraq
war. During the height of violence in 2006 and 2007, some conservative bloggers complained that the traditional media covered only the violence and failed
to tell their audiences about the successes of the U.S. military and the Iraqi
government. "What's important," according to one conservative blogger, "is to
fill in both sides of the story or multiple sides of the story."[73]

Although the watchdog role is critical of the media, bloggers suggest their
goal is not to destroy the traditional media, but to reform it.[74] According to
Joshua Micah Marshall, the critique that comes from blogs like his is intended
to "get people to practice better journalism."[75] Similarly, Markos Moulitsas
argued that the country needs a press that "acts like a check on government,
that acts like it's working in the public interest, as opposed to just trying to
ingratiate themselves with the people in power and get invited to the right
cocktail parties."[76]

Pitting Elites against Non-elites within News Media

In addition to a general competition with traditional media, blogs also are affecting intra-media competition between two levels of journalism: elites (prestige
newspapers, newsmagazines, networks, etc.) and non-elites (regional and local
newspapers and broadcast stations). Traditionally there is a unidirectional relationship whereby the elite press, particularly through wire services and syn-
dicates, becomes the source of content for non-elite publications. Non-elite
journalists also pick up cues from national media and then add a local angle.
Much less common is movement in the other direction, that is, elite media
gather stories from non-elite press and include them in their content.

Blogs are providing an opportunity for non-elite press to affect elite news content. According to Moulitsas, non-elite journalists use the blogs to attract the attention of the elite press to a story. By pitching the story to an A-list blog, which is an easier information source to reach than the elite press, non-elite sources can send the story to a national audience, perhaps to be picked up by elite journalists who read the blog.[77] Although blog sources primarily are drawn from the elite press as well, blogs have a wider array of sources they use, including the non-elite press.[78] This trend may help the non-elite press shape the news agenda as their content moves indirectly to elite media.

However, this scenario assumes that elite media actually draw from blogs to get stories. Later in this chapter we will test that assumption. But past examples suggest that news media are reluctant to repeat blog content. One example is a story that broke in October and again in December 2007 concerning an alleged affair between John Edwards and a video producer who worked on the Edwards campaign. On both occasions, the initiating newspaper was a non-elite source, the *National Enquirer*. The tabloid, which played a role in a sex scandal involving Democratic presidential front-runner Gary Hart in the 1988 presidential race, ran a story charging Edwards with impregnating the woman and then covering it up by blaming the incident on a staffer. The Drudge Report repeated the story in blaring headlines, and some A-list blogs mentioned it as well. But despite plenty of cover from the A-list blogs, the traditional media did not use the story and it did not break out of the blogosphere at either time. Only later, after Edwards was no longer a presidential candidate, did the story finally break in the traditional media causing Edwards to admit to an affair, but deny he was the father of the child.[79]

Competing for a Niche Political Audience

Another impact on journalism is new competition for a niche audience. Traditional media have faced increasing competitive pressures from new information sources. Twenty-four-hour news channels and Internet news sites offer the most politically interested segments of news audiences the information sources that satisfy their seemingly insatiable demands for political news. The political blogosphere is the latest entrant in that competition for the eyeballs of political junkies.

However, the contest begins with the traditional media competing under a handicap of audience expectations. News media organizations provide news across a broad spectrum of topics: politics, sports, entertainment, weather, etc. Even within political news, news media rarely devote their broadcasts primarily to one topic. The audience anticipates stories on varying topics because they expect to be informed about a range of news occurring that day. Bloggers, on the other hand, don't have the same obligation to report the news of the day. Any particular blog can, and will, ignore the vast majority of stories the news media cover and home in on one or two topics for a post, a day, or even several days, if they wish. Blogs can specialize, and politics is the specialty of political blogs. This distinction in roles can be seen in the Trent Lott story. Whereas the blogs could devote time to this story, news media had the responsibility to report other news, such as the resignation of Paul O'Neill, secretary of the treasury, and Larry Lindsay, the White House chief economic advisor, as well as a close election for U.S. Senate in Louisiana.[80]

But bloggers also view themselves as competitors of specialized political media such as opinion magazines. The *New Republic*, the *National Review*, the *Nation*, and similar magazines are in competition with their respective ideological blogospheres. Markos Moulitsas wrote on his blog, "New Republic is mortally wounded and cornered, desperate for relevance because it has lost half its circulation since the blogs arrived on the scene."[81]

So far the niche audience primarily is supplementing by using both blogs and traditional media as information sources, as we will see later. But there may be indications that the niche audience will gravitate to news sources that more neatly fit their news interests. That may leave the traditional media with a less politically interested audience and traditional news outlets increasingly competing with *Entertainment Tonight* or *20/20* rather than CNN, Fox News, or the blogosphere.

De-bureaucratizing Writing

With its roots in personal journals, the blogosphere still values individualistic writing characterized by the absence of editing by another individual. In their comparison with news media, bloggers point to the absence of a news hierarchy as a distinct advantage in the quality of their writing. They argue that they do a better job of writing because they don't have the bureaucracy of traditional news media that "turns even the best prose limp, lifeless, sterile, and homogenized."[82]

In response to the blogosphere's perceived freshness as a medium in contrast with a bureaucratic news organization approach, individual journalists have started their own blogs, sometimes separate from organizations. And news media organizations have created blogs in order to capture interest in blogs among their readers and meet the imperatives of a new medium; staff writers frequently blog there. The style is much more real-time, informal, and opinion-laced, much like the blogosphere generally. One editor for the *New York Times* Web site explained the role of the newspaper's blog as a vehicle for "insights that might not rise to a full article but are worthy of reporting."[83]

News organization blogs also offer more space for news, news that won't fit in the hard copy.[84] This is especially true of short pieces, news notes that don't justify article-length treatment. Due to the looser space restrictions, stories or short news notes can go into a blog when they would not meet the threshold for the print edition. One reporter for the *Washington Post* noted, "The bar is lower than getting something in a newspaper."[85]

Ideally blogs would be an opportunity for news media to spend more time on substantive issues. For example, during a presidential campaign a newspaper could add depth to stories about issues and candidates instead of focusing on the horse race that dominates media coverage.[86] But blog content is more likely to be shorter versions of what already appears in the print edition, or perhaps even more inside gossip than extensive policy discussion.

The blogosphere is creating new dilemmas for news professionals on their own Web sites. One is the transparency of the news-gathering process. By example blogs show print media that reporting can be open and transparent, with an emphasis on public development of information.[87] Bloggers sometimes even actively encourage readers to provide information to them. Joshua Micah Marshall of Talking Points Memo has urged readers to do research for him and communicate their findings to his audience.[88] Blogs are not the only forces moving journalism in this direction. Home video, Internet-based reporting, and the twenty-four-hour news cycle also play a part.

News organizations' adoption of journalist blogs potentially makes the news-gathering process public because reporters can post pieces online as they gather news; they need not wait to distribute a final product in the form of a printed newspaper article or a television news story. One reporter-blogger said he will inform his readers of what he's working on and what information he has before he even writes the story. It illuminates the news process and even invites reader reaction in the formation of the story.[89] But does it also lead to confusion and misinformation? The release of information from one source may be contradicted by later sources. Yet the reporter has distributed the information as if it were confirmed fact. Or could part of the story lead to inaccurate conclusions by a reader, particularly one who does not go back to read the full product?

Blogs also raise the question of the role of editing. Should journalists' blogs be edited? Is it a violation of the norms of the blogosphere that an individual's writing is edited by someone else? Or are those norms changeable as the blogosphere acquires new members who seek to adapt the medium to their uses? Editing is fundamental to the journalistic process and antithetical to the original blog culture. This dilemma is exemplified in the case of a reporter for a California newspaper who wanted to post a strongly critical statement about a gubernatorial candidate but was forced to run copy past the editor first. Bloggers complained about the news organization's decision to edit the journalist, and the newspaper eventually overturned its decision.[90] But then some of the reporter's colleagues complained about the new double standard of editing: print stories are edited but blog posts are not.[91] The dilemma for the news organization is that regardless of who the blog writer is, the news organization still holds responsibility for what is written by a journalist on the newspaper's blog.

Approaches to editing vary. For example, the *New York Times* blog is edited,[92] but others are not. Those organizations may share the view of one editor at a newspaper where blogs were not edited that editing was not necessary because the journalist-bloggers were longtime reporters who "apply the tenets of good journalism to their Web logs."[93] But what happens when a generation of journalist-bloggers does not share those experiences? Will editing then be necessary?

Including the Public

Blogging has presented another dilemma for traditional media. How should they handle increased public involvement in the news presentation? Bloggers challenge media claims that the news presentation must be dominated by trained professionals. They bristle at the assumption that the news media product is more legitimate because it is written and edited by trained professional journalists. One blogger opined, "Just because you don't get paid for writing a blog doesn't mean you're any less authoritative."[94]

Traditional journalists have developed an aura of professionalism via journalistic education, professional societies, and codes of ethics. Bloggers have none of those. Many are amateurs in the processes of news gathering and reporting. Some journalists have disparaged the amateurism of blogging. One reporter said the power of blogs was "like C-SPAN in the hands of a 19 year-old."[95] Despite this kind of criticism of bloggers, news media organizations are responding to the capability of and the demand for public involvement. They are opening up the news presentation, particularly online, to more voices than those offered by news professionals. One example is the creation of newspaper blogs. As mentioned earlier, major media publications—including elite newspapers, network news divisions, and national newsmagazines—have started their own blogs.[96] In addition, blogs have proliferated among regional media such as the *Houston Chronicle*, the *Atlanta Journal-Constitution*, and the *San Antonio Express-News*.[97] These blogs clearly are dominated by the news professionals, but they typically include a comment function. These comments appear directly underneath or at least along with the story. Thus nonprofessionals are offered an opportunity to participate in the news presentation provided to online readers.

One drawback of this increased interaction with readers is the potential for journalists to confuse the blog posters with the broad readership. News professionals may become obsessed with responding to those who read the blogs and make comments rather than a broader but silent audience. One photojournalist obviously paid attention to the comments when he noted, "Thirty years ago if somebody didn't like a picture I had in the paper, I got some letters passed on by my editor a few weeks later; now I get a hundred bloggers calling for my blood before I even see the paper."[98] Reporters unused to such criticism can be thin-skinned and too quick to respond. They may lash out at their critics. But they also may begin to tailor the news presentation in response to those who are vocal, despite the fact those critics may be a distinct minority.

Such responses may even lead journalists to discard news judgment in order to increase online readership.[99] With the emergence of a new amateur online journalism, professionals may view amateur approaches as more valid than their own. For example, one journalist blogger asserted, "My readers know more than I do."[100] Although the remark may suggest a humility that any group with power should share, it seems odd in another sense. Some individuals in the audience may know more than the journalist (or others who respond to stories may give the impression they know more), but that hardly translates into general knowledge by the audience. The fact that journalists receive the news before their audience and filter what they gather before it gets to the audience suggests that journalists have more knowledge than their audience.

Freeing Journalists

Blogging began as a public personal expression, much like writing a personal diary that is photocopied and handed out to perfect strangers. One survey of bloggers (both political and nonpolitical) found that the most common reason for blogging was to "document their personal experiences and share them with others." And the most common topic of blog writing, these bloggers said, was their "life and experiences.[101] That style carries over into political blogs. A-list political bloggers broadcast their personal thoughts to hundreds of thousands of people. Joshua Micah Marshall lamented, "In a way I've lost my ability to have my own private reflections. I've gotten in the habit of just putting everything out there."[102]

Through most of the past century the professional norms of journalism were diametrically opposite to this personalized approach in news writing. As a vehement reaction to the partisan press of an earlier age, journalists were required to hide their personal feelings behind the mask of objectivity. Over the past several decades, the preeminence of objectivity has been eroded by successive challenges from the "new journalism" movement, advocacy journalism, and public journalism. Moreover, public opinion about the news media has become more critical of journalists' assertions that they maintain objectivity. Most Americans perceive at least a fair amount of political bias in the news they get.[103] Blogs are the most recent addition to the anti-objectivity trends of the past half-century.

But blogs are different from these previous movements because they come from outside of journalism. They offer journalists an alternative method of writing that combines the elements of previous movements, such as critical analysis and advocacy journalism, with an emphasis on the human nature of the reporter over the model of the journalist as an interchangeable professional. One blogger explained that blogs "tend to be impressionistic, telegraphic, raw, honest, individualistic, highly opinionated and passionate, often striking an emotional chord."[104] By adopting blog writing, journalists have been freed from the constraints of objective journalism. When blogging they are more likely to express personal views, make unsubstantiated assertions, and abandon their reliance on sources to make points.

The blog world's norms are beginning to carry over into and reshape the norms of journalism. Journalists can act more like bloggers and less like objective journalists. In fact, adherence to the standard format of news writing on a media blog would evoke criticism from the blogosphere and, at least in the current blogosphere, chase away readers. This liberation, however, leads to the question of how far it will extend into journalism. Will the blog writing style become the style incorporated outside the blogosphere, in journalists' traditional formats of news presentation? The answer, probably, is no. Objective journalism took some time to establish itself as the paradigm for news presentation. It is not likely to disappear quickly. Moreover, audience expectations are still relevant, and the vast majority of the traditional audience still expects a press that provides news that is devoid of a particular point of view.[105]

What does that mean for individual journalists? It creates a tension for individual journalists who both blog and continue to work as daily reporters covering beats. Perhaps blogging can be viewed as a release—the liberation discussed above. For a brief time in their daily routine, reporters can break out of their set patterns and express personal opinions and, frankly, be themselves. But will that eventually affect their traditional writing?

Maybe an even more important question is whether journalists will be trusted as neutral descriptors of events once their personal views about those same events are expressed on blogs. Does the liberation undermine journalists' credibility? The question is particularly important given the decline in credibility already experienced by the press.[106] Will blog expression, as attractive as it may be as release, harm journalists' ability to perform their main function as news gatherers and reporters?

Following the Blogs' Agenda

Another impact of the political blogosphere on journalism is the new dilemma of what to do with blog stories. Bloggers view themselves as a vital component of the news-gathering process. One of the predictions by bloggers is that increasingly they will be viewed as the first source that journalists will then follow. One common line is, "If journalism is the first draft of history, blogs might just be the first draft of journalism."[107]

Journalists are not likely to be accommodating in standing aside to let bloggers write the first drafts of their stories. Following the blogs' agenda places journalists in a secondary position in terms of news dissemination. Journalistic culture thrives on the notion that journalists are first with information. They have the news before anyone else, and they get to decide what the public also will get to know. As discussed earlier, that gatekeeping function is under attack now. Nevertheless, the primacy of the journalist as the source of information disseminated to the public is a position journalists are reluctant to relinquish.

But there are other limitations besides pride on any journalistic rush to adopt the blogs' agenda. One is the fact that blogs have a reputation for getting things wrong. Many spread rumors and gossip without any compunction about reliable sourcing or effects on their reputation. Bloggers would respond that they do not play the role of producing a finished news product; rather, they disseminate bits and pieces here and there. Some of it will be true; other parts won't be. But nothing has been withheld and the whole process eventually sorts itself out. Journalists cannot afford the luxury of an eventual sorting out. The public will not tolerate unsubstantiated stories when they have become accustomed to reliable news. Moreover, blog stories may not fit news values. For example, political bloggers typically focus on stories that would be considered "inside baseball" by the vast majority of the public. News media serve that larger, less politically interested audience that political bloggers do not.

Nevertheless blog stories are out there, and some of them possess elements of newsworthiness. What if some other news outlet uses the blog story and scoops everyone else as a result? Blog stories cannot be completely ignored. Yet neither can they be incorporated into the news product without being subject to professional standards of news judgment and reporting. Later we will discuss how journalists are handling that dilemma.

Journalism's Effects on Blogs

Bloggers suggest they are changing journalism, or reforming it. Yet the effects are not unidirectional. Journalism is shaping the evolution of blogging as well. As a practice in its infancy, blogging does not have its own traditions to shape the approach of participants to the creation and dissemination of blog content. Hence the development of blogging can be heavily influenced by other forces with a more entrenched history. And as bloggers go mainstream, other forces have strong incentives to cast blogging in certain directions. For example, politicians, party organizations, or interest groups may seek to annex blogs to serve particular individual or group goals.

The most powerful source of influence over blogs is likely to be journalism. Journalism shares the same objectives as blogging: both seek to disseminate news and information to a particular audience. And the integration of journalists into blogging increases the opportunities for influence on this yet undeveloped activity. That integration is more pronounced by the fact that blogging has emerged at the same time that newsrooms are downsizing. Journalists who still want to practice their craft may find blogs an available alternative.

Establishing Blogger Standards

Bloggers are being held to standards of professionalism that journalists created in the first place. For example, sourcing needs to be used, and those sources must be reliable. Information also should be timely and interesting and should meet the reader's needs. The blogosphere is divided over whether to accept journalistic standards. One blogger worried, "If you try to put the rules of mainstream journalism onto blogs, you end up sucking the life out of them."[108]

Nevertheless, the most successful bloggers of the future in terms of audience and impact in and out of the blogosphere will be those who adhere to standards of journalism. For example, the Media Bloggers Association, the association of journalist-bloggers, currently seeks journalist status: credentialing for journalists, equal access to sources, and coverage under shield laws. The differences between journalist-bloggers and the rest of the blogging community essentially will create a two-tiered blogging world. One part of that world will be bloggers who subscribe to a code of ethics and become journalist-like. The other will be everyone else, bloggers who wish to retain blogging's peculiarity. That division will become the equivalent of the difference between the evolution of large corporate-based newspapers and the single-person, small-town newspaper run on a shoestring budget. It is important to remember that the latter model largely disappeared. The corporate model, which wholly dominates traditional media today, is likely to become the model governing influential blogs of the future.

Defining a Relationship

By providing information to news reporters, and in turn relying on those same journalists for information, political bloggers have forged a relationship with the journalistic community. By adopting the role of commentator on traditional media content, they became dependent on the very news organizations they often inveigh against. And as journalists began to pay attention to that commentary, and bloggers became conscious of that fact, the dependency relationship deepened. Journalists' usage of blogs, news coverage of the blogosphere, and reliance on bloggers as occasional news sources (much as they rely on politicians and interest group representatives) all contributed to the dependency. Bloggers felt recognized, appreciated, and useful in affecting traditional politics. Even for an established journalist like Andrew Sullivan, the attention had to be surprising and gratifying. But for those who were unknown, such as Markos Moulitsas, Duncan Black, and Glenn Reynolds, it had to be a truly heady experience.

Once the adulation, or at least acknowledgment, occurred for bloggers, it was impossible for them not to want it to continue. But maintaining the relationship required adapting to it. To continue to be read and quoted and courted, top political bloggers had to adjust to the needs of the audience—journalists—by becoming similar to those journalists in norms and practices and providing content that would attract the attention of news media professionals.

A Symbiotic Relationship

Bloggers often describe their relationship with journalists as a competitive one. Some bloggers have suggested that the blogosphere will replace traditional media. They envision a future where traditional media no longer serve a useful function. As blogs bypass traditional media filters and news consumers get their own direct information, there will no longer be a need for traditional news media sources, some bloggers predict.[109] For their part, journalists often criticize bloggers as wannabe journalists who lack the professionalism requisite for the title. Bloggers have even been called parasitic, accused of drawing on the media's work but making no original contribution in news generation.[110] Some journalists respond with silence, suggesting the blogosphere is not worthy of reply. They may pretend political blogs do not exist, or they acknowledge their existence but insist that blogs have no relationship to journalism.

Certainly competitive elements exist in the relationship. They compete because they are alike in many ways. They both gather and disseminate news. Bloggers want to be first with the story, as do journalists. Bloggers and journalists tussle over the media's agenda. Bloggers want media coverage to reflect more bloggers' priorities. Journalists, however, naturally seek to maintain control over that agenda. They compete because they overlap in the nature of their content. Both deal with straight news reporting and commentary. A-list political blogs often report current events as well as comment on them. The degree to which they do so varies significantly. For example, The Huffington Post features hard news coverage with lengthy late-breaking wire service stories, while others, such as Hugh Hewitt and Eschaton, typically ignore the latest breaking news. Similarly, traditional media have included commentary and analysis in the news presentation. Newspapers editorialize on their editorial pages and allow others, both columnists and readers, to express opinions on the same pages. And broadcast news programs have included commentary at times in segregated segments either during the news hour or at other times.

The overlap between the two media, therefore, is hardly complete. That is common sense. If blogs had duplicated journalism, there would have been no appeal. It is precisely because they did not that they have acquired an audience. They offer a facet of news that is underplayed in news reporting by journalists. Blogs emphasize commentary with some straight news, while news organizations offer straight news with some commentary. That is why competition is too narrow an explanation of the relationship between journalists and bloggers.

What has developed is a symbiotic relationship. That symbiotic relationship defines and predicts the relationship between journalists and bloggers. Such relationships form because both parts receive mutual benefits, but they also entail particular costs. Both bloggers and journalists have developed a dependency on one another. Blogs have become integrated into the news reporting process. Journalists pay attention to them; they read blogs and occasionally they even use blogs as news sources.

Journalists and bloggers benefit in the sense that they rely on one another to provide a facet of news each has difficulty offering. For journalists who embrace objective reporting, opinion and commentary occupy an uneasy place in the journalistic profession. Moreover, the type of commentary some blogs engage in—inside gossip—is outside the bounds of respectable journalism. Bloggers, on the other hand, have no difficulty with commentary; in fact, they revel in it. Their problem is an inability to match the news media's surveillance capability. Therefore bloggers, like everyone else, must rely on the news media for news. For national political bloggers, that means particular dependence on national media such as the *New York Times*, the *Washington Post*, and CNN.[111] They read media stories every day and use them as springboards for blog posts.

Although critical of traditional media, some bloggers admit their dependence on traditional media. Markos Moulitsas said the media are allies: "I don't want to do the reporting....I need the media to do its job and provide the raw data, the raw information that then we can use to decide what's the best course for our country."[112] John Hinderaker has articulated the respective roles: "I don't think that the press has a special role in constitutional terms. I think they have a special role in our economy, and that is as primary news gatherers and news disseminators. We bloggers and others in the field of commentary can do anything that journalists can do. Sometimes we do it better; sometimes maybe we don't do it as well. But we can do it. But we don't have staffs of full-time reporters and budgets to send reporters to far-off parts of the world and so on. Somebody needs to carry out that primary news-gathering and news-reporting function."[113]

Bloggers rely on news media for their own news. As mentioned earlier, blog posts are replete with references to traditional media stories that bloggers have found. It is no surprise that bloggers themselves admit that the traditional media constitute a vital source of information for them. Moulitsas admitted he gets his news mostly from newspapers.[114] Joshua Micah Marshall said his ideas come from the media: "In general, I'll read an article, then I'll start thinking about it, and I'll have this reflex to write about it."[115] A reporter described a visit to the office of Talking Points Memo, Marshall's blog: "A pair of interns wearing fat headphones monitor three flat-screen televisions mounted along a wall. Two of them are turned to MSNBC and CNN....The third is tuned to

C-SPAN, which is about to broadcast a Senate Foreign Relations Committee hearing. If anything interesting—or interestingly false—gets said during that hearing, the interns can use TiVo to post a short video excerpt online, along with text commentary."[116]

In fact the very legitimacy of the blogs has been enhanced by the presence of journalists among bloggers. Blogs by former or even current journalists legitimated blogs for other journalists. When journalists first examined blogs to determine whether they were worth their time to read, they saw writing by former colleagues and well-known peers. This established a level of trust in the new medium that was not shared previously by discussion groups or chat rooms and has continued to attract readers. As a result, the blogosphere now includes a journalistic audience that has reported on blogs for a non-blog-reading audience and offers the potential of magnifying the influence of the blogosphere beyond its own borders.[117]

One aspect of this symbiotic relationship is the implicit division of labor between these two entities. The division reflects the weaknesses of both: journalists' eschewing of commentary and bloggers' inability to collect hard news. When bloggers argue that their contribution is a substantial part of the consumer's news package, they are acknowledging this division of labor. Notice that Moulitsas called the news product "raw data." The implication is that without the blogs the information provided by the news media is incomplete. It lacks the analysis—the interpretative frame—that blogs provide. Without blogs, the reader gets only descriptive information without an understanding of meaning and context.

It is important to note that the blogs' addition is one that is not new to journalism. Even before blogs, journalistic analysis tentatively had emerged out of objective journalism and been granted a role in the process of news reporting. Journalists today are more likely than their counterparts a generation ago to include analysis in their reporting and to write separate analysis pieces that do not fit the descriptive model. However, bloggers have a point that the vast majority of the news is dedicated to stories that are highly descriptive in nature. The journalist is not encouraged to inject personal feelings or an overtly subjective frame into the story. That does not mean journalists cannot create a frame for the story, but the norms of the profession compel them to find someone else to say what they would like to say. The bloggers' contribution in this symbiotic relationship is to say what journalists do not say but would like to say. For example, journalists reporting a story about the absence of weapons of mass destruction in Iraq after the Bush administration went to war on that premise might want to add that the president either lied to the public or was incompetent in seeking the truth. The blogger can, and does, assert that.

Nevertheless one can question the value added by bloggers in terms of commentary. Isn't there already plenty of commentary on editorial pages that serves the same function as blogs? Are blogs any different from the newspapers' editorial pages? In sheer numbers they are. There are only a handful of newspapers with national scope or that are read by elites outside of their geographic region (such as the *Los Angeles Times* and the *Chicago Tribune*); in contrast, there are many blogs to choose from, even among the influentials.

Another value of blogs is their ability to broadcast a perspective emanating from outside traditional journalism. Reaction to news now is filtered through journalists interviewing journalists. Journalists can be accused of being too insular when they turn to each other for reaction to events. But theoretically bloggers allow journalists to see reaction from outside the journalistic community. Because bloggers spend little time in news rooms or briefing rooms or press galleries, their reaction becomes another perspective, one that may be seen as the public's reaction or at least a response by people who are more like the public than journalists are. Of course, as we have seen, that assumption is flawed because some of the influential bloggers are affiliated with traditional media or at one time themselves were journalists. Even those who were not journalists look far more like elites than they do the general public.

The act of gauging that reaction also is a profoundly subjective one. The two broad camps of the blogosphere—as well as the range within it—allow journalists potentially to pick and choose which blogs they seek to use in order to frame the story. Bloggers potentially become another source for the journalist using sources to say what the journalist cannot. Moreover, the blog analysis appears faster than editorials. Newspaper editorials appear once a day, whereas blog commentary can be nearly instantaneous. Within minutes of the announcement of Harriet Miers's nomination, blogs were commenting on it—typically unfavorably. For journalists on a twenty-four-hour cycle with constant deadlines, the blogs offer reaction much faster than other news sources. Of course, the instant analysis can lead to questions about whether the reaction is thoughtful and reasoned. But that is not the real question; in fact, one might argue that the more emotional the reaction, the more newsworthy the blog post.

The symbiosis goes beyond straight news versus commentary. It is also breadth versus depth of reporting. News media possess the capability to conduct surveillance across a broad array of events. With news bureaus in various parts of the country and the globe, national news organizations are capable of drawing event-driven stories into the press, typically in short segments. Television news stories are one example, but so are newspaper stories that, with the advent of *USA Today* and the Internet, have become shorter over time. Blogs, by contrast, lack that capability and are not expected to play that role. They can perform a complementary function of burrowing down more deeply into details of more specific events at a level that general-interest media rarely reach. Wilson Lowrey suggested that bloggers "produce content based on stories that have been abandoned by traditional journalism organizations."[118] But the capability to do so does not mean they actually do so. As discussed earlier, bloggers vary considerably in their depth of substance. Many blogs, such as Instapundit, consist of numerous brief posts, rarely going beyond brief discussion, or even bare mention, of issues or events. The minority are those who feature lengthy posts with extensive exposition of a particular topic. Journalists, in turn, rely on blogs for information that would be more difficult for them to collect on their own. This is especially true for highly specialized blogs written by experts. These specialty blogs may be valuable journalistic sources for knowledge that journalists themselves don't possess.[119]

This description of a mutually beneficial relationship with repeated interaction may ring hollow to many journalists, and perhaps even bloggers. And they may be correct. The existence of a symbiotic relationship in a general sense does not mean every individual journalist or blogger is part of that relationship. Indeed, there are journalists who do not use blogs or pay attention to them. As individuals, they do not participate in the relationship, although they may still be affected by its existence. And there are political bloggers who rely on the media for news to varying extents, some doing so only marginally. However, they are not likely to be influentials because readers of the influential blogs are people who pay close attention to traditional media. Most likely they read blogs in order to place that information in an interpretive frame that corresponds to their views. Those audience uses are discussed in the next chapter.

Again, the existence of a symbiotic relationship does not mean that journalists and blogs do not compete at times as well. The competition may well be an important component of the symbiosis. It helps establish the independence of the two entities, thus preventing absorption. And that independence is particularly emphasized by blogs. Bloggers relish asserting their autonomy by embarrassing the press. They note that news media missed a story or a news organization or individual journalist made a major mistake. Moreover, the competition may lead to displacement. As bloggers fight for press credentials, they may well dislodge journalists for coveted spots at hearings, trials, and even in press pools. Similarly, news organizations may replicate blog offerings in an attempt to stave off use of blogs for news analysis.

Nevertheless the journalistic community as a whole has formed this new association. It is a relationship that exists despite the expressed hostility on the part of many bloggers and the public disdain or seeming neglect on the part of journalists. As long as journalists see bloggers as potential news sources, and bloggers rely on the traditional media for news, their work will be inter-twined rather than distinct. The journalists' role in that relationship is our next subject.

Journalists' Use of Blogs

Ultimately bloggers' potential influence on individual political journalists is contingent on whether journalists are aware of blogs, read blogs, and actually incorporate blog reading into the news-gathering and -reporting process much as they would other regular sources of information. But do they really do that? A-list political bloggers believe they're being read by political journalists. For example, Glenn Reynolds said, "There's not much doubt that most political journalists read a lot of the blogs."[120]

However, journalists' own assertions about how much they pay attention to blogs, and whether blog content is important, vary from individual to indi-vidual. Walter Shapiro of *USA Today* said he reads political blogs, sometimes more than once a day. Ryan Lizza of the *New Republic* said he reads ten to fifteen blogs daily. Adam Nagourney of the *New York Times* said he doesn't read blogs regularly because there's too much out there to read, but Mark Halperin, ABC News political director, said he reads political blogs regularly. Ron Brownstein, the *National Journal* columnist, said he reads campaign blogs but doesn't find them useful: "I feel like we're talking to ourselves with most of that stuff."[121]

Do journalists really pay attention to blogs? Do they read blogs, and if so, is it more than just occasionally? How often do they read them? How much time do they devote to them? Is it a cursory read, or do they devote a significant amount of time to finding out what the blogs are saying? Which blogs do they read? Is there an ideological bias in blog reading? Are they like other political blog readers and favor the A-list blogs, or are there other blogs they follow? Why do they read blogs? Is it curiosity? Is it pleasure? Or is blog reading more important than that? Is blog reading an element of news gathering? Do they use blogs to help find sources, gather story ideas, obtain news they don't get elsewhere? How often are blogs used in the news-gathering process?

This section answers those questions through a review of the results of a national survey of political journalists conducted in the spring of 2007. (For a discussion of the survey, see the appendix.) The survey asked journalists about their political blog use, their media use generally, and what role blogs played in how they gathered news.

Reading Blogs

Journalists do read blogs—and they admit they do. As table 6.1 shows, a majority of journalists said they read political blogs at least several times weekly. Only a small minority (9 percent) said they never read political blogs. At the other end, over a third said they read political blogs on a daily basis. Clearly, blog reading has become part of a regular ritual for political journalists. This is particularly significant because it is such a recent change. Because political blogs did not exist until 2000, and it was several years later before an array of A-list political blogs emerged, the rapid adoption of blogs as a reading habit in such a short time is remarkable.

Some journalists adopted blog reading fairly quickly. One survey of journalists in late 2004 found that 29 percent read blogs daily. But in the same survey, nearly 50 percent said they never read blogs.[122] The number of journalists reading blogs daily has grown generally, but the greatest growth seems to be among those journalists who have decided they need to pay at least some attention to political blogs.

Also, it is noteworthy that journalists have carved out so much extra time in the day (often up to thirty minutes) to read political blogs. Fifty-seven percent said they read blogs on average between five and thirty minutes a day. Another 16 percent said they spend more than thirty minutes a day reading blogs. Most journalists are devoting at least some time each day to blogs; some are devoting a significant block of time in a busy day. Somehow they are adding to busy days an extra activity that didn't exist only a few years ago.

But it is important to remember what blog reading has not done. Clearly, it has not supplanted reporters' use of other media sources. According to table 6.1, the vast majority of political journalists include several news sources in their

Table 6.1   Frequency of Journalists' Use of News Sources

Frequency of use	Online news	Talk radio	Nat'l newspaper	Local newspaper	Network news	Local TV news	Blogs
Never	1%	23%	1%	1%	2%	11%	9%
Several times/year	2	24	1	2	2	21	16
Several times/month	5	19	4	1	13	20	19
Several times/week	14	16	14	2	18	20	20
Daily	78	18	80	94	58	29	36

daily information-gathering routine, including local newspapers, national news-papers, online news sources, and network broadcast news. In fact, traditional media still dominate as the preferred sources of political journalist information. This is particularly true of print media. More than 90 percent of journalists paid attention to national and local newspapers; 75 percent said they watched network broadcast news at least several times a week.

But the dramatic change in this picture from a similar survey twenty years ago is the use of online news sources—not as a replacement, but as a supple-ment for traditional hard copy news stories. In this survey, online news sources were used as frequently as national newspapers. This study doesn't reveal which online news sources journalists are using. However, it is likely that these sources are the online versions of traditional news sources such as CNN, Fox News, the *Wall Street Journal*, and the *Washington Post*. Given the practice of updating Web sites of traditional media throughout the day, these journalists may be reading the print version in the morning and the online versions throughout the day.

One of those online news sources is the political blog. But when discuss-ing political blog reading by journalists, it is important to use the plural. Most political journalists who read blogs read more than one. And fifty-four percent said they read three or more blogs per week. They may be sampling across blogs to avoid relying too much on the perspective of a single blogger, or they may see different blogs as serving different information niches. The dilemma may be choosing which of the many blogs, even just among the influentials, to devote precious time to reading. With a routine that includes reading several blogs regularly, journalists may suffer information overload.[123]

The type of political blog journalists read is a general politics blog such as the influentials we have been looking at throughout this study. Fewer use blogs devoted to specific policy areas, such as foreign policy, education, or energy. Sixty-six percent said they read blogs that are about politics generally, while 27 percent reported they read blogs that were devoted to a specific policy area.

The survey asked journalists if they were familiar with any of fifteen popular political blogs (see table 6.2).[124] About 50 percent of the journalists were famil-iar with seven of the highest ranked political blogs. Daily Kos and Wonkette, blogs that have received extensive attention from the press in news stories, were familiar to 77 percent of the journalists. The blogs journalists had heard of ranged across both ideological blogospheres. Of the seven blogs with which journalists were familiar, three (Daily Kos, Wonkette, and Talking Points) are in the liberal blogosphere, and four are more to the right (Andrew Sullivan, Michelle Malkin, Instapundit, and RedState).

Table 6.2   Journalists' Familiarity with Popular Political Blogs, in Percentages

	Heard of	Read in past week
Daily Kos	77	32
Wonkette	77	30
Andrew Sullivan	69	20
Michelle Malkin	59	17
Instapundit	57	19
RedState	55	29
Talking Points Memo	49	37
Hugh Hewitt	35	11
Power Line	33	25
Crooks and Liars	29	29
Volokh Conspiracy	23	31
MyDD	19	44
Eschaton	17	36
Talk Left	14	42
Little Green Footballs	8	40

To assess what blogs journalists actually read on a regular basis (as opposed to those they had just heard of) they also were asked what blogs they had read in the past week. Not surprisingly, journalists had heard of more blogs than they actually read. But a surprising finding was the fact that the blogs they were most familiar with were not necessarily those they actually read. For example, although 59 percent of the journalists had heard of Michelle Malkin, only 17 percent had read the blog in the past week.

Another study found that journalist blog reading leaned heavily toward top political blogs.[125] The top ten blogs accounted for 54 percent of the blogs read by journalists. Elite journalists were even more likely to center their attention on a small handful of blogs; those ten blogs accounted for 74 percent of blogs referenced by elite journalists. The most-read blogs by journalists were almost exclusively those in the liberal blogosphere. Of the top five blogs in terms of journalistic readership, four—MyDD, Talk Left, Talking Points, and Eschaton— were A-list liberal blogs. Another indication of the tilt toward the liberal blogosphere was the preference for blogs to the left when journalists were asked to list the blogs they read. Of the 203 journalists who listed one or more blogs they read, there were 308 mentions of blogs read in the past week. Fifty-two percent of those mentions went to blogs that were to the left politically, despite the fact that of the fifteen blogs asked about, only six were left-leaning blogs.

Journalists are aware of blogs in both ideological blogospheres, but they spend their time actually reading the blogs in the liberal blogosphere. These reading patterns suggest that journalists may be getting primarily one view of the blogosphere. It also could affect what blogs are mentioned in news stories. Additionally, when journalists take story ideas from blogs, those ideas naturally will come from blogs they read.

Using Blogs as News Sources

Seventy-four percent of journalists surveyed said they read blogs mainly for work-related reasons; only 9 percent said they did so mainly for personal interests. So what role does blog reading play in journalistic news gathering and reporting? To answer this question, journalists were asked how often they use blogs to do three things: get information about news they can't find elsewhere, identify sources for stories they are writing, and, perhaps most important for agenda setting, get story ideas.

As table 6.3 shows, the most common use of blogs by journalists (59 percent) is to get news that isn't covered elsewhere. Journalists are looking for stories not provided in the traditional media. Unlike traditional media outlets that cover a wide range of news designed to appeal to an audience not strongly interested in politics, political blogs are specialized sources. Because journalists also cover this specialized topic, it makes sense that they would seek out news from outlets that provide information that is not covered or is under-covered in other traditional media.

If blogs are acquiring much of their information from traditional media, then the information the journalists get from blogs would seem to be repetitive of what they are seeing in their own search of the traditional media. Indeed, in many cases it may be. A journalist covering national politics may have already read the *New York Times* and the *Washington Post* before turning to the blogs. Yet journalists also are using blogs to collect information from media sources. A reporter for the *San Diego Union-Tribune* said he uses blogs to get access to pertinent articles from the Capitol publication *The Hill*.[126] Blogs may well have become a supplement for journalists' own surveillance of news outlets.

Table 6.3   Frequency of Use of Blogs in Elements of News-Gathering Process

Frequency of use	Find news	Find news sources	Get story ideas not elsewhere
Regularly	13%	6%	3%
Sometimes	46	25	25
Rarely	24	42	44
Never	16	28	28

The line is drawn, though, on journalists saying they use blogs for news gathering. Most journalists (70 percent) said they had rarely or never used blogs to find sources for stories. Only six percent said they did so regularly. Given the time devoted to reading blogs, it seems odd that journalists would not say they used them to gather news. There may be several reasons for this response. Political blogs typically cite traditional news media as their sources. Many of these may be articles journalists are already familiar with, or journalists may be reluctant to cite such sources themselves since they are paid to gather news and not to repeat it from another traditional media source. Another reason may be trust-related. Journalists may be unsure that the sources they see listed in blogs are ones that they should use. They may be seeing news in the blogs, but then turning to the original source provided by the blog as their actual source. Hence the credit would go not to the blog but to the confirming, and more reliable, source. Or it could be that the top political bloggers themselves are not adequate sources since they are not experts on policy, electoral campaigns, public opinion, or other topics.

Journalists also say they don't use blogs for story ideas. Seventy-two percent said they rarely or never do so, and only 3 percent said they do so regularly. Again, this finding seems incongruous. If journalists are spending time reading blogs at least several times a week (with some doing so far more often), and they are doing so for work-related reasons, why would they not actually use their blog reading for possible stories? One possible explanation is that story generation is not in their purview. They cover stories assigned to them by an assignment or desk editor. However, that explanation may be true in some cases, but not generally. Political or policy reporters typically have a broad mandate to originate stories, rather than merely report what an editor gives them. Another explanation is that they feel confident of their own story ideas and aren't looking at blogs as a generator of ideas. That also may be partially true, but journalists search for news. Why do journalists spend so much work-related time reading blogs if they are in the business of gathering news and blogs do not provide that news? Still another explanation, which is discussed below, is the trust factor again. It may well be that journalists do not fully trust the information they are receiving on blogs. Although blogs are interesting to read, the credibility of the information is questionable enough to not qualify for inclusion in news.

Yet it is noteworthy that blogs have come to play a role for some journalists in some critical elements of news gathering. The fact that 31 percent of the journalists have used blogs to find sources and 28 percent have used them to get story ideas suggests that a minority of journalists employ blogs for purposes that directly relate to news gathering. It is important to remember that ten years ago the number would have been zero.

The most important use for political blogs by journalists is to obtain reaction. Fifty-three percent said they read blogs to gauge public reaction to events. This could include a State of the Union speech, a congressional vote, a terrorist attack, or other events reported in traditional media and commented on by the blogs. Blog reaction is an outsider response that can be more easily gauged than calling twenty-five undecided voters, doing person-on-the-street interviews, or conducting a scientific poll. Using blogs for reporting reaction by a small group of political activists is one thing, but a problem arises when reaction is extrapolated from bloggers' posts and online comments to the general public. That leap requires an assumption that the political blogosphere is representative of the larger public—an assumption without evidence.

Another, perhaps safer use of blogs is to read commentary on the news from bloggers; fifty-nine percent of journalists said they read blogs to do this. The blogs provide what traditional media partly do: offer analysis on events. Whereas journalists are expected to adhere to the norms of journalism, bloggers can offer lively, partisan, even biting interpretation of current events. This level of usage of blogs is not surprising because so much of blog content is not the transmission of hard news, but the expression of bloggers' own commentary or the dissemination of commentary by others. Absent from this category is media content, which is already in the traditional media. There may not be much in blogs that is original for journalists to use as news.

Depending on the blogger, analysis may attract journalists because it is incisive. Blogs by lawyers may offer the journalist more context for a Supreme Court decision or other legal opinion. A blog post on The Huffington Post by a national political reporter or an elections expert may provide journalists with more in-depth analysis of a primary or caucus vote than they can obtain elsewhere.

Blogs have become a news-gathering tool for journalists. They want to hear commentary on what traditional media are saying. They want to see how others are reacting to news events. And they use blogs to gather news that traditional media sources are not covering, such as political stories that may be too "inside baseball" for traditional media. What is missing in most cases, however, is an admission of a direct linkage to the news product produced by the journalist. They said they aren't using blogs to find sources or, most important, get story ideas. The journalist is the filter for blog effect. Most journalists seem to be reluctant to pass on directly the information they obtain from blogs to their audiences.

Trusting Blogs

Why are journalists mainly acting as filters rather than as conduits for blog agendas and content? The answer may lie with journalists' perceptions of their own role. Journalists see themselves as filters for other news sources—politicians, candidates, institutions, organizations. Why would blogs be treated differently?

But perhaps blogs are treated differently. Certainly White House Rose Garden ceremonies and congressional press conferences do form the news content for journalists. Story ideas are gleaned from press briefings and interviews, not to mention actual events. Journalists admit that they receive press releases and advisories that influence story generation. Yet journalists say that story ideas are not gleaned from blogs. Why?

The difference may well be credibility. Whereas other sources may be viewed as legitimate and credible, in the eyes of the public as well as the press, blog content still may be suspect in the eyes of journalists. Fifty-two percent of journalists said that they felt information they read on blogs was less accurate than what is in the mainstream media, and an additional 32 percent said it was much less accurate. Only 16 percent felt it was as accurate. None believed it was more accurate than traditional journalistic sources. Apparently journalists don't quite trust the content they read on blogs. Reporting public reaction is well and good because it can be couched as "This is what the blogs are saying." But actually trusting the information blogs provide for story ideas or as actual news is another thing altogether.

If journalists completely discounted blog information, then it is likely they would not waste their time reading blogs. But journalists were split on the general credibility of political blogs. Fifty-two percent felt they were at least somewhat credible, but 48 percent believed they were not very credible or not credible at all. Because many fellow journalists dismiss blog credibility, use of blogs may suffer even by those who view blog content as at least somewhat credible. The division may well lead journalists to treat blog information cautiously. These findings suggest that journalistic treatment of blogs is fluid and that blogs may well acquire increased acceptance by journalists as time passes.

Comparing Agendas

There has been little analysis of agenda setting between political blogs and the traditional media. Kevin Wallsten looked at the issue congruence between blogs that were not A-list and traditional media coverage. He found that the degree of influence of the traditional media on political bloggers depends on the frequency of activity of the blog. Blogs with daily (or more often) postings had the highest correlation with media topics.[127] This finding suggests that bloggers who are seeking regular topics for expression look to traditional media sources to find them. This would support the hypothesis that political bloggers are influenced by traditional media.

Another study found that newspaper and blog coverage of major Democratic presidential candidates was highly correlated. Both media covered the candidates negatively. There was a strong correlation between blog coverage and editorials, but no correlation between blog coverage and letters to the editor. Also, newspaper stories and blogs were similar in emphasis on the horse race. In terms of treatment of candidates, A-list blogs act more like news media than like the writings of average people.[128]

To determine the influence of media on one other's agendas, the blog content discussed earlier was compared with newspaper stories. Stories appearing on the front page of four major newspapers—the *New York Times*, the *Washington Post*, the *Washington Times*, and the *Wall Street Journal*—were content-analyzed during the same month as the seven blogs (September 2006). Altogether, 548 stories were analyzed. (For a more detailed discussion of method, see the appendix.) But before we examine competing agendas, there are other important findings about the interrelationship between newspapers and blogs.

First, it is clear that blogs notice newspapers far more than newspapers pay attention to blogs. In these four elite newspapers, blogs were rarely mentioned—either by name or generally—during this period. Of 548 front-page stories, only eight (1.5 percent) mentioned a specific blog by name. Only 12 (2 percent) mentioned a blog as a source of information in the story. Only 3 percent mentioned the word "blog" in the story, and a similar percentage mentioned a Web site as a source.

Even when blogs are mentioned, it is often not in a positive context. This may well reflect what journalists think (and perhaps what they think the public thinks) about blogs. For example, a *Wall Street Journal* story mentioned blogs along with "a glut of gossipy tabloids" as changing the New York fashion scene. A *Washington Times* story on 9/11 conspiracy theories concluded, "Internet bloggers circulated reams of unsubstantiated assertions." Blogs are mentioned when they actually are a part of the story. For example, a *Washington Post* story profiled bloggers. A *New York Times* story discussed the culture of politicians making verbal gaffes and then publicly apologizing; the piece mentioned blogs as part of that culture.

In the few other cases when blogs were mentioned, it was in a way that suggests the journalist used a blog for information in writing the story. For example, a *Washington Post* story on social networking sites mentioned information drawn from Facebook's blog. A *Wall Street Journal* article mentioned content on the blog of the prime minister of Hungary, and a *New York Times* story did the same in referring to information gleaned from the blog of a congressional candidate. Such overt references are rare, but they do indicate that at least some journalists at these elite newspapers are reading blogs specifically to elicit information for stories. The odds are low that these journalists would visit the blog of the Hungarian prime minister or a congressional candidate just for entertainment. These small references raise the question of how much blog content is being used without reference to the blog directly. Due to the ambivalence about blogs among journalists, as well as the public perception that blogs are a haven for extremists and shrill partisans, it may be that journalists are tiptoeing forward in the use of blogs.

Even if they are not explicitly used as sources, do blogs still impact news media agendas? The study of blog posts and news media stories conducted for this book found an overlap between the two media, but not as large as might be expected (See table 6.4). The newspapers emphasized discussion of general domestic policy, ranging across health care, education, energy policy, and housing. As discussed earlier, the midterm elections were a popular topic for the blogs. The two also differed substantially on coverage of international relations and foreign policy, news of the blogosphere, economic news, and coverage of the news media itself. Whereas the newspapers devoted 31 percent of their coverage to either domestic or foreign policy areas, the blogs' coverage constituted only 9 percent of all posts. Bloggers rarely covered economic news (business news, stock market, labor and commerce statistics and news, etc.). For newspapers, the economy was the fifth most covered topic.

The blogosphere had its own favored topics. The newspapers rarely had interest in the happenings of the blogosphere, or even the news media themselves. Bloggers, however, dedicated 18 percent of their posts to news of the blogosphere and 5 percent to events or issues regarding the news media. The contrasting agendas can be explained to a great extent by the difference in roles of the two media. Newspapers become the source for general news about the events of the world, particularly since the previous issue. Blogs serve no such purpose. Blog readers have no expectation that they will get a survey of a range of news—tornadoes in Kansas, the stock market, unemployment figures, as well as elections in California and the latest White House news.

The newspaper and blog agendas were similar in some respects. The midterm elections and the war on terror were significant components of the information

Table 6.4   Topic Agenda: Newspapers and Blogs Compared, in Percentages

Topic	Newspapers	Blogs
Midterm elections	12	18
War on Terror	11	16
Blog news	0	13
General domestic policy	19	5
Iraq war	6	6
International relations/foreign policy	12	4
News media-related	0	5
White House/Congress	3	4
Other scandals	<1	4
Middle East	3	3
Economic	8	1
Celebrity news	1	2
Iran	2	2
Republican House scandals	1	2
Defense Department	<1	1
CIA leak	<1	1
Immigration	3	<1
Miscellaneous	13	13
Total	100	100
Total number of articles/posts	606	2,828

portrait presented by both newspapers and blogs. The newspapers' coverage was less than that of the blogs due to their attention to other topics, yet both placed these topics at the top of their agendas. Both devoted the same amount of coverage to the Iraq war, the Middle East, and Iran. They similarly largely ignored issues such as the Valerie Plame CIA leak, the Department of Defense and Donald Rumsfeld, and even the Republican House scandals.

The expectation was that the substance of bloggers' posts would be what they draw from traditional media and then comment on with their own spin. Certainly that occurs, but in the vast majority of cases, it does not. When the posts of these bloggers occurring the day before, the day of, and the day after a news story were analyzed for topic comparison with that day's news coverage in front-page stories of the four elite newspapers under study, only 8 percent of posts matched the topics discussed in the stories.[129]

During the period under study, bloggers discussed the wars in Iraq and Afghanistan, Senator Joe Lieberman's bid to retain his U.S. Senate seat, Hezbollah's war with Israel, and many other topics. All of these also were covered by the front-page stories of these newspapers, but not necessarily at the same time as the blogs. One explanation for this discrepancy is that the conservative blogs dragged down that percentage. These blogs may ignore traditional media because they view them as liberal. (However, two of the newspapers in the sample take more conservative editorial positions and seemingly would be magnets for the attention of conservative bloggers and potential material for their posts.) Conservative bloggers might be assumed to have their own agendas that do not acknowledge the traditional media's agenda.

Indeed, liberal and conservative bloggers do have their own agendas. For example, Eschaton, Wonkette, Crooks and Liars, and Daily Kos together had ten posts about Republican Representative Bob Ney pleading guilty to charges of corruption; Wonkette alone had half of those. There were forty-five blog posts about the George Allen and Jim Webb race for the U.S. Senate in Virginia. Most of those posts covered controversies about Allen, such as his "macaca" statement, his Jewish ancestry, and his association with reportedly racist organizations. All but six came from liberal blogs. The three conservative blogs did not discuss Ney's guilty plea at all, nor did they spend much time on Allen's controversies. However, 33 percent of the posts about terrorism or the war on terror came from the three conservative blogs.

Even though the two sets of bloggers have separate agendas in many cases, their approach to the traditional media's agenda is similar. The conservative blogs were slightly less likely to cover the same topics as those discussed in the traditional media (7 percent) compared with the liberal blogs (9 percent), but the difference was hardly dramatic. The differences among blogs in their attention to the media's agenda may stem less from ideology and more from bloggers' own sense of integration with the political and media mainstream. Thirteen percent of Daily Kos posts matched news stories. Similarly, 11 percent of Michelle Malkin's posts and 10 percent of Crooks and Liars' posts covered the same topics as those discussed by the newspapers. Eschaton, on the other hand, had only a 4 percent overlap.

These findings suggest that the news media and the blogosphere have largely separate agendas. Even when there is a topic overlap between news stories and blogs, it does not mean that either drew from the other. Instead, it is more likely that the overlap is related to a third party that served as the source for both. This could be an event or, more likely, the efforts of a publicist. For example, both the *Washington Times* and Instapundit covered a story on cancer treatment success. Instapundit's story, which appeared after the *Washington Times* story, cited *Science News*. The newspaper story cited the journal *Science*. Both may have received their own news releases on the research finding. In other cases, the appearance of similar topics likely was more serendipitous than planned.

For example, Crooks and Liars posted on the lack of success in the wars in Afghanistan and Iraq. The next day a *New York Times* story appeared about the failure of U.S. troops to make secure a part of Afghanistan known as "Little America." Daily Kos also discussed and linked to an Associated Press story on the upsurge in violence in Afghanistan. Although discussing the same topic, none of the three linked to each other or cited the same sources. Daily Kos did use traditional media, an AP story, although Crooks and Liars relied on two liberal blogs.

Agenda-setting efforts seemed to occur in a few circumstances. One surrounded the airing of an ABC docudrama titled *The Path to 9/11*. The program, which aired on the fifth anniversary of the September 11, 2001, attacks, stirred controversy because former Clinton administration officials, including the former president himself, and other Democrats complained that the program was riddled with historical inaccuracies. The blogosphere covered the story extensively. From September 1 until the show aired, bloggers were discussing it. The liberal bloggers Daily Kos and Eschaton were using their blogs to highlight inaccuracies they saw in the script as well as efforts by former Clinton administration officials to urge ABC to make changes or cancel the series. Daily Kos termed it a "right wing docudrama." Additionally, they urged their readers to contact ABC to lobby against the program's airing. Conservative bloggers, bemused by the liberal bloggers' distress, joined the discussion to counter the pressure from the left on ABC.

Three percent of the blog posts addressed this topic (compared to 7 percent on topics related to the Iraq war). All the blogs, with the exception of Little Green Footballs, discussed the upcoming miniseries and the various facets of the story, including a letter from President Clinton's attorney asking ABC to correct the film or shelve it, congressional Democratic leaders' threats to review television licenses, petition drives by the Democratic National Committee, and the conservative blogosphere's reaction to the fury exhibited over the program by the liberal bloggers. However, the blogosphere's exhaustive discussion barely penetrated the traditional news media's agenda. Only one traditional news story during the month covered what the blogosphere spent days covering. It was not even a story the elite press generated; rather, it was an Associated Press story appearing in the *Washington Times* on September 8.

Half of the blog posts appeared before the newspaper story did. They discussed the scheduling of the film, the possibility of changes in the script, and the fact that the details of the film had been given to right-wing supporters and bloggers but not to those on the left. All of these could have led to news media coverage. Yet the actual news peg of the story was a letter written by Bruce Lindsey, President Clinton's attorney. The letter pointed out inaccuracies in the film and demanded corrections. Although some of the bloggers discussed this angle as well, it is likely the AP story originated from a public relations effort by President Clinton and others in his administration to affect ABC's treatment of the docudrama.

However, the blogosphere did have an impact on the news story. The AP story also mentioned that the program, though praised by conservatives, had "drawn fire from liberal blogs" and that one blog claimed it had caused 25,000 of its readers to complain directly to ABC. The AP story did not appear to be a direct result of bloggers' efforts to revise or scuttle the show, but the reporter was aware of bloggers' efforts. The extent to which they contributed to the story's appearance is unknown. The prominent news features highlighted in the story were the change in ABC's stance on the program and the pressure applied by prominent Democrats.

This example illustrates the interaction among potential agenda setters and the blogosphere. The blogosphere needed legitimacy from other players, in this case President Clinton and others formerly in his administration, to get the press to notice the blogosphere's issue. Whether the blogosphere played a role in prompting the Clinton administration officials' actions or ABC's, or whether the two events were parallel but unrelated, is unknown. However, the example shows that even an item discussed by both the liberal and conservative blogospheres over a several-day period may not become a traditional media story without intervention from outside the blogosphere.

One topic that did appear extensively in both the blogs and the news media simultaneously was coverage of the Mark Foley scandal. The Florida representative resigned abruptly on September 29, 2006, after salacious e-mails and instant messages he had written to House pages were circulated in the blogosphere. The blog StopSexPredators posted e-mails by Foley on September 24. According to a Wonkette post on September 27, someone sent the post to Wonkette, which repeated it. The blog did not name the source or offer much credence to the story. Wonkette added, "Oh, of course they're not real. But let's all pretend, ok?" Late on September 28, ABC News posted the story on the news organization's blog, but it was not picked up by the newspapers until Foley resigned the next day. Three of the four newspapers had stories about the resignation on September 30. The blogs had reported the story the previous day. But these blogs did not originate the story; they cited the ABC News blog as the first to break the story, although Crooks and Liars also cited another blog as the source of information about the scandal.

This was an atypical case in which multiple news media sources and several bloggers covered the same topic at the same time. Yet the agenda was set primarily by traditional media. Even though the story circulated on some blogs prior to the ABC News story, it was not taken seriously until it had been legitimated by the news media. Nevertheless this case does serve as an example of efforts to set agendas in reaction to the event. The bloggers' take on the scandal varied depending on how they wanted subsequent discussion on larger issues to evolve. For example, in its second post on the topic, after relating the latest on the story, Crooks and Liars added, "Sounds like the leadership in Congress really needs to be asked some serious questions about this." Michelle Malkin, which didn't discuss the incident until late in the evening, did not mention congressional leaders' foreknowledge or treatment of Foley; instead, that blog warned parents to teach their children about the dangers of sexual predators.

The image of bloggers linking to major stories in the traditional media and then commenting on them is more characteristic of some political blogs than others. Typically bloggers who do so use the press as a foil. One example is a post on Little Green Footballs that addressed a front-page *Washington Post* story of the same day. The story, which discussed the tendency of some conservative Muslims in the United States to isolate themselves from the larger society, was the topic of a Little Green Footballs post at 8:53 that morning. The post called the piece "today's episode of the Washington Post's amazing public relations campaign to help us stop worrying and learn to love Islam." The blog then quoted some of the story and linked to the rest.

Repeating and commenting on the news media's daily product does not necessarily maintain an audience. Bloggers need a value-added component to make their product appealing. That means providing news and commentary that is not already available to their audience. As we will see in the next chapter, blog readers already are highly exposed to traditional media sources, including national newspapers; many will have read those stories already. A blog that repeats those stories may offer analysis that adds to the traditional media product, but not much else that would interest the reader. Rather, bloggers often turn to sources that may not be readily apparent to their blog audience in order to set their own agendas. These include other news stories that they may feel are under-covered by the traditional media. The blog posts include news stories, but they tend to be those that are shorter, less obvious news items that bloggers want to point their audience to, just in case they missed them. Additionally, sources may be news media that their audience may not already frequent, such as regional newspapers or specialized media. Blog posts cited the *Rocky*

Mountain News (Denver), the *Daily Mail* (London), the *New York Observer*, the *Knoxville (Tennessee) News Sentinel*, and the *Australia Herald-Sun*, to name a few of the media that the vast majority of readers do not routinely read.

A blogger who concentrates on the media's agenda acknowledges the media's role in agenda setting. Finding what the press does not cover, or at least does not emphasize, does not acknowledge the news media's agenda-setting role. Instead, it challenges that role and asserts the blogosphere's role as a new agenda setter.

In summary, the blogosphere slightly overlaps with and draws from the news media's agenda; however, it does not merely replicate it. Conversely, the traditional media are even less likely to follow the lead of the blogosphere. The major stories in traditional media can make it into the blogosphere, but, as indicated by the *Path to 9/11* coverage, big stories in the blogosphere rarely make it into the important stories of the traditional media. That does not mean the blogosphere may not affect content in other ways. It could be the blogosphere's role is as a gauge of what is going on without particular mention of blogs. Information on blogs may find its way into print, but only after another source also has the story; that source becomes the direct agenda setter and the explicit source in the story, not the blog. This is easier to do in cases where the blog itself cites an original source. The blog then becomes a transmitter of information about possible sources rather than the actual source.

The blogosphere may not play an agenda-setting role yet because journalists are unsure about whether political blogs can be trusted. If the blogosphere ever gains that trust, it will be because it acquires a sense of legitimacy that equates with news media expectations for reliable sources. This transformation may be achieved by the blogosphere becoming professionalized, including establishing a code of ethics for gathering and reporting news, credentialing by government, and adhering to established standards of accuracy. The blogosphere may not be expected to abandon partisan bias. Opinion magazines long have been known for partisanship. Newspaper editorial pages are one-sided., And broadcast media in recent years have become associated with partisan leanings. However, blogs may be expected to establish a firewall between the news dissemination and opinion expression functions to enhance the credibility of their news presentation.

Blogs and the Journalistic Process

Political blog reading has become a part of political journalists' routines for keeping informed. Blogs have not acquired the level of attention journalists give to newspapers or network news, but blogs have found a niche in journalists' news gathering. Nevertheless, these findings suggest some ambiguity among political journalists about the role of blogs. That ambiguity is at the crux of the relationship between journalists and bloggers. It can be expressed something like this: Journalists are willing to invest time in reading blogs and examining their content for news. And there are several reasons journalists would be inclined to read blogs. One is the attention so many others outside the blogosphere are paying to this new online medium. The message journalists hear over and over (and even repeat themselves) is that blogs are important and those outside the blogosphere should pay attention to them. Bloggers obviously feed such conceptions to magnify their importance. Press coverage, particularly coverage that suggests momentum toward greater blog influence, potentially helps blogs. It may increase readership and enhance bloggers' status vis-à-vis journalists and politicians. Journalists undoubtedly hear that message and may turn to blogs to see what's going on. Journalists' use of blogs is still a very new phenomenon: 58 percent of the journalists surveyed said they had been reading blogs for two years or less.

Another reason journalists read blogs is that blogs have uncovered stories the traditional media missed. Even though blogs may not be valuable on an ongoing basis as direct news sources, perhaps a journalist will miss that rare major story that the blogosphere breaks and other journalists miss. The journalist would not want to be the last to know about it.

Still another reason for journalistic attention is that blog content cites traditional media and even comments extensively on specific news stories. Many journalists are interested in what is being said about the work of journalists generally, but also their own work specifically. In fact, 31 percent of the journalists said one reason they read blogs is to gauge reaction to their own stories.

However, there are equally compelling reasons not to use blog content in news. A major barrier is the fact that because blogs do not adhere to professional standards of journalism, their information may be inaccurate. A journalist who picks up such a story, particularly in the rush to be first, may end up embarrassed and discredited. Blog proponents may counter that journalists get stories wrong as well, yet other journalists and the public still use them. Indeed, that is true. But that argument may be little consolation to a journalist whose reputation is damaged by accepting a false blog story as truth and repeating it. Also, blogs have a reputation for extremism. As mentioned in chapter 2, the culture of the blogosphere is rougher, more partisan, and shriller than is tolerated in traditional media and political discourse generally. Can blog content in that atmosphere be considered legitimate, worthy of citing?

Still another limitation for using blog content is the appeal to the audience. Blog content is specialized in nature. When political stories are pushed aside for entertainment or celebrity pieces, is there a market within journalism for "inside baseball" news that appeals to a small minority of the traditional media audience?

Where does this leave blogs' role in journalism? The problem for the future is determining whether blog use will continue to grow. Are those journalists who use blogs for news—the minority at present—the vanguard of a new development in journalism? Will journalists eventually wholeheartedly embrace political blogs as news sources? Or will there be continued reluctance to use blogs, given their inherent weaknesses in current form. Blogs may have to prove their worth to journalists in order to pass the newsworthiness test.

The original question was whether the preconditions for blogs' role in media agenda setting exist: Do journalists read blogs and do they use them in news gathering? The answer is yes and no. They read blogs and view them as a news source for themselves, but they don't yet see them in the same light as they do current sources. Nor does the blog agenda shape the news media agenda. And, as we have seen, the news media agenda shape, but do not wholly determine the agenda of the blogosphere.

7

The Audience

The final player to discuss is the political blog audience. As mentioned earlier, traditional news media audiences intermingle with other players in agenda setting. But do blog audiences do so as well? Before answering that question, it is important to understand who this audience is. Are they unemployed twenty-somethings who spend their days hunched over a computer screen reading the latest gossip about a presidential candidate or smirking over the blogosphere's report on still another media failure? Are they social outcasts who live in a virtual world disconnected from others? Or are they mainstream voters, average Americans? Do they represent the broad spectrum of social life—truckers, physicians, accountants, manicurists, and PhDs as well as high school dropouts, voters and nonvoters? Are they ordinary people seeking more information in order to make decisions about issues and candidates? What are their attitudes about traditional media? Have these readers given up on mainstream media? Or are they supplementing blog and media news sources? And why do they read? What motivates them to spend time reading someone else's political opinions? Is it pure entertainment? Or do blogs offer news they don't get elsewhere? What is the relationship between blogs and their audience? Are they affected by what they read? Do they read blogs in order to glean information, but also, perhaps, to shape opinions as well?

Relatively few surveys of blog audiences exist; even fewer have been conducted for political blog audiences.[1] The Institute for Politics, Democracy & the Internet, the Pew Internet and American Life Project, and Harris Interactive, among others, have polled blog audiences.[2] To answer many of these questions, a survey of political blog readers was conducted. The details of the survey are in the appendix, but, in brief, the survey sample initially included 2,729 people who were part of an Internet survey panel developed by Knowledge Networks. Of those, 653 people who read political blogs at least several times a month became the primary sample.

Three Types of Blog Readers

From the assertions made about the reach of political blogs, one might assume that political blog reading is a universal activity. That is not the case. A majority of Americans do not read political blogs, and most of those who do read them are not regular readers.[3] However, a significant minority of the population have read political blogs at some point. Forty-one percent of adults say they read political blogs at least several times a year. However, nearly half of those said they read blogs *only* several times a year. This likely means they have read a political blog or two at some point in time. Perhaps they received an e-mail from someone they know referring them to a political blog post or stumbled on a political blog while browsing or looked at one but decided not to go back. Because political blogs change daily, sometimes hourly, these people are not political blog readers.

Actual political blog readers—those who read blogs with some consistency—are a smaller percentage: 23 percent read political blogs at least several times a month. Nearly half of those, however, said they read blogs only several times a month. Those we'll call "occasional" readers. They may have blogs on their "favorites." They may go to blogs when there is a story they want more news about and that extra information is not available in traditional media sources. They may enjoy reading blogs but do not have time to do so on a regular basis. Another 7 percent said they read political blogs several times a week but not daily. We'll call them "regular" readers. The last group constitutes 5 percent of adults online. They are the "daily" readers and are the most active blog readership. Although not measured, some portion of this group of readers probably attends to blogs even more frequently than daily. The continual updating of influential blogs throughout the day assumes that some readers return to blogs periodically in a day's time.

These figures are quite similar to results of other recent studies that found daily readers are a small percentage of the population. Two studies of adult Americans, not just those online, found that political blog reading was a habit of relatively few. A CBS/*New York Times* survey in March 2007 found that 4 percent of Americans said they visited political blogs frequently, 14 percent did so occasionally, and 24 percent did so rarely. A Harris Interactive survey similarly found that 4 percent said they read political blogs daily, 7 percent did so several times a week, and 10 percent did so several times a month.[4]

These figures suggest that political blog reading still is not an activity familiar to most Americans, even those online. The vast majority of Americans online are not even occasional readers of political blogs. Those who say they never read blogs and those who probably have seen a political blog or two at some point constitute three of every four adults online. Obviously, if all adults are included—such as the 27 percent of Americans who are not even online—the percentage of those who read political blogs among the general public falls even lower.[5]

The active political blog–reading community—the daily readers—constitute only one in twenty of online Americans. Even the regular readers make up only 12 percent of those online. This is a far cry from the claims sometimes made about the size and impact of the political blog audience. And it is a considerably smaller audience than the one for traditional media. Seventy percent of Americans say they regularly watch local television news, just over 50 percent say they read a daily newspaper, and nearly 50 percent say they are regular watchers of national nightly network news programs.[6]

One response to these numbers is that any judgment of blogosphere impact is premature. The blogosphere is yet in its infancy and perhaps has not realized its full potential as an information medium. As the argument goes, the number of Americans using blogs will increase significantly as time passes. Indeed, it is true that any analysis should examine not just a current snapshot of readership but also consider the future growth of the blogosphere, both audience size and the scope of blogs that eventually will reside there. Obviously it is impossible to do anything but speculate on future growth. But it is possible to examine the rate of growth in audience size and predict the future by comparing blog audience size today with the recent past.

Indeed, that examination is illuminating. The number of devoted blog readers has not changed significantly since 2004, when 4 percent of adults said they regularly read blogs. But the number of less frequent blog readers has risen. In 2004 only 5 percent of blog readers said they read blogs "sometimes."[7] If that equates with our regular and occasional readers, then the number of such readers has more than tripled in three years.

Why would one group grow significantly and the other stagnate? It is possible that those most interested in reading blogs daily quickly found this medium and joined the audience some time ago. That group may not grow larger since it requires a number of traits that the vast majority of adults do not possess, such as intense interest in politics, time to devote to political news retrieval, and enjoyment of the blog culture. However, those who read less frequently could grow in size if the blogosphere begins to appeal to that larger potential audience. Such a scenario could play out like this: As blogs are talked about more in the news or in interpersonal discussions, increasing numbers of Americans will explore political blogs to see what is going on there. These people may go to blogs when they are prompted by others or as they pursue a link from some other online source. Or they may go to political blogs when a story is breaking that blogs are the first to respond to.

But the appeal of these blogs will still be limited, as is true with other forms of specialized political-oriented media. General news blogs, whose appeal transcends those interested in politics, could capture a larger audience. But because political blogs cover a specialized topic that has greatest appeal to a small minority of Americans they will not be popular.

And the nature of online readership militates against political blogs acquiring a less politically oriented viewership. For example, television news program viewing may be as passive as staying tuned after the conclusion of an entertainment-oriented program. As a program sandwiched between entertainment programming, a news broadcast may attract an audience that is inadvertent. Even more inadvertent is the audience for television political advertisement viewing, which is interspersed in entertainment programming and is too brief for many viewers to bother to pick up the remote and change the channel.

By contrast, political blogs require active choice to join the audience. Individuals rarely go there by mistake. In fact, a political blog reader must go online and make several clicks to get to the blog and read it. Those whose interest in politics is occasional or slight to begin with will rarely make that effort. Even if the blog link is e-mailed to the individual by someone else, the perusal of the link does not mean that an individual lacking significant political interest will become a regular reader of the blog.

But there is a significant minority who will pay at least occasional attention to political blogs. They may be drawn to blogs when others prompt them, or when a controversy erupts when political blogs are part of the story, such as in the case of the *60 Minutes II* National Guard memo piece or blogs' role in Barack Obama's statement about "bitter" rural Pennsylvanians. Blog reading for this group, however, is not the same as reading the newspaper or watching television news on a daily basis. They may not be seeking a substitute for their traditional media habits, yet they are interested in keeping informed, at least periodically, about what is going on in the blogosphere.

There are other important differences among the three groups of political blog readers, particularly between the daily readers and the other two groups. One is the length of time they have been reading political blogs. While 58 percent of occasional readers said they had been reading political blogs for two years or less, 44 percent of daily blog readers said they had been blog readers for four years or more. Many daily blog readers found blogs some time ago, perhaps due to their need for the kind of information blogs provide. Their interests, and perhaps their longing for information separate from that provided by the traditional media, drew them to blogs. They also may have been in social circles—e-mail lists, interest group affiliation, etc.—where information about or from political blogs was circulated. Others, perhaps the less frequent readers, may have found political blogs through news media stories about blogs or stories where blogs were mentioned as a source in the story or through Internet browsing. These readers—a large group compared to the daily readers—are new to blogs and have not incorporated blog reading into their daily news information routines.

Daily political blog readers also differ from less frequent readers in their involvement in the blogosphere. One measure of this engagement is the amount of time spent reading political blogs. The median time spent reading blogs in any given day is twenty-two minutes. However, 29 percent of all political blog readers devote thirty minutes or more to blog reading. They are far more likely to be the daily blog readers; nearly 50 percent of *daily* blog readers spend 30 minutes or more reading political blogs. Those who have made blog reading a part of their daily news gathering routine, admittedly a small portion, have carved out a significant block of news-gathering time to this activity.

Still another measure of involvement is the act of posting blog material. Although the vast majority (80 percent) of blog readers only read and do not comment, those who do comment are most likely to be the daily readers. Twenty-eight percent of daily readers had commented at least once on someone else's blog, and a majority of those had done so four or more times. Only 18 percent of regular and occasional readers had done so, and, of those, a majority had commented only once or twice.

Daily political blog readers are also most likely to be bloggers themselves. Only 11 percent of occasional readers and 14 percent of regular readers had their own blog, but 25 percent of daily readers were bloggers. Daily blog readers also are somewhat more likely to use blog rolls, moving from blog to blog, discovering new blogs as they go. Thirty-nine percent of daily blog readers said they find new blogs through links from blogs they read; 30 percent of regular readers and 20 percent of occasional readers found new blogs that way.

That leads to another cleavage between the groups: the number of political blogs they read. Daily readers read more blogs in any given week than regular or occasional readers. While 84 percent of occasional readers and 59 percent of regular readers read two or fewer blogs, 64 percent of daily readers read three or more blogs.

Also, daily blog readers place a higher priority on what they read on political blogs than do other blog readers. Compared with other blog readers, daily readers are more likely to believe what they read on blogs is more important than what they read in the mainstream media. Twenty-nine percent of daily readers felt blog content was more important than what they read in traditional media sources. Only 11 percent of regular readers and 13 percent of occasional readers shared that view.

Are Blogs Replacing Traditional Media?

As shown earlier, some bloggers view blogging as the successor to traditional media. Even if traditional news organizations do not disappear, there is often an attitude among bloggers of superiority toward traditional media. Traditional news media, they claim, hide their bias, miss important stories, and are too cozy with elites and defend them in their coverage. Given this assault on traditional media's role, one might assume this rhetoric would have turned political blog readers, particularly daily readers, against the traditional media. But findings suggest that is not the case. It is not even true for daily blog readers. (See table 7.1). With the exception of reading a national newspaper (which is a habit for relatively few Americans), the vast majority of blog readers—regardless of frequency—are also traditional media users.[8] There does not seem to be a lot of difference across types of blog readers, again with that exception of national newspaper reading; 40 percent of daily blog readers said they read a national newspaper as well.

Rather than abandoning traditional media, political blog readers, particularly the daily readers, seem to be the most media-dependent. They use traditional media at rates well above those of other Americans. In fact, their national newspaper reading far exceeds that of the public generally. According to a study by the Pew Research Center, only 12 percent of Americans read a national newspaper online.[9]

Table 7.1   Blog Readers' Use of Media Sources

	Blog-reading frequency		
	Occasional	Regular	Daily
Local newspaper	59%	54%	61%
Local TV news	80	78	69
National newspaper	21	28	40
Network TV news	75	72	72

Note: Table lists percentages of those who use media source at least several times per week.

The explanation for media dependency, particularly the greater interest in national newspapers, undoubtedly lies with these readers' keen interest in politics, particularly national politics. Political blogs—with their emphasis on national issues such as the Iraq war, presidential campaigns, and White House gossip—offer the same diet of political news as national newspapers. It is no wonder blog readers who are most addicted to political blogs would also be the most likely to read a newspaper such as *USA Today*, the *New York Times*, or the *Wall Street Journal* that provides more of the kind of news they want than any other traditional news source.

Another explanation may stem from the political blogs' reliance on national newspapers as sources of text and commentary for their blog posts. Daily readers share bloggers' fascination with traditional media content. Whether readers have been influenced by bloggers to read national newspapers (an ironic assumption) or they already have a national newspaper reading habit cannot be determined from these data. But the correlation suggests a current common reliance on media sources that are often disparaged by both bloggers and the readers who comment on blogs.

These data do not tell us whether media use habits have changed over time. They do indicate that, at present, blog readers are supplementing their traditional media use with blogs rather than abandoning the traditional media, as might be concluded from the blogosphere's stated dissatisfaction with traditional media. That finding suggests that bloggers and their audiences share a reliance on traditional media sources.

Another indication that blogs and traditional media coexist for blog readers, even the most avid ones, is the paucity of blog readers who view blogs as their primary news source (see table 7.2). Only 3 percent of daily blog readers said

Table 7.2   Primary Source of News for Blog Readers

	Blog-reading frequency		
	Occasional	Regular	Daily
Television	40%	33%	18%
Newspaper	16	18	9
Internet	27	34	56
Blogs	0	1	3
Radio	13	10	11
Newsmagazines	3	1	2
Other	1	2	1
Total	100%	99%*	100%
N =	306	199	148

Note: * = rounding error.

they get most of their news from blogs. Most blog readers are using traditional media—television, newspapers, or radio—as their main news source.

These findings show that daily readers rely heavily on the Internet for news and information. However, that does not prove that traditional media are losing this audience. Online news sources are quite likely to be traditional news media in online form. It could be that "Internet news sources" means FoxNews.com, CNN.com, WashingtonPost.com, or some other online version of a traditional media source. In fact, according to the Pew Research Center, half of the most viewed online news sites are traditional media sites, including the MSNBC. com, CNN.com, the *New York Times*, and local newspaper sites.[10]

Despite their reliance on traditional news media for information, particularly as a primary news source, daily blog readers are somewhat wary of these media outlets. Of the three groups, not surprisingly, daily blog readers are most suspicious of the traditional media and, in turn, the most trusting of blogs. When asked whether blog content was more or less accurate than traditional media information, 30 percent of daily blog readers said blogs were the more accurate source (see table 7.3). Only 17 percent of regular readers and 10 percent of occasional readers felt that way. Occasional readers were much more likely to say that blogs were less accurate (24 percent), compared with 13 percent of regular readers and 8 percent of daily readers.

It is interesting to note that even though blog readers obviously pay attention to blogs, they were not quick to grant blogs they read the superiority over news media that is often suggested by bloggers. Nearly 50 percent of the occasional and daily readers felt blogs were no more accurate than the traditional media.

Another interesting finding is the number of occasional and regular blog readers who weren't sure which was more accurate. For them, blogs were not

Table 7.3   Perceptions of Blog versus Media Accuracy

	Blog-reading frequency		
	Occasional	Regular	Daily
Accuracy of blogs over media			
More accurate	10%	17%	30%
About as accurate	24	28	40
Less accurate	24	13	8
Not sure	41	42	21
Total	99%*	100%	99%*

Note: * = rounding error.

the clear truth-finding source compared to the traditional media. They may have felt they were unable to judge the two types of content separately, even though they read both. Moreover, there may be an overlay of traditional and blog content in the minds of blog readers. This occurs because of the intermingling of traditional news media in blog content. Also, because these readers are extensive users of both types of media, the source of the information may become confused in their minds, particularly when a significant amount of the content on blogs emanates from traditional media.

On the other hand, the vast majority (72 percent) of blog readers, regardless of the level of their reading, believed that traditional media tended to favor one side in their reporting. Yet they were less sure that such bias routinely made its way into media content and affected the veracity of the reporting. Only 47 percent believed that mainstream news reports "are often inaccurate."

Clearly there is some ambivalence about the traditional media. Blog readers are concerned that they are not getting the whole side of the story in their regular news sources. They suspect habitual bias in the traditional news content, and they may be turning to the Internet, however slightly, in terms of news retrieval, although that still may be a reliance on traditional media. However, given their higher than normal usage of traditional media, that decline still places them well above non-political blog readers in terms of media dependence.

Yet there may still be respect for the professionalism of journalists. These readers' news retrieval habits suggest they still highly regard the traditional media. This is despite the fact that those same media are often disdained by the bloggers they read. (Of course, as was noted earlier, those same bloggers also rely heavily on traditional media.) Perhaps most surprising, in the face of withering criticism of the traditional media, is that even a majority of their most avid audience—the daily readers—were not quick to place blog content above media content, as bloggers often claim they should.

What Blog Readers Are Like

We've concluded a few things about blog readers so far. There are fewer blog readers than bloggers claim, but their ranks, at least those who sometimes read blogs, are growing. We know they use traditional media. We know some of their attitudes about those media. They are ambivalent about traditional media, but some of them think quite highly of blogs. Are blog readers typical Americans demographically? Are they predominantly male? Are they white or racially diverse? Are they less or better educated than others? In what ways are they similar to or different from those who don't read blogs, others who are online, or even the general public?

Previous studies have suggested that the political blog audience is more male than female, older than Internet users generally, well educated, and fairly affluent. They're also more partisan than those who don't read blogs. And they are politically engaged.[11]

Table 7.4 provides information on what this audience is like. First, we see that there is a profound gender gap in the political blogosphere. Men are heavily overrepresented among blog readers, particularly daily readers. Although there is parity among those who have seen a political blog, actual readership divides on gender lines, and the divide grows as the frequency of readership intensifies.[12] This gender gap corresponds to one among top political bloggers, where men heavily predominate.[13] Matthew Hindman found that there is also a gender gap in the ideological blogospheres. Males are more likely to read conservative blogs such as Instapundit, Little Green Footballs, and Michelle Malkin, while liberal blogs attract roughly even percentages of men and women, although some attract more women than men.[14]

We can speculate what it is that attracts males to and seems to repel females from reading political blogs. One explanation may be the characteristics of online discussion. These findings mirror other studies of gender usage of online political discussion forums.[15] The traits of these forums—verbal attack, conflict, competition—may be more attractive to male readers. Blogging can be much like that, although nothing inherent in any online discussion forum mandates that approach. Another possible cause is the dearth of female voices among the top political bloggers currently. As discussed in chapter 3, few women are on the A-list of political bloggers. And Michelle Malkin's fiery rhetoric may or may not appeal more to women than men. Women simply may find few relevant voices in the political blogosphere that would attract them. Still another explanation may lie with the problem of time. As mentioned earlier, the male-female divide is broadest among the daily users, those who are spending the largest chunks of time online reading blogs. Women may not take that time away from other activities to read political blogs. It is important to remember that, unlike the general blog audience, these women are more likely to be middle-aged or older. They may have children, jobs, household chores, or other responsibilities that limit their time online.

The crucial component of this finding is that the political blogosphere tends to be a male-oriented forum dominated by male bloggers who in turn attract an audience that is largely male. That male dominance may make attracting female blog readers difficult. It would affect the type of discussion as well as its

Table 7.4   Blog Readers versus Non-Readers

	Blog-reading frequency				
	Never read*	Have read**	Occasional	Regular	Daily
Gender					
Male	44%	50%	57%	54%	61%
Female	56	50	43	46	39
Race					
White	78%	73%	75%	71%	67%
Black	7	11	8	10	10
Hispanic	10	10	8	9	14
Other	6	7	9	9	9
Education					
Less than high school	10%	5%	6%	13%	5%
High school degree	31	22	19	15	17
Some college	28	35	34	24	28
Bachelor's or higher	32	37	41	48	50
Marital status					
Married	60%	59%	53%	52%	50%
Single	22	26	29	32	34
Divorced	12	11	10	13	10
Widowed	4	3	6	3	4
Separated	1	2	2	1	2
Income					
Under $25,000	20%	19%	26%	20%	19%
$25,000–49,999	31	25	24	30	22
$50,000–74,999	21	26	18	22	23
$75,000–99,999	14	15	16	14	22
$100,000 and up	14	15	14	14	14

Note: * = This category includes 1,550 individuals in the original sample of 2,729 respondents who said they had never read a political blog. ** = This group includes 526 individuals in the original sample of 2,729 respondents who said they read blogs several times a year.

style. It also may mean that the blogosphere as a gauge of the broader general public is flawed.

Blog readers are slightly more likely to be unmarried than non-readers. The difference is most stark with daily blog readers. That gap might be related to the time factor; singles may have more time to devote to online discussion, not to mention the social component of interacting with others online through political blogs.

Table 7.4 shows that daily political blog readers are not less likely to be minorities. In fact, they are slightly more likely to be African American or

Hispanic. As chapter 3 pointed out, bloggers generally tend to be more racially diverse than the general population. Because the blogosphere offers a broad array of blogs, it could well be that racial and ethnic minorities find voices in the blogosphere that are not available in the traditional media.

Studies of blog readers generally find them to be younger than the general public. According to the Pew Internet and American Life project, 54 percent of bloggers are under the age of thirty.[16] But other studies found that political blog readers are not the same as blog readers generally. Matthew Hindman found that political blog readers are not disproportionately young: 50 percent were forty-five or older. A Harris Interactive poll also found blog readers are older: 50 percent were forty-four or older.[17] Our study also found that political blog readers are not predominantly in the under-thirty group that fits the stereotype of blog readers. The mean age for political blog readers was forty-six, and 40 percent of political blog readers were fifty or older. By contrast, a Pew study of the blog audience generally found only 16 percent fell in that age category.[18] The age gap between the blog audience generally and those who read political blogs may seem unusual given the perception of blogging, but it shouldn't be. Political scientists have long known that older citizens are the most frequent voters. Interest and involvement in politics is more common generally in older people, up to a certain point when physical disability intervenes. Moreover, interest in news and politics has declined among younger people.[19] That these trends would spill over into blog reading should not be surprising.

Political blog readers also are better educated than those who do not read political blogs. Whereas 50 percent of daily and regular political blog readers hold at least a four-year college degree, only 33 percent of nonreaders did. These findings match those of other politically interested groups, including others who discuss politics online.[20]

One might expect that higher educational backgrounds would mean higher income levels for political blog readers. That was the case, as table 7.4 shows, for the most avid readers, the daily readers. Thirty-six percent of daily readers made $75,000 or more, whereas only 28 percent of non-readers did so. Similarly, at the lower end, 51 percent of non-readers were in the under-$50,000 income bracket, and only 41 percent of daily readers were.

Daily political blog readers differ from non-readers. They are more likely to be well educated, more affluent, single, and male. But the expectation does not fit in the area of race: the daily blog reader is not more likely to be white. This profile mirrors the known political online discussion audience. The culture of political blogs may reflect the expected audience. While those who are occasional readers are more like the general population, the more one reads, the more different one looks from others who are online.

But what are they like in terms of political ideology and partisanship? We know the talk radio phenomenon became a forum for conservative Republicans to be reinforced. Despite attempts by liberal groups, conservative shows and audiences have dominated that medium. However, political blogs on the left have proliferated. They are viewed by liberal bloggers as a mobilization tool. Yet there is also a conservative blogosphere and, given the audience size of some conservative political blogs, similarly has acquired a devoted niche audience. Which are political blog readers—liberals and Democrats or conservatives and Republicans?

Table 7.5 tells us that the daily reader audience includes more conservatives than liberals: 40 percent of the daily readers called themselves conservatives, and 34 percent self-identified as liberals. The rest of the blog audience was more evenly divided, although conservatives still had a slight edge. There is not a clear dominance for either ideological persuasion. That may explain why the two ideological blogospheres thrive and why both top the charts for influence across the blogosphere and audience size.

Table 7.5 tells us something else, although it is not surprising. Blog readers are more ideological than non-readers. Whereas about 66 percent of the blog readers (excluding daily readers) viewed themselves as liberal or conservative, only 58 percent of non-readers so identified. The daily readers, not surprisingly, are the most ideologically polarized of all, and they are far more ideological than the non-readers. Whereas 41 percent of non-readers saw themselves as moderates, only 25 percent of daily readers identified as moderates. It should not be surprising that an ideologically polarized political blogosphere, peppered with content that heavily reinforces ideological cohesion and skewers those of the opposite ideological persuasion, would attract a political blog readership of a similar mind-set.

One would expect this audience to be Republicans. That is not the case. Fifty-eight percent of daily blog readers identified themselves as Democrats. Only 35 percent said they were Republicans. What accounts for that? Perhaps it is the unpopularity of calling oneself a Republican near the end of a term of an unpopular Republican president and when the Republican Party lost control of both houses of Congress and Republican self-identification in the electorate dipped.[21] However, the Democratic bias in blog reading was true several years ago. In 2004 Kerry voters were slightly more likely than Bush voters to read political blogs.[22] Another possible explanation is that more conservative, or at least moderate, Democrats are attracted to some political blogs. Blogs such as Daily Kos have been critical of establishment Democratic leaders and support-ive of efforts to recruit candidates who match electoral districts rather than

Table 7.5   Partisanship, Ideology, and Blog Reading

	Blog-reading frequency				
	Never	Have read	Occasional	Regular	Daily
Ideology					
Liberal	25%	35%	31%	31%	34%
Moderate	41	34	34	37	25
Conservative	33	31	35	31	40
Total	99%*	100%	100%	99%	99%
Partisanship					
Strong GOP	16%	13%	14%	11%	19%
Weak GOP	14	12	12	10	5
Leans GOP	15	11	17	14	12
Undeclared/Independent	5	5	3	7	7
Leans Democrat	19	21	20	17	22
Weak Democrat	15	17	16	18	9
Strong Democrat	16	22	17	21	27
Total	101%*	100%	100%	100%	100%
N =	1,550	526	306	199	148

Note: * = rounding error.

imposing a one-size-fits-all ideological stamp on Democratic candidates. That pragmatic approach may be appealing to more moderate Democrats.

One consistent and clear point is that, like their ideological persuasions, blog readers are stronger in their partisanship as well. Thirty-two percent of those who never read blogs said they were strong partisans, whereas 46 percent of daily blog readers so identified. Again, the difference is primarily among Democrats. This is particularly true of the daily readers: 16 percent of nonreaders identified as strong Democrats, but 27 percent of daily blog readers did so. On the Republican side, the distinction was less stark; daily readers were slightly more likely to be strong partisans and other readers were less likely.

Political blog readers possess higher than average levels of political knowledge: 86 percent of blog readers knew which party controlled the U.S. House of Representatives, compared to 76 percent of the general public.[23] That isn't surprising since these readers are heavy media users and read blogs strongly oriented toward political themes. But they're also more distrustful of government than the general public. According to the National Election Studies, 47 percent of the general public believes the government in Washington can be trusted to do the right thing at least most of the time.[24] Only 16 percent of political blog readers (and 9 percent of daily readers) felt so. And only one percent of the public said the federal government can be trusted none of the time, whereas 17 percent of blog readers (and 29 percent of daily readers) agreed with that statement. Blog readers also may be more likely to accept conspiracy theories, such as those related to 9/11.[25]

Blog readers are not only more politically knowledgeable, but they are also more politically active than the general public. This is especially true of the daily readers, as shown in table 7.6, which compares blog readers to the general public. Occasional and regular blog readers were about as likely as the general public to attempt to persuade someone else to vote for or against a party or candidate. However, daily blog readers were significantly more likely to do so.

The differences between blog readers and the general public were more apparent for two other measures. Blog readers, particularly daily readers, were more likely to attend political meetings and give money to candidates. Daily readers were the most politically active; more than 25 percent said they had attended a political meeting in the past year, compared with only 7 percent of the general public. Similarly, 28 percent of daily readers had given money to a candidate in the past year; only 13 percent of the public had done so. It is possible that exposure to blogs is stimulating political activity on the part of those who are politically interested. Or it could be that daily blog readers are already politically active and these findings reflect a level of political interest that spurs both political blog reading and political involvement. It is impossible to tell from these data. But we can conclude that political blog readers, particularly the daily readers, are unlike the general public in their level of political involvement.

Table 7.6   Political Activity: Blog Readers versus General Public

Political activity*	General public	Occasional reader	Regular reader	Daily reader
Attempted to persuade someone else to vote for/ against party/candidate	48%	48%	46%	56%
Attended political meetings	7	12	16	29
Gave money to a candidate	13	16	15	28

Source of "General public" information is American National Election Study, 2004, at www.electionstudies.org.
* = Political activities engaged in at least once during the past year.

The Visible Blog Audience

There is a third group between bloggers and their audiences, a small subset of the audience who become both readers and bloggers. These are the blog readers who comment on the blogs. Unlike readers, they are a visible presence in the blogosphere.

Commenters do have a secondary status on a blog. It takes more clicks to see their comments, and only by clicking on the comment link can readers see the millions of comments that are posted across the blogosphere. Some political blogs do not allow commenting, further restricting the role of commenters.

Because commenters are visible, one might assume they are just the audience speaking. In other words, perhaps their comments are reflective of those held by the blog readership generally. But is this true? The question becomes more important when we consider that the A-list political bloggers tend to be much like the elites they often deride. The commenters, then, would seem to be the closest thing to public opinion expressed by a mass audience. Are they?

Defining commenters as those who posted a comment to a blog at least twice in the past week, we find they are unlike other blog readers in several respects. Commenters are more politically active than the rest of the blog audience. They're more likely to try to persuade others about candidates or parties. They also approach blogs somewhat differently than does the rest of the audience. Those who comment frequently are somewhat more likely to agree with the blogs they read. Twenty-six percent of those who comment five or more times said they agree with blogger they read most of the time, whereas only 15 percent of those who never commented felt that way. This special group of blog readers also put higher stock in the role of blogs than even other blog readers. Fifty-three percent said they rely on blogs for the latest information, whereas only 33 percent of other blog readers felt that way. And they are significantly more likely to consider news they read on blogs to be more important than what is in traditional media. The commenters are more distrustful of traditional media than other readers are. Forty-two percent of those who had commented agreed with the statement that the mainstream media doesn't give accurate information, whereas only 21 percent of those who had never commented agreed. They also were more likely to believe that news media are biased.

The visible blogosphere of commenters is not reflective of the blog audience generally. They believe blogs more, trust the media less, and seek to be opinion leaders and engage in political activism more than other blog readers do. Using comments as a gauge of blog readers' sentiments may lead to inaccurate conclusions about the blog audience, not to mention the general public.

Uses and Gratifications of Blog Reading

Why do people read political blogs? What do they get out of blogs that they can't get from exposure to traditional media? When tens of millions of Americans read political blogs at least occasionally, something must attract their interest. And for those millions who do so daily, the attraction must be compelling.

One possible theory is that blog reading is a sign of dissatisfaction with existing news sources. According to Barbara K. Kaye, many blog readers enjoy blogs because they dislike and distrust the media.[26] Yet that does not account for the fact that the blog audience still uses existing news sources. Even the most avid blog readers do so; in fact, as we have seen, they are the most media-dependent. Kaye also suggests that traditional media act as a foil for the blogs. Political blog users read traditional media, but then turn to the blogs for the counterpoint commentary on shared media content.[27] Our earlier discussion suggests that happens to some extent, but not as much as one might expect.

One need of the blog audience that may not be met as much by traditional news media is access to the latest political news. As table 7.7 shows, 55 percent of daily blog readers said they are more likely to hear about the latest news from blogs than from the mainstream media. Although traditional media sites update periodically throughout the day, blogs do so incessantly. Readers may perceive that it is the blog rather than the traditional media that will tell them

Table 7.7   Reasons for Reading Blogs

	Blog-reading frequency		
Reason	Occasional	Regular	Daily
Blogs are entertaining.	61%	51%	53%
I'm more likely to hear about latest news from blogs.	31	34	56
Mainstream media do not give full information.	29	31	42
Blogs give me information I don't get elsewhere.	30	43	44
Mainstream media do not give me accurate information.	21	19	41

Note: Numbers represent percentage of respondents who agree with statement. Respondents could list more than one reason for reading.

what has happened most recently. Hence turning to the blog satisfies a need to be up to date.

Another real need is accurate news and information. Two studies of blog readers found that users of political blogs rate bloggers as more credible than traditional media.[28] In our study, blog readers similarly were critical of the traditional media. Thirty-nine percent agreed that the mainstream media do not provide accurate information. Nor do they feel they are getting the whole story from traditional media sources. When asked whether they agreed with the statement that the mainstream media aren't giving them full information, 43 percent of daily blog readers said yes. Only 29 and 31 percent of occasional and regular readers, respectively, agreed. Unlike traditional media, blogs apparently fill that need, particularly for daily readers. Forty-five percent of daily bloggers agreed with the statement "Blogs give me information I don't get elsewhere," whereas only a little more than 33 percent of other blog readers agreed with that statement. Blog readers, particularly daily readers, seem to want something more. The fact that so many daily blog readers also read national newspapers suggests that they already have received much of the news that the blogs would give them. Readers are getting something beyond what they receive from the news media.

Another reason blog readers give for reading blogs was their entertainment value. A majority of blog readers agreed that blogs are entertaining. As noted earlier, blog content is more lively and less controlled by journalistic norms than traditional media stories. Bloggers are openly biased and resort to ad hominem attacks, much like talk radio. Interestingly though, it is the least frequent readers who were most likely to agree that blogs provide entertainment for them. For the regular and daily readers, blogs may be more serious business. For them—and here the regular and daily readers are in sync—blog reading offers important information.

Is blog reading a reinforcement mechanism? Do people go to blogs to be confirmed in the opinions they already hold? Does Daily Kos or Michelle Malkin or some other blog reassure them that their views are correct? One measure of reinforcement is the nature of the particular blog a reader will gravitate to. We would expect that more liberal blogs attract liberals and that conservatives are drawn to more conservative blogs. For the most part, that is the pattern. One measure of this is reader familiarity with various blogs. Liberals were more likely to have heard of liberal blogs, and conservatives were more likely to have heard of conservative blogs (see table 7.8).

Another piece of evidence of reinforcement can be found in examining which blogs people actually read. Among respondents, 113 said they had read

Table 7.8   Blog Readers' Familiarity with Ideological Blogs

| | Blogs by ideology | | | | | | |
| | Liberal blogs | | | | Conservative blogs | | |
	Daily Kos	Wonkette	Eschaton	Crooks and Liars	Instapundit	Michelle Malkin	Little Green Footballs
Ideology of reader							
Liberal	46%	50%	46%	54%	45%	34%	30%
Moderate	21	20	19	21	19	16	16
Conservative	34	30	35	25	35	49	53
Total	101%*	100%	100%	100%	99%*	99%*	99%*

Note: Numbers represent percentage of respondents who have heard of blog. * = rounding error.

Table 7.9   Ideology and Blog Reading

| | Ideology of reader | | |
	Liberal	Moderate	Conservative
Blog ideology			
Exclusively liberal	70%	52%	31%
Exclusively conservative	10	22	45
Read both	20	26	24
Total	100%	100%	100%
N =	46	23	42

at least one of the seven blogs under study. Of those, 51 percent reported they had read only liberal blogs; another 26 percent said they had read only conservative blogs. In total, nearly 77 percent of blog readers said they read only blogs that were of a certain ideological persuasion.

When considering the ideology of the reader, the gap between the spheres is largest for liberals. Seventy percent of readers who self-identified as liberals said they read exclusively liberal blogs; only 45 percent of conservatives said the same regarding conservative blogs (see table 7.9). Conservatives were far more likely than liberals to read liberal blogs. Moderates also were more likely to read liberal blogs than conservative ones. Only 26 percent of moderates read both.

These findings suggest that, for the most part, blog readers are gravitating to those blogs that reinforce their views. One blogger described this phenomenon: "I have 3,000 people who listen to what I say and, judging from the posted comments, many of them pretty much agree with me."[29] However, the reinforcement applies more to liberals than conservatives because conservatives are more likely than liberals to be exposed to views in opposition to their own. Whereas conservatives may have other sources of reinforcement, such as talk radio, liberals may view the blogosphere as their haven from contrasting views.

Another measure of reinforcement is the level of agreement with the opinions they read on political blogs. The greater the devotion to blog reading, the higher the agreement with the bloggers. Thirty-three percent of daily readers said they agreed with the opinions of bloggers whose blogs they read at least most of the time, whereas only 20 percent of regular and only 13 percent of occasional readers felt that way.

Agenda Setting and the Blog Audience

The audience's needs in reading blogs are not lost on bloggers. They have strong incentives to be concerned. Attracting readers is the method by which common blogs become influential or A-list blogs. It is also the way the most popular blogs gain status against each other in the blogosphere.

One example is the rise of The Huffington Post. The blog was only begun in 2005, but within two years it had made the A-list. It had outpaced longer lasting blogs and become financially successful. In one year, revenue nearly doubled. Arianna Huffington and her two cofounders approached the blog from a business model of creating online communities around types of news content—politics, but also entertainment, style, and business.[30] Huffington found, cultivated, and maintained an audience based on determining what audiences wanted rather than merely what she wanted to say.

For the influentials, keeping, or better yet growing, an audience is important because of increasing competition for that audience. If new blogs such as The Huffington Post can emerge suddenly, existing political blogs may lose their own audiences. If the blogosphere grows, as some predict, then audience gain may be across the board, although at varying levels. However, if the audience for the political blogosphere doesn't grow, then political blogs may be in cutthroat competition to acquire a relatively limited audience.

Another, related reason for being concerned about audience is the effect on advertising. Because bloggers do not collect subscription fees, they rely on advertising to make a full-time living at blogging. Few influential bloggers can afford a decline in audience size that subsequently reduces their income. One example is the controversy over Markos Moulitsas's unsympathetic statements about four American contractors who were killed brutally in Iraq, as mentioned in chapter 3. The controversy led to a campaign to embarrass his advertisers.[31]

Income dependence is even more acute when the blog moves beyond a one-person affair, as has become the case with blogs such as Daily Kos, The Huffington Post, and Power Line. As popular bloggers hire staff to help manage the blog, commercial pressures also increase. In fact, those pressures may even lead a political blog to seek a larger audience. The Huffington Post, for example, has an array of topic areas designed to grow the audience beyond the limited appeal of political topics.[32]

The audience holds the key to the success of bloggers, both would-be influentials and those already on the political blog A-list. Without their audiences, influential bloggers are no longer important. Far from reaching the A-list, common bloggers might as well be silent if no one is paying attention. Even most common bloggers seek some kind of audience, however small.[33]

Bloggers acknowledge the role of audiences in their content formation. One blogger expressed the distinction this way: "Blogging is not about writing posts. Heck, that's the least of your challenges. No, blogging is about cultivating a mutually beneficial relationship with an ever-growing online readership, and that's hard work."[34] Moreover, bloggers claim that their interaction with their audience is much more frequent and sustained than is true for traditional media. In most cases, bloggers allow the audience to comment on every post. Audience members sometimes are invited to become bloggers as well. Daily Kos hosts blogs for readers called diaries and regularly highlights some of the diary entries on its main page. The bloggers also created the Yearly Kos Convention of liberal bloggers.

Readers are even encouraged to respond to blog posts. This could be to form a team of investigators pursuing pieces of information. For example, in 2006, Wonkette asked its readers to get a photograph of a birthday cake for U.S. Senate candidate Katherine Harris that reportedly had the candidate's image on it: "Can someone find us a picture of this cake? Or find out the deal with this song? Because the song sounds pretty great too." It was the interaction with readers that led to exposure of the National Guard memos as well as the determination of which senators had put a secret hold on the federal spending database bill discussed earlier.[35] Readers also may be asked to report on events in their area to share with all of the blog's readers. On Crooks and Liars readers were asked if they had voted on a day when primaries were held in some states.

Then they were encouraged, "Give us updates from the races in your area. We'll keep updating the thread." This content addition reinforces bloggers' claim that blog content is an evolving process. That process contrasts with news media stories that end when the story is broadcast or published. And it is not just the regular updating of an original post, which occurs frequently, but the presence of an opportunity for readers to help shape the blog's content.

Bloggers also use open threads to facilitate reader discussion. The open thread is a time when a blogger posts an invitation to readers to make comments. Typically readers set the agenda without direction from the blogger. For example, John Amato on Crooks and Liars started an open thread by merely writing, "Have fun…"; Daily Kos often began threads with "blah, blah, blah." The rhetoric sometimes suggests that the blogger enjoys a personal rapport with readers. A Daily Kos post opened up a thread with the invitation, "Chat away and tell us what you're up to on this three-day weekend."

But even open threads can be agenda setting, at least within the thread. Sometimes a blogger will direct the open thread by prefacing it. On the fifth anniversary of 9/11, Little Green Footballs wrote at the beginning of an open thread titled "Where Were You on 9/11?," "[This is] an open thread for *LGF* readers to post their memories of where they were, and what they did, on the day Islamic terrorists struck at the heart of America." A Daily Kos open thread started with the direction, "This is an open science thread. What's bubbling atop your Labor Day Bunsen Burner?" Crooks and Liars included a post on how difficult it is to talk to a conservative and ended, "So I turn it over to you: How do you talk to a Conservative? How do we start bridging over the divisive rhetoric to start rebuilding what's been lost?"

One question, then, is whether readers can only reinforce agenda items already offered by the blogger or can change the agenda. Bloggers do urge readers to send post topics to them, and some bloggers will acknowledge in a post that the idea or the source came from a reader. A parenthetical reference at the end of the post on a topic post from several readers, such as "(hat tip: LGF readers)" or "(h/t: Deanna)," recognizes the audience's role in the post's creation.

Bloggers will repeat readers' analyses of news items. For example, when writing about riots in Hungary, Wonkette noted, "Many readers note that Hungarians are rioting because the prime minister was caught telling lies." Daily Kos asked readers to translate a German newspaper column and then thanked readers the next day for sending in translations.

What is unknown is the gatekeeping role of the blogger in filtering post topics coming from readers. That may be unknowable because only the blogger will know what tips or responses he or she receives from readers. Will the blogger discard story ideas that do not fit his or her agenda? Will analyses that do not correspond to bloggers' own perspectives receive attention? The culture of the blogosphere supposedly welcomes that interaction. Bloggers say that their readers are their editors. The information product, according to bloggers, is the result, at least partly, of the interaction with readers rather than the news media model of the dissemination of a final product that readers take or leave. Whether or not political blog readers are explicit agenda setters, audience expectations weigh heavily in the minds of bloggers who seek to retain their audience. One blogger suggested that readers' expectations can be placed in three categories: content, evaluation, and value.[36] A blog that offers too little content (or too many posts), rehashes news available elsewhere, or veers into topics of little or no interest to the audience runs the risk of losing that audience. That means a blog about politics that becomes primarily entertainment-oriented may lose an audience craving political news. One that is conservative and becomes liberal (or less conservative) similarly may become unpopular with its audience. Bloggers' new topic interests that are not shared by readers may cause audiences to look elsewhere.

All of this suggests that audiences have the potential of shaping content, not with their feet, but with their mouse. Failing to return to a blog (or unsubscribing from its RSS feed) offers enormous power for the audience to shape the content of the blog. But even for those who remain with the blog, interaction through commenting is significant because bloggers believe they should listen to their audience, and they know that, ultimately, whether they still have an audience depends on how willing they are to meet their readers' needs.

Conclusion

Despite the early predictions that blogs would transcend traditional media, ignite popular political participation, and revolutionize politics, blogs actually have avoided widespread dismissal as a brief phenomenon sustained primarily by hype. Instead, the political blogosphere has acquired a small but significant niche in American politics. The blogosphere has joined in a transactional relationship with others that allows it to occasionally affect agendas as well as the actions of other agenda seekers, the press, and the public. That association with these players offers blogs an opportunity to be part of agenda setting.

The agenda-setting role is hardly the one envisioned by some early bloggers. News media do not follow the blogs' agenda. When the agendas overlap, it is more likely the news media who have set bloggers' agendas. It is true that blog content is very much the result of bloggers' originating their own content, including their own set of topics, and then sharing that information with each other.

In terms of agenda setting beyond the blogosphere, and the interplay of these actors, it is the blogs who are incorporating traditional media agendas more than the other way around. Blogs are far more likely to join an existing topic thread created by media than the media are to pick up a thread initiated in the blogosphere. Blogs like to emphasize their successes—Trent Lott, Rathergate, Obama's "bitter" comments—but these are anomalies rather than the norm in terms of agendas.

Yet blogs also follow their own agendas. That fact may explain why blogs have occasional success in setting media and public agendas. Without separate agendas they would not be able to do so. Even when they do follow media agendas, they can seek to frame that agenda in a way that may lead blog readers to a new interpretation of the media's agenda.

Amplifying Media Coverage

Clearly blogs are not mere repeaters of media agendas. They often amplify media coverage, however. They expand the scope of one news organization's product beyond that outlet's audience reach. For example, a story in the *San Francisco Chronicle* repeated by a national blogger can reach an audience far beyond the circulation of the paper, even the online edition. It has the potential of becoming a story read by other journalists who then can incorporate it into news stories, either as a primary topic or as a facet of a larger related story. Blogs' role as amplifier may not even be mentioned by the news organizations who are utilizing blog content in this way. The blogosphere also can extend the life of a story beyond a brief mention in the press. The classic example is the Trent Lott story. Originally picked up by traditional media, bloggers then continued to discuss the story until other news outlets covered it as well.

In some instances, blogs can become an echo chamber for media stories and create an echo that reverberates for some time after news media have lost interest. One example is Howard Dean's scream in 2004, which was repeated in the blogosphere as much as or more than in traditional media.[1] Others, such as the House Republican corruption scandals in 2006, the Larry Craig scandal in 2007, and the resignation of New York governor Eliot Spitzer in 2008, also serve as examples of stories originating in the news media but receiving repeated attention in the blogs. According to Gracie Lawson-Borders and Rita Kirk, that echo chamber expands the shelf life of some news stories as repeated blogs comment on it: "Messages go in and rattle around far longer than a news story in the more traditional news outlets."[2]

The amplification role has the potential of enhancing democratic discourse. In an era when media coverage of policy is increasingly superficial, amplification would seem to provide the opportunity for the public to move beyond sketchy discussion of policy. Indeed, the blogs seem well positioned to do so. They supposedly possess unlimited space that allows them to offer extensive treatment of current policy issues. In fact, their advantage is greater than political talk radio because they have more space than hosts have time, and they can link their readers to detailed policy treatises that expand on the topic.

Alas, that potential has not always become reality. Amplification does not necessarily mean more substantive discussion. Top political blogs are quite similar to one another in their emphasis on politics rather than extensive policy discussion. Policy, domestic or foreign, is not the most popular topic on blogs. Rather, the latest scandal, the current event, the verbal battle between candidates or partisans—these are more frequent topics. Any expectation that blogs would improve on the media by providing more extensive issue discussion isn't being fulfilled.[3]

The failure to offer more in-depth issue discussion than is available in traditional media may be due to several factors. One is that A-list bloggers are politically interested people rather than policy wonks. They follow politics. They enjoy reading, talking, and writing about it; they are generalists. Some may fill a more specific niche, such as Little Green Footballs' emphasis on the war on terror. Others may have a legal bent, such as the Volokh Conspiracy. But their appeal is not as specialists, but as generalists who range across a panoply of subjects, such as the war in Iraq, U.S. foreign policy, campaigns and elections, current legislation in Congress. What unites these subjects for bloggers? Typically, it is their political dimension.

Bloggers who specialize in specific policy areas do exist. A few even gain a significant audience among the issue networks that address that topic, as well as journalists who cover particular policy areas. However, those bloggers do not reach the A-list because the audience they serve, with their narrow interests, is so small. Admittedly, these blogs are readily available to anyone who would like to read them. Not unlike a public library that provides easy access to a wide range of books but attracts to certain sections of the library only those interested in those subjects, narrowly focused policy-specific blogs are unable to compete in audience reach with broad blogs devoted to general politics.

That leads to another explanation of the nature of blog content, that is, the appeal to blog readers. Traditional news media audiences have become accustomed to increased brevity in the news presentation. For example, the creation of *USA Today* as a new national newspaper in the early 1980s did not signal expanded treatment of policy or even current events. Instead, the paper offered shorter treatment accompanied by extensive graphics. Fast, shorter coverage isn't a function of media choice as much as it is a response to the lifestyle of the audience. The audience for blogs also is in a hurry. One reason for the rush is increased demand for information gathering. More and more information sources exist, but the time constraints remain the same. Blogs have been added to the mix, but, for most blog readers, nothing has been subtracted. Blog readers apparently still attend to traditional media but also carve out time for blog reading. This means both sources must compete for a severely time-limited audience. Not surprisingly, the writing style of blogs conforms to that rushed approach. The popular style is frequent short posts covering a variety of topics rather than a smaller number of posts developing an argument or offering greater detail on legislation, policy proposals, or theses.

The fact that posts can come quickly seems to mean they must. That is a technological advantage of blogs over traditional media—the rapidity with which information can be transmitted. As a result, blogs have become media on fast-forward. News stories, both broadcast and print, are shorter than they used to be, but blog posts are shorter still. Print and broadcast editions appear, in their regular formats, once a day. Blogs are updated several times a day. In this study, posts on one blog were added, on average, nineteen times a day.

But rapidity militates against depth. Bloggers quickly are on to the next issue with the next post. Topics shoot across blogs with a speed faster than the rapid-fire delivery of television news. When a blogger's agenda is driven by the latest news story, opinion article, or fellow blog post, then the result will be a quick and light handling of a broad array of topics on the latest events rather than an exhaustive treatment of policy issues.

Blogosphere Agendas

For the most part, bloggers have their own agendas. A separate agenda is essential to creating a niche among the audience's information sources. Without some added value offered by a blogger, the reader will see no need to continue reading the blog. The blogs' agenda is to offer what is not already available to the reader. Blog readers expect blogs to address topics that are not in the newspapers or on television news, or at least not emphasized there. This may well give readers the sense that they are gaining exclusive access to information that is being ignored or, worse, hidden by the traditional media.

Even when blogs follow news media agendas, they still provide the frame that likely satisfied many of their readers. Political blog readers are already heavy traditional media users as well. One added value of blog content is the transformation of that news into information that conforms to readers' worldview. The frame bloggers place on events or issues, such as conservatives viewing media coverage of discrimination against Muslims as yet another sign of liberal bias among journalists, is important particularly when the media are setting the agenda for discussion.

Agendas beyond the Blogosphere

To the extent that the blogosphere sets its own agendas, they typically are limited to the blogosphere itself. Blogs repeat material on other blogs, and the discussion waxes and wanes within the blog community, and more particularly within a particular camp of the blogosphere. The interesting question is why there are times when the blogosphere's agenda breaks beyond its confines and reaches a wider audience. Why do journalists occasionally pick up blog stories and move them on to the press's agenda?

A necessary condition for blogs' role is that news media organizations miss or underplay a story that bloggers report. An example is the Eason Jordan story, in which journalists adhered to "off the record" rules and skipped the story about a CNN executive commenting that journalists were targeted by U.S. troops. Journalists mentioned Jordan's comments only after they appeared in the blogosphere. This situation can occur due to a couple of circumstances. One is that professional practices of journalism restrict reporters' news gathering. In the Jordan case, the session where he spoke was off the record; according to journalistic practice, "off the record" means journalists cannot attribute, even indirectly, what was said. Because bloggers have no such standard, they were able to break the story when journalists could not. Once the blogosphere had done so, journalists were free to report Jordan's comments. The blogosphere, then, can provide an opening for journalists to report a story they are constrained from reporting by journalistic standards.

Still another constraint on reporters that provides an opening for blog agenda setting is the symbiotic relationship between sources and journalists. Journalists, particularly those on specific beats who depend on the goodwill of their sources, operate in an atmosphere of satisfying sources' needs in order to preserve the relationship. The conventional wisdom is that the Watergate story never would have been broken if the assigned reporters were on the White House beat. Bloggers who have no such relationship are freer to use information they glean without concern about affecting sources. For example, the conservative blogs who uncovered the false documents used by CBS News in the National Guard story had no need to rely on the goodwill of Dan Rather or CBS.

Another result of that symbiotic relationship, and similarly a journalistic constraint that occasionally advantages blogs in agenda setting, is the journalistic acceptance of elites' attitudes and behavior in informal settings. The Trent Lott case is an example. Although many journalists attended the event, only ABC News reported Lott's statements. Even that reporting was essentially buried in the middle of an online report.

Journalists also may miss a story because they are not invited to be present where news is made, but where one or more bloggers do appear. An example is the case of a blogger who attended a Barack Obama fund-raiser and blogged about Obama's comment that rural Pennsylvanians are "bitter." The event was closed to the press; the invitation came to the blogger not because she was a blogger but due to her status as an Obama donor.

This speaks to the confusion over whether a blogger is a journalist or plays some other role. If a blogger is a journalist and receives press credentials, does the press exclusion include him or her? If bloggers do not have press credentials, can they attend and report the information as if they were journalists? Journalists would consider themselves uninvited to such events. Should bloggers who are read by journalists and may well report on the event similarly forgo attending? Will closed events in the future specify journalists as well as bloggers? Until a resolution occurs, if it does, bloggers will continue to have an advantage in attending events that are closed to the press but not to them. And that advantage will result in occasional stories that move from the blogosphere to the larger media agenda because of the newsworthiness of the information.

Another reason for blog story breakout is the absence of other sources in a highly competitive environment where news is at a premium. This was the case with the John Edwards campaign suspension. The rush to get the story first—and the absence of other sources (or the disbelief in them)—resulted in a blogosphere story bursting into the traditional media for a brief moment. Still another reason is an environment of information overload for journalists coupled with increased journalistic reliance on citizen journalists. The pickup of the blog story about Cindy McCain's recipes on the McCain campaign Web site is a case in point. Journalists would not have examined the recipes to determine their source; it was a chance search by a citizen that led to information being transmitted to a blog and then to journalists.

Sensing the overwhelming nature of information as well as the opportunity to employ citizens as eyes and ears for news stories, news organizations encourage their audiences to help them gather news. News tips are solicited by both television news and newspapers. And television news programs now routinely air amateur video clips submitted by viewers. Blogs have become still another citizen journalist source.

As indicated by this study of blog and news media content, however, blog news rarely enters the journalistic mainstream. Even a story that circulates widely in the blogosphere can be ignored unless it receives confirmation outside the blogosphere. One prerequisite seems to be confirmation by a newsmaker of the blog news' existence. This occurred when the introduction of Bill Clinton into the story of the *Path to 9/11* program prompted a front-page news story when repeated blog posts had not. In another case, in the 2004 presidential campaign, Swift Boat veterans targeted Democratic nominee John Kerry with a video questioning his war record long before news organizations picked up the story. The story of the anti-Kerry campaign ran through the conservative blogosphere, but news media failed to pick it up. Only when the presidential candidate's campaign responded to the claims did news organizations feel the story was legitimated and they could cover it.[4]

Interactions with Other Players

Journalists

Journalists and bloggers have entered a symbiotic relationship. Andrew Sullivan admitted bloggers' dependence on journalists: "There will always be a critical need for good reporting, and I don't think bloggers will ever be able to replicate that."[5] In turn, journalists have become blog readers and blog users. They use blogs for some facets of news gathering. As acceptance of blogs as news sources grows, blogs will become more integrated into news gathering. In forging a relationship, both journalists and bloggers have changed each other.[6] According to Sullivan, bloggers also possess their own significant role in the relationship: "Blogs depend on the journalistic resources of big media to do the bulk of reporting and analysis. What blogs do is provide the best scrutiny of big media imaginable—ratcheting up the standards of the professionals, adding new voices, new perspectives, and new facts every minute."[7]

Bloggers have forced journalists to be more accessible, to be interactive, to be more willing to include the public in news making, and even to view news gathering as a more transparent process. Journalists, in turn, have become a model for bloggers who want credibility as news outlets: the need to establish ethical standards, the imperative of accuracy, and the consequences of writing first and thinking second. Journalists have even shown bloggers how to get political players to pay attention to them.

Journalists also rely on blogs as a gauge of public opinion. Blogs become a simple method of going beyond elites to assess reaction to current events. No need to make phone calls or walk into the street; just click over to blogs and read the posts. Howard Fineman, a political correspondent for *Newsweek*, said he reads blogs so he can get a "feel for the conversation going on in the country about politics."[8] Karen Tumulty of *Time* said that blogs are a "good indicator of what's in the political bloodstream at any given moment."[9] However, this reliance contains serious flaws. As shown earlier, bloggers and their audiences are not representative of the general blog audience, not to mention the general public. Their comments are not likely to be an accurate gauge of public discussion going on around the country about politics.

Agenda Seekers

The blogosphere also has formed a relationship with other agenda seekers— policy makers, groups, and candidates. These agenda seekers have found that, given journalistic use of blogs, the blogosphere may be a means for capturing journalists' attention and subsequent coverage. Even without the role of the traditional media, the blogosphere's own audience size, as well as the likely political activity and influence of blog readers, recommends it as a mechanism for reaching certain constituencies. These seekers now consider blogs to be part of public relations strategies and act to shape blog coverage. This occurs through the forms familiar to press relations operations—press releases, interviews, press conferences—but also through other means, such as paying bloggers or hiring bloggers as staff.

The financial exigencies of blogging, coupled with the lack of authoritative status accorded the blogosphere, offers these agenda seekers an opportunity to form mutually beneficial relationships, much as partisan editors did in the early 1800s. And, much like the partisan press of an earlier age, those relationships are not difficult to establish. Many bloggers are available to be co-opted. For nearly all political bloggers, blogging is not financially lucrative; at best it may provide a living for an individual blogger and a small staff. Bloggers who already possess strong partisan leanings are a willing audience for individuals and groups who share those leanings and seek blog support to promulgate their views.

The Public

Unlike political journalists, the general public largely avoids political blogs. Blog influence is limited to a relatively small minority of the population who are politically interested and active. These are the daily or regular readers for whom blog reading has become a habit.

For the vast majority of the general public, political blogs are something they've heard of, perhaps even read a time or two, but otherwise pay no attention to. The happenings of the political blogosphere become real only when news media cover them or others, a friend or a coworker, direct them to a specific political blog. In order to reach this audience, bloggers need traditional media. They need to break out of the blogosphere and acquire media recognition. Journalists rarely cooperate. Nor is that reticence to publicize blog content likely to change anytime soon.

The size of the habitual blog audience is not increasing; only the irregular blog audience has grown in recent years. That growth does provide an opening, though, for blog influence. Blogs may be able to impact the larger audience under circumstances where blogs become news. Those are the occasions when the non-blog reader may turn to the blogosphere to determine what is going on.

Impacting blog content is not limited just to elites—the agenda seekers. There is a subset of the general public that does interact with bloggers in affecting the content of blogs. This occurs not just because the blogosphere facilitates direct posting of comments by the audience, but also because political bloggers have become conscious of the need to attract and maintain an audience in order to be influential.

The Future of Political Blogging

A Revolution?

In his book *The Revolution Will Not Be Televised*, Joe Trippi predicted that the Internet, including blogs, would revolutionize American politics.[10] The blog revolution has been envisaged by bloggers as well.[11] Others, however, have shied away from such a prediction.[12]

The definition of a revolution is debatable, but typically a revolution is associated with the overthrow of an existing regime. This book has shown that rather than overthrow politics, blogs have become integrated into the political system. They have formed relationships with other players that give them a potential role in agenda making. Those connections place them more in the mainstream of political life than at the barricades where bloggers have viewed themselves.

Some might argue that the assessment is premature. The political blogosphere has had a short life. Aren't blogs just getting their legs? Couldn't this revolution occur eventually? As the political blogosphere expands in size, readership, and influence, will the much-vaunted revolution ultimately occur? The answer is no.

Why is a revolution unlikely? The political blogosphere audience is relatively small. It is unlikely to grow enough to rival the Internet audience or the traditional media audience. Political blogs, like opinion magazines and twenty-four-hour news channels, have a limited appeal to typical Americans. Public interest in a blog may increase temporarily when it becomes part of the news story, but on the whole, political blogs will remain popular only to a small segment of the population.

However, the blogosphere may be able to impact that small group of political activists and aficionados who read blogs regularly. In the course of a presidential campaign, that will not be a large number of voters compared to the electorate generally. Michael Turk, who directed the e-campaign for the Bush reelection campaign, concluded, "The blogosphere is likely to have the greatest influence in the primaries."[13] And that influence may be even weaker in primaries than in caucus states, where participants constitute a small percentage of the electorate and are primarily those who are most politically interested.

As a result of the nature of the audience, the influence of the political blogosphere can be more powerful than audience size would intimate. Journalists and opinion makers have the potential to set agendas and influence one another's opinions, even if blog influence on that power seems uncommon. Journalists, however, are still wary of blogs—a wariness that will wane only as blogs become more like traditional journalism. Of course, that means the revolutionaries will become part of the very political system they seek to overthrow.

Indeed, A-list political blogs have gone mainstream. Traditional players are co-opting bloggers. The financial vulnerability of bloggers also will produce consolidation and the rise of blogging networks and conglomerates. If Ana Marie Cox can be hired to blog for $18,000, other bloggers similarly can be employed to blog in certain niches of the political blogosphere. Bloggers for hire already characterize A-list political blogging.

As those developments occur, blog posts will become less the province of the "pajamadeen" and more the product of corporate structures governed by profit-making. The outward appearance of the political blogosphere may not change at first. The audience may be attracted to blogs that appear autonomous, edgy, and countercultural. But like radio stations where the station's format is designed to fit a certain genre and appeal to a particular audience, blog content will be the outcome of a marketing decision rather than an eclectic choice by a single, local blogger.

The changes in the blogosphere have led to criticism of bloggers' willingness to become close to those they write about. One blogger, and a critic of blog co-option, argued, "Once you get a taste of money and fame and power and adulation, how do you stay true to what got you there in the first place?"[14] The criticism will be common as the blogosphere transforms from the Wild West environment imagined by its early participants into a corporate enterprise filled with large conglomerates.

Won't the blogosphere increase public participation? What about all those people who have become bloggers? Although this study cannot speak definitively about how people become political bloggers, the probability is that political bloggers are those who already possessed a strong interest in politics when they created their blogs. That's why they created a political blog rather than some other kind of blog.

What about blog readers? Hasn't the blogging phenomenon stimulated them politically? Again, this research doesn't answer that question. Future studies will have to do that. But as the findings in chapter 7 show, regular blog readers are already highly politically interested, while those who are irregular readers or non-readers are not. Did blogs create that difference? It is unlikely. Rather, blog reading probably reflects those differences rather than creates them.

Rather than revolutionary, the blogosphere in fact looks much like traditional politics. Certain people with resources are advantaged. The most influential bloggers are drawn from an elite group of well-educated individuals who contrast with rather than reflect the general public. Meanwhile, minority voices are underrepresented among the most influential bloggers. For example, Hispanic bloggers feel the blogosphere reflects the real world in the sense that in neither context do Hispanics have much of a political voice.[15] And African American bloggers admit that there is a "black blogosphere" and that most of the other bloggers they interact with also are black.[16]

Agenda seekers vie for one another's attention. Blog content is shaped by candidates, groups, policy makers, and the press—the very targets of the revolution. Some bloggers even become the paid operatives ("consultants") of these agenda seekers. Partisan divisions in the blogosphere, not surprisingly, reflect current political cleavages. Partisanship has become more intense in American politics over the past quarter-century or so.[17] The blogosphere reflects, and perhaps amplifies, that trend. But it has not altered it.

Also, commercial interests increasingly are becoming paramount in the blogosphere. Blogging may be like any other journalistic activity. The individual who owns a blog is the one who actually possesses freedom of the press, not the writer. In the early days of blogs, that distinction was irrelevant, but it will become clearer as a few blogs become corporate enterprises with hierarchical structures. Although relatively few blogs will become corporate entities, those few will be the most widely read.

Blog content, like traditional media content, is becoming what the audience wants to read. Competition for audience size already shapes the nature of blog content. That trend will accelerate as blogs become units of conglomerates determined to extend their reach into the blogosphere. Moreover, that competition among blogs will become more intense as growth in readership slows and top blogs compete for a more or less stable politically-oriented audience. Increasingly, blogs will cooperate less and compete more in order to maintain their audience share.

Division of Labor?

Might blogs and journalists settle into a division of labor that offers each a niche in news dissemination? Might news media offer the traditional hard and soft news functions, while blogs offer commentary? This division has the advantage of allowing both to focus on what they do best—traditional media as the source of reporting and blogs as the commentator.

Traditional media could benefit from that division. Audiences are suspicious of journalists when they offer analysis and commentary. Audience dissatisfaction with media has risen at the same time journalists have moved away from the strictly descriptive role toward a more narrative and interpretive form of reporting. The recurring fads of journalism—advocacy journalism, public journalism, citizen journalism—send the signal to the public that journalism is in need of reform. One such reform would be a return to reporting that lacks analysis or interpretation but adheres to description.

Blogs, on the other hand, lack news-gathering capabilities. Blogs do rely on readers, but those readers usually lack access that is accorded journalists. Readers may be able to provide a first-hand account of FEMA's response to a natural disaster, but they don't participate in White House or congressional press briefings. They don't sit in the press section of Air Force One when the president comes back to chat.

Blogs' role as commentary source would free blogs of the effort to compete with news media, particularly in conveying late-breaking news. Without the pressure to post frequently, bloggers could become more thoughtful and more reflective in their analysis. Bloggers' approach to sustained argument is spotty. For example, Instapundit's posts are short, sometimes less than a sentence, and rarely include sustained thought and argument. Other blogs may develop arguments and even provide evidence, but the medium does not encourage it. Rather, the dominant feature is quick response to unfolding events. This is not an insignificant advantage; one print columnist lamented that in the time it takes him to write a column, the topic can be presented by several blogs.[18]

The blogosphere has been criticized for being obsessed with the very latest news. One journalist suggested, "The blogosphere, at its worst, values timeliness over thought."[19] But the technological capability to be first doesn't require blogs to do so. Bloggers' role as primarily commentators might reduce the number of posts, and their speed, but allow more time for consideration of current events rather than duplicating journalists' immediate response to breaking news.

Another advantage of blogs taking over commentary is the flawed nature of media commentary. Media criticism too often becomes cynical as politicians receive general disapproval. The tone of coverage of presidential campaigns, for example, is primarily far more negative than positive, and newspaper editorials are rarely designed to stimulate people to become engaged in politics. As partisans, blogs may be able to motivate audiences in a way that journalists cannot. Because blogs are openly partisan and sometimes use their content to make direct appeals to action, they may be more effective than news media at motivating partisans to become engaged in politics rather than act merely as spectators. One journalist described the blogosphere as "a potpourri of opinion and little more."[20] But even if it were only that, the blogosphere would have a place in the media of public discourse. Opinion may well spur positive action rather than cynicism.

Displacement, Absorption, or Cohabitation?

As discussed earlier, initial claims about the blogosphere were that it would replace traditional media. Blogs have acquired a niche, but displacement of other media is unlikely. Like other new information forums, the blogosphere will cause existing forms to shift somewhat to accommodate it but also retain their own places. When radio appeared, radio news did not doom the newspaper; instead, newspapers adapted. They published fewer editions because radio provided the late-breaking news. Nor did newspapers fold after the advent of television. The audience for newspapers shifted, but they did not disappear.[21]

Each new medium found its niche audience, or it did not survive. Audience use of media changed, but the audience assured that there would still be space enough for a variety of media. Radio would be for those who want quick, brief reports; newsmagazines for people who don't want to read a daily newspaper; television for people who like visual news. Yet these audiences are hardly mutually exclusive. Audiences expand their use of media to accommodate new media. This is true as well for the relationship between traditional media and blogs.

Displacement is unlikely for several reasons. First, blogs rely on the traditional media for content. Although bloggers portray themselves as news gatherers, particularly collecting and disseminating news that traditional media ignore or downplay, blog content actually is heavily determined by traditional media content. Second, the political blog audience is not a mirror of the traditional media audience. Traditional news media attract a range of readers and viewers and listeners who have limited interest in political news. Political blogs naturally thrive on political news. The audience for political blogs is more likely to be similar to the audience for heavily political news media such as the twenty-four-hour cable news channels and elite newspapers. That audience is a fairly small slice of the total media audience; therefore they are not a threat to the continuance of traditional media such as television news, newspapers, or even newsmagazines. Third, the audience for political blogs is more likely to supplement than supplant. Audiences realize that political blogs are not substitutes for traditional media. Blogs may provide analysis and entertainment, but they are not regularly news gatherers. They provide a value added to the news product, but their role is not possible without the existence of the news product (which they rarely produce) in the first place.

Nevertheless, at least one blogger would like to make displacement a reality rather than speculation. Arianna Huffington of The Huffington Post intended to turn her blog into an online newspaper. With 3.7 million unique visitors in early 2008, the blog had an online audience that surpassed most other online news sources.[22] Only sites like the *New York Times* had more online readers. Like print newspapers, her blog would cover the gamut of news subjects— sports, entertainment, business, the arts, and politics. In addition, Huffington planned to add local news for major metropolitan areas.[23]

However, displacement could occur in the opposite direction. News media possess the potential to absorb blogs. Traditional media have online resources capable of duplicating blogs, particularly with the type of audience where blog growth is most likely to occur. Whether newspapers can compete to take readers away from the existing blogs or, more likely, attract the bulk of new blog readers is a question still to be determined.

News media outlets have the advantage of holding a traditional and recognized brand as news, information, and commentary sources. Similar to the appeal of alternative newspapers, some blog readers will prefer independent media. But those alternative publications have limited appeal. Readers may be more attracted to a known one-stop site for news and commentary. This will be particularly true of those who are accustomed to the brand name of traditional media and still wish to use such media for their source of online commentary. Newspapers can provide conservative blogs, liberal blogs, and other blogs in between. The question is whether news organizations will so adapt. It is a question that news organizations will have to ask themselves. The answer may well determine the future of newspapers as well as the future of blogs.

The absence of displacement on either side does not suggest blogs have not and will not influence American politics and journalism in the future. As mentioned earlier, blogs already have influenced the shape of journalism. Blogs have affected news reporting. They have forced journalists to decide whether their journalistic norms are relevant in an age when blogs exist. They have raised questions about whether speed outweighs confirmation and reliability. They have questioned the value of an editorial process that offers quality control but blandness, in contrast to one that is feisty and lively, although deeply flawed. The blogosphere has shaped the news-gathering process. It has prompted journalists to look for news from sources that did not exist a decade ago. It has changed news gathering habits as journalists supplement traditional media use with blog perusing. Blogs have even confronted journalists with the question of what constitutes a journalist. Can a blogger who engages in little reporting, expresses overt partisan opinions, endorses candidates, is self-employed, and has a minuscule audience be considered a journalist?

The future of blogs may be one of cohabitation with other players in the kind of relationship described earlier. Such an existence may not satisfy some bloggers. There is still an adolescence about blogging—a penchant to braggadocio. As one journalist put it, "Skepticism, restraint, a willingness to....put one-self in the background—these would not seem to be a blogger's trademarks."[24] Bloggers have beat their chests to call attention to themselves. When they have made a difference, it is broadcast as a cataclysmic event.

Despite bloggers' rhetorical protests, there is historical precedent for the formation of a relationship with other players. The practice is similar to eighteenth-century printers taking payments from politicians and party organizations to become their mouthpieces. Only later did publishers of newspapers achieve financial independence from politicians and parties.[25] Bloggers may experience a similar pattern. Their reliance on politicians is related to their financial insecurity. Bloggers rarely earn a living from blogging; therefore they must find ways to supplement their income. Consulting with or even working for politicians is one way to do that. Like their counterparts of an earlier age, a handful of bloggers may achieve financial independence, particularly through advertising revenue, and subsequently carve out their own autonomous niche. The corporate nature of new blogs enhances the probability of that scenario.

Additionally, time may be on their side. The greatest growth in the blog audience will be among traditional media readers who gradually move to the online product of news dissemination. This group includes those who already use the traditional media format but supplement or replace it with the online one. Growth also will occur in another group, that is, younger media consumers, who are less likely to use traditional media today than were their predecessors.[26] They are prime targets for blog attention, either from the traditional media or existing blogs. This audience already uses new media, such as television talk shows (including the *Daily Show*), Internet news, and social networking sites. Whether they will include political blog components in their news consumption is another question.

If traditional media have incorporated blogs and aggressively courted this audience, they may be able to absorb most bloggers. However, some blogs may be able to establish their own audience base and reputation as news sources in competition with traditional journalism. The Huffington Post may well be the model for such a site. By incorporating traditional media's descriptive news content as well as commentary, this kind of blog may survive the one-stop model that news organizations provide.

Even if news media offer a blog product that attracts the blog audience, niche blogs will not automatically disappear. Just as national news magazines and opinion magazines coexist in a media environment dominated by television and newspapers, specialized political blogs will continue to be read by a narrow audience. Nevertheless the future of political blogging may well be one that looks more like the traditional media environment we have long known and less like the political blogosphere that was intended to revolutionize politics.

Appendix

Methodology

The study of political blogs is in its infancy in social science research. That isn't surprising given the newness of blogs themselves. Academics only recently have applied systematic analysis to the study of blogs. Some studies have focused on analysis of blog content.[1] Others have centered on surveying and understanding the audience.[2] A few have done both.[3] Rarer still is the study that compares traditional journalism and blog content.[4]

This project sought to determine both the nature of the content as well as the composition of the audience, including a specialized audience of journalist-readers. The content analysis had two components: analysis of the content of political blogs and analysis of elite media content. The survey research also had two components: an elite survey of political journalists and a political blog audience survey. All these methods will be discussed below.

Content Analysis

Content analysis is a tool designed to examine systematically the manifest content of communication.[5] Content analysis can be both quantitative (counting words, phrases, sentences, etc.) as well as qualitative. This study used both approaches by using aggregate data as well as individual examples in order to enrich the description of the quantitative data.

Blogs

For academic researchers specializing in content analysis, a blog has the advantage of being much like traditional print media. It is a written format, there is quite a bit of content (usually several posts per day), and many blogs (particularly the A-list ones) provide archives to help locate past writing.

This content analysis focused on prominent political blogs. Prominence was determined by their appearance among the top fifty blogs on both of two lists of blogs regularly updated on www.technorati.com and www.truthlaidbear .com. The former is the most comprehensive listing of blogs based on the number of links from other blogs.[6] The latter determines the size of the audience by measuring the number of daily site visits, which is an indication of readership. Both measures were employed to prevent inclusion of a blog that was popular with readers but not with the blogosphere generally or one that had influence with other political blogs but a limited readership itself.

A blog was defined as political if the main subject of discussion was national politics. There was overlap on the two lists, and the determination of "political" was made by visiting each blog where the political nature was unclear (typically blogs that did not already have a reputation as national political blogs) and determining whether the content primarily addressed national politics.

Through this filter, seven political blogs were included in the sample because they appeared among the top fifty blogs on both lists. The blogs in the sample were Daily Kos, Wonkette, Eschaton, Crooks and Liars, Instapundit, Michelle Malkin, and Little Green Footballs. This sample had an additional, although unplanned, advantage of representing ideological diversity. The first four blogs are viewed as part of the liberal blogosphere, while the last three are in the conservative blogosphere.

A one-month period, September 2006, was selected for analysis. That period was outside of a presidential election period but within the midterm election of 2006. That time period provided the advantage of viewing blog discussion during an election but also at a time when that election would not have dominated all the attention of the blogs. Election coverage was one aspect of the content, but not the dominant feature. During the month of September, these seven blogs were downloaded and archived into Word files and then retrieved for coding.

One factor in organizing coding is the unit of analysis. Blogs consist of multiple posts by an author or authors, much like separate diary entries. A post is a discrete entry in the blog that is defined by time and date. Entries may be short (a line or two) or lengthy (nearly a page). Each post may well focus on a separate topic or it may continue a previous topic with a new point. Either way, each post potentially has its own separate identity. Therefore the best unit of analysis was not the blog as a whole—or a daily collection of posts—but the individual post.

During the thirty days of September, the total number of blog posts over the seven blogs was 2,951. The number of posts by blog is displayed in table 4.1. In addition to topic, blog posts were coded for use of links to other sources, the nature of other sources (Web sites, news media, other blogs), the presence of comments, etc. (The comments themselves, however, were not coded.)

To test for inter-coder reliability, each blog post was coded three times, each by a different coder. On the dichotomous variables, 71 percent of the coding was unanimous across the three coders and 26 percent had two-thirds agreement. The topics coding resulted in 86 percent unanimous agreement and 12 percent two-thirds agreement. The topics agreement was higher than expected because most of the blog posts are brief and consist of one easily discernible topic.

News Media Sites

To compare blog and news media agendas, news stories from four national newspapers were coded over the same time period (September 2006). The four selected are widely recognized elite newspapers and represent an ideological cross-section based on editorial direction: the *Wall Street Journal*, the *Washington Post*, the *New York Times*, and the *Washington Times*. All of the front-page stories were coded. The sample included 548 stories: *Wall Street Journal*, 95; *Washington Post*, 166; *New York Times*, 168; and *Washington Times*, 119. The stories coded were limited to those that appeared on the front page of the paper. The rationale was that these stories were considered the most important due to their placement. Also, these stories would not primarily be technology stories or stories about blogs where discussion of blogs would be paramount to the story. Rather, they would reflect what news professionals had decided were the priorities for readers.

The newspaper coding was more limited in scope. The stories were coded only for topics discussed in the story, the types of sources used, and whether blogs generally or specific blogs were mentioned in the story. To check intercoder reliability, 100 of the stories were coded twice. The agreement between coders was 86 percent. For dichotomous variables, agreement was 97 percent, and agreement for nondichotomous variables was lower, at 74 percent.

Survey Research

Few studies exist of the blog audience, particularly the readers of political blogs. The Pew Research Center has devoted its survey research to understanding the

Internet audience, including the blog audience. But scholars are just beginning to analyze this group.

One of the major difficulties in conducting survey research of the political blog audience is identifying who reads political blogs. The least expensive approach, particularly when done in cooperation with bloggers, is to conduct a self-selected sample survey that is created by soliciting readers through posts on blogs. However, this approach is problematic because it is not a random sample. Generalization becomes difficult, and therefore the application of the study is limited.

Another approach is a telephone survey of the general public with a screen for political blog readers. That approach is time-consuming and expensive because the vast majority of American adults are not political blog readers, even as infrequently as several times a month.

A third approach is to use an existing panel administered by an existing polling firm that has been collected for online research purposes. The advantage of this approach is the reduced cost of identifying and surveying participants. The disadvantage is the representative nature of the online panel. The online panel consists of people who have self-selected into the sample and already are very familiar with the Internet. However, the survey data are weighted to reflect the demographic composition of the general public, thus enhancing the validity of the sample.

Journalist Survey

A survey of current journalists was conducted during the spring of 2007 to determine the nature of blog use and attitudes toward political blogs. Polimetrix administered a survey of journalists. Names of journalists were culled from the *News Media Directory* published by Leadership Directories. The sample drawn included only those journalists whose specialty was national politics or policy. Over the course of several months, 874 journalists were e-mailed, mailed, or faxed invitations to go to a Web site to complete the survey. A total of 203 journalists completed the survey.

This approach is flawed in the sense that those who respond may be more interested in blogs and new information technology than those who do not. Elite surveys are difficult because response rates are dependent on respondent interest in the topic. Therefore, these findings need to be considered in light of that limitation.

Journalists were asked about whether they read blogs; which blogs they read; whether they read primarily for work or pleasure; how familiar they were with popular political blogs; and whether they use blogs for a variety of purposes, such as finding late-breaking news, identifying potential sources, getting story ideas, gauging public reaction to events, etc. They also were surveyed about their attitudes toward blogs, such as their accuracy and overall credibility as news sources.

Audience Survey

The audience survey was conducted in April 2007 by Knowledge Networks using their online panel. On April 6, individuals in the panel were sent an e-mail requesting that they go to a Web site and complete the survey. The e-mail was sent to 3,676 individuals, of whom 2,729 took the survey over the next ten days. Of those, 653 individuals qualified to participate in the study. Qualification occurred if the individual read political blogs at least several times a month. That filter was designed to include only regular political blog readers.

The survey asked readers which political blogs they read, how often they read them, how many minutes they spent reading blogs, whether they comment on blogs, whether they had heard of particular blogs and read them, etc. They also were asked about traditional media use, political knowledge, attitudes about government, ideology, and other related questions. The results were weighted.

Notes

Introduction

1. David D. Perlmutter, *Blogwars*, New York: Oxford University Press, 2008, p. 62.
2. Daniel W. Drezner and Henry Farrell, "The Power and Politics of Blogs," paper presented at the annual meeting of the American Political Science Association, Chicago, September 2–5, 2004; Mallory Jensen, "A Brief History of Weblogs," *Columbia Journalism Review*, September/October 2003, p. 22.
3. Drezner and Farrell, "The Power and Politics of Blogs"; Gracie Lawson-Borders and Rita Kirk, "Blogs in Campaign Communication," *American Behavioral Scientist*, 49 (December 2005), p. 549.
4. "State of the Blogosphere," 2008, at http://www.technorati.com/blogging/state-of-the-blogosphere/; "State of the Live Web April 2007," at http://technorati.com/weblog/2007/04/328.html.
5. John B. Horrigan, "Home Broadband Adoption 2008," Pew Internet and American Life Project, July 2008, at http://www.pewinternet.org/pdfs/PIP_Broadband_2008.pdf
6. Maggie Griffith and Susannah Fox, "Hobbyists Online," Pew Internet and American Life Project, September 19, 2007, at http://www.pewinternet.org/PPF/r/221/report_display.asp.; Lee Rainie, "The State of Blogging," Pew Internet and American Life Project, January 2, 2005, at http://www.pewinternet.org/PPF/r/144/report_display.asp.
7. Amanda Lenhart, Deborah Fallows, and John Horrigan, "Content Creation Online: 44% of U.S. Internet Users Have Contributed Their Thoughts and Their Files to the Online World," Pew Internet and American Life Project, February 29, 2004, at http://www.pewinternet.org/PPF/r/113/report_display.asp; Rainie, "The State of Blogging."
8. "State of the Blogosphere," 2008, at http://www.technorati.com/blogging/state-of-the-blogosphere/.
9. Norman Makatgo Su et al., "Politics as Usual in the Blogosphere," *Proceedings of the 4th International Workshop on Social Intelligence Design* (SID 2005), at http://cache.search.yahoo-ht2.akadns.net/search/cache?ei=UTF-8&p=politics+as+usual+in+the+blogosphere&fr=yfp-t-501&u=www.ics.uci.

edu/%7Eyangwang/papers/SID05.pdf&w=politics+usual+blogosphere&d=Wi
u2FjWxQzBd&icp=1&.intl=us.

10. "Entertainment, Technology, and Hurricanes Dominate the 2005
Blogosphere, According to Intelliseek's BlogPulse.com," *PR Newswire,*
December 23, 2005, p. 1.

11. Rebecca Reynolds, "Political News Blog and Newspaper Coverage of
Democratic Candidates in the 2004 U.S. Presidential Election," paper
presented at the annual meeting of the International Communication
Association, New York, May 26–30, 2005.

12. Joseph Graf, "The Audience for Political Blogs: New Research on Blog
Readership," Institute for Politics, Democracy, and the Internet, October
2006, at http://ipdi.org/UploadedFiles/Audience%20for%20Political%20Blogs.
pdf.

13. Matthew Klam, "Fear and Laptops on the Campaign Trail," *New York Times
Magazine,* September 26, 2004, p. 43.

14. Rachel Smolkin, "The Expanding Blogosphere," *American Journalism Review,*
June/July 2004, at http://www.ajr.org/Article.asp?id=3682.

15. Matthew Hindman, *The Myth of Digital Democracy,* Princeton, N.J.: Princeton
University Press, forthcoming, chapter 6.

16. See, for example, Jerome Armstrong, "A Victory for People-Powered Politics,"
Christian Science Monitor, November 9, 2006, at http://www.csmonitor.
com/2006/1109/p09s01-coop.html; "Who Deserves the Credit for Tuesday's
Victories," November 10, 2006, at http://downwithtyranny.blogspot.
com/2006/11/who-deserves-credit-for-tuesdays.html; Michael Lazzaro,
"Daily Kossack Responds to Jonah Goldberg's Critique of Progressive
Bloggers," *Los Angeles Times,* May 20, 2007, at http://www.latimes.com/
news/opinion/la-oew-lazzaro20may20,0,6888342.story?coll=la-opinion-
center.

17. Matt Welch, "Blogworld and Its Gravity: The New Amateur Journalists Weigh
In," *Columbia Journalism Review,* September/October 2003, p. 21.

18. Hindman, *The Myth of Digital Democracy.*

19. Andrew Sullivan, "A Blogger's Creed," *Time,* September 27, 2004, p. 37.

20. Quoted in J. D. Lasica, "Blogs and Journalism Need Each Other," *Nieman
Reports,* Fall 2003, p. 71.

21. Joyce Y. M. Nip, "Exploring the Second Phase of Public Journalism,"
Journalism Studies, 7 (April 2006), pp. 212–236.

22. Quoted in Paul Burka, "That Blog Won't Hunt," *Texas Monthly,* March 2005,
p. 12.

23. Stephen Coleman, "Blogs and the New Politics of Listening," *Political
Quarterly,* 76 (April 2005), pp. 272–280.

24. Welch, "Blogworld and Its Gravity," p. 21; J. D. Lasica, "Blogging as a Form
of Journalism," *USC Annenberg Online Journalism Review,* April 29, 2002, at
http://www.ojr.org/ojr/lasica/1019166956.php.

25. Quoted in Dan Balz, "Bloggers' Convention Draws Democrats," *Washington
Post,* June 11, 2006, p. A5.

26. "Trends in Political Values and Core Attitudes: 1987–2007," Pew Research Center for the People and the Press, March 22, 2007, at http://people-press.org/reports/pdf/312.pdf.

27. Balz, "Bloggers Convention Draws Democrats," p. A5.

28. See Joe Trippi, *The Revolution Will Not Be Televised: Democracy, the Internet, and the Overthrow of Everything*, New York: William Morrow, 2004.

29. Svetlana V. Kulikova and David D. Perlmutter, "Blogging Down the Dictator? The Kyrgyz Revolution and Samizdat Websites," *International Communication Gazette*, 69 (2007), pp. 29–50.

30. Michael Keren, "Blogging and the Politics of Melancholy," *Canadian Journal of Communication*, 29 (2004), p. 8.

31. Keren, "Blogging and the Politics of Melancholy," p. 16.

32. Geoffrey Sheagley, "Blogs as Information Sources: The Impact of Source Credibility and Partisan Affiliation," paper presented at the annual meeting of the Midwest Political Science Association, Chicago, April 12–15, 2007; Thomas Kunkel, "Express Yourself," *American Journalism Review*, December 2006/January 2007, at http://www.ajr.org/Article.asp?id=4232.

33. Perlmutter, *Blogwars*, p. 15.

34. Coleman, "Blogs and the New Politics of Listening."

35. Armstrong, "A Victory for People-Powered Politics" p. 9.

36. "Markos Moulitsas Zuniga," *Current Biography*, 58 (March 2007), p. 67.

37. Lenhart and Fox, "Bloggers: A Portrait of the Internet's New Storytellers."

38. Bara Vaida, "Blogging On," *National Journal*, October 6, 2007, p. 26.

39. Quoted in Gregg Sangillo, "Bloggers: A Who's Who," *National Journal*, January 21, 2006, pp. 37–39.

40. Lenhart and Fox, "Bloggers: A Portrait of the Internet's New Storytellers"; Lisa Guernsey, "Telling All Online: It's a Man's World (Isn't It?)," *New York Times*, November 28, 2002, p. G1.

41. Perlmutter, *Blogwars*, p. 12.

42. Armstrong, "A Victory for People-Powered Politics."

Chapter 1

1. Liriel Higa, "United Bloggers? Depends on the Issue," CQ *Weekly*, October 16, 2006, p. 2745.

2. Stephen Dinan, "Bloggers Will Join Bush in Bill-Signing Ceremony; Pressed Congress for Spending Database," *Washington Times*, September 26, 2006, p. A4.

3. Dinan, "Bloggers Will Join Bush."

4. David D. Perlmutter, *Blogwars*, New York: Oxford University Press, 2008, pp. 69–70; Tom Bevin and John McIntyre, "The 'Old Media' Meets the 'New Media,'" *The Masthead*, Spring 2005, pp. 10–11; Sue MacDonald, "Drudge Report, DailyKos, and Instapundit Grab Most 'Buzz' among Political Blogs, Says Intelliseek," *Business Wire*, October 27, 2004, p. 1.

5. Bernard Cohen, *The Press and Foreign Policy*, Princeton, N.J.: Princeton University Press, 1963, p. 13.

6. Maxwell E. McCombs and Donald L. Shaw, "The Agenda-Setting Function of the Mass Media," *Public Opinion Quarterly*, 36 no. 2 (Summer 1972), pp. 176–187.

7. Maxwell McCombs, Juan Pablo Llamas, Esteban Lopez-Escobar, and Federico Rey, "Candidate Images in Spanish Elections: Second-Level Agenda-Setting Effects," *Journalism and Mass Communication Quarterly*, 74 no. 4 (Winter 1997), pp. 703–717.

8. Sei-Hill Kim, Dietram A. Scheufele, and James Shanahan, "Think about It This Way: Attribute Agenda-Setting Function of the Press and the Public's Evaluation of a Local Issue," *Journalism and Mass Communication Quarterly*, 79 no. 1 (Spring 2002), pp. 7–25; Spiro Kiousis, Philemon Bantimaroudis, and Hyun Ban, "Candidate Image Attributes: Experiments on the Substantive Dimension of Second Level Agenda Setting," *Communication Research*, 26 (August 1999), pp. 414–428.

9. Fay Lomax Cook et al., "Media and Agenda Setting: Effects on the Public, Interest Group Leaders, Policy Makers, and Policy," *Public Opinion Quarterly*, 47 (Spring 1983), pp. 16–35.

10. Daniel Schorr, "Ten Days That Shook the White House," *Columbia Journalism Review*, July/August 1991, pp. 21–23.

11. Wayne Wanta and Yu-Wei Hu, "The Effects of Credibility, Reliance, and Exposure on Media Agenda Setting: A Path Analysis Model," *Journalism Quarterly*, 71(Spring 1994), pp. 90–98.

12. Joe Bob Hester and Rhonda Gibson, "The Economy and Second-Level Agenda Setting: A Time-Series Analysis of Economic News and Public Opinion about the Economy," *Journalism and Mass Communication Quarterly*, 80 no. 1 (Spring 2003), pp. 73–90; Lutz Erbring, Edie N. Goldenberg, and Arthur H. Miller, "Front-Page News and Real-World Cues: A New Look at Agenda-Setting by the Media," *American Journal of Political Science*, 24 (February 1980), pp. 16–49.

13. Yariv Tsfati, "Does Audience Skepticism of the Media Matter in Agenda Setting?" *Journal of Broadcasting and Electronic Media*, June 2003, pp. 157–176.

14. James P. Winter and Chaim H. Eyal, "Agenda Setting for the Civil Rights Issue," *Public Opinion Quarterly*, 45 (Autumn 1981), pp. 376–383; Roy L. Behr and Shanto Iyengar, "Television News, Real-World Cues, and Changes in the Public Agenda," *Public Opinion Quarterly*, 49 (Spring 1985), pp. 38–57.

15. Russell J. Dalton et al., "A Test of Media-Centered Agenda Setting: Newspaper Content and Public Interests in a Presidential Election," *Political Communication*, 15 (1998), pp. 463–481.

16. John Tedesco, "Issue and Strategy Agenda-Setting in the 2000 Presidential Primaries," *American Behavioral Scientist*, 44 no. 12 (August 2001), pp. 2048–2067.

17. Marilyn Roberts and Maxwell McCombs, "Agenda Setting and Political Advertising: Origins of the News Agenda," *Political Communication*, 11 (1994), pp. 249–262.

18. Jeffrey S. Peake, "Presidential Agenda Setting in Foreign Policy," *Political Research Quarterly*, 54 no. 1 (March 2001), pp. 69–86.

19. Marion R. Just et al., *Crosstalk: Citizens, Candidates, and Media in a Presidential Campaign*, Chicago: University of Chicago Press, 1996; Dalton et al. "A Test of Media-Centered Agenda Setting"; Charles M. Tidmarch, Lisa J. Hyman, and Jill E. Sorkin, "Press Issue Agendas in the 1982 Congressional and Gubernatorial Election Campaigns," *Journal of Politics*, 46 (November 1984), pp. 1226–1242. For an opposing view, see Behr and Iyengar, "Television News."

20. Howard Rosenberg, "Network Anchors Pull Up Anchors," *Los Angeles Times*, March 7, 1986, p. 26.

21. See David H. Weaver et al., *Media Agenda-Setting in a Presidential Election: Issues, Images, and Interest*, New York: Praeger, 1981; Young Jun Son and David H. Weaver, "Another Look at What Moves Public Opinion: Media Agenda Setting and Polls in the 2000 U.S. Election," *International Journal of Public Opinion Research*, 18 (2006): 174–197; John C. Tedesco, "Intercandidate Agenda Setting in the 2004 Presidential Primary," *American Behavioral Scientist*, 49 (September 2005), pp. 92–113.

22. "2004 National Election Pool (NEP) Exit Polls," Roper Center for Public Opinion Research, University of Connecticut, 2004.

23. See, for example, C. Anthony Broh, "Reporting the Polls in the 1976 Presidential Election," *Public Opinion Quarterly*, 44 (Winter 1980), pp. 514–529; Thomas E. Patterson, *The Mass Media Election*, New York: Praeger, 1980; Robert Andersen, "Reporting Public Opinion Polls: The Media and the 1997 Canadian Election," *International Journal of Public Opinion Research*, 12 (Autumn 2000), pp. 285–299.

24. See, for example, Doris Graber, *Processing Politics: Learning from Television in the Internet Age*, Chicago: University of Chicago Press, 2001.

25. Dalton et al., "A Test of Media-Centered Agenda Setting," p. 474.

26. "Journalist Q & A—Andrew Sullivan, Time.com," *PR Week*, January 15, 2007, p. 14.

27. Jim Kuhnhenn, "Obama Photo in Turban, Robe Causes Stir," *Boston Globe*, February 25, 2008, at http://www.boston.com/ae/theater_arts/articles/2008/02/25/obama_photo_causes_stir/.

28. See Shanto Iyengar, *Is Anyone Responsible?* Chicago: University of Chicago Press, 1991; Robert M. Entman, *Projections of Power: Framing News, Public Opinion, and U.S. Foreign Policy*, Chicago: University of Chicago Press, 2004.

29. David Glenn, "The (Josh) Marshall Plan," *Columbia Journalism Review*, September/October 2007, at http://www.cjr.org/feature/the_josh_marshall_plan.php?page=all.

30. Ryan Chittum and Joe Hagain, "Student's Suicide Sets Off Explosion of Theories by Blogs," *Wall Street Journal*, October 13, 2005, p. B1.

31. T. Neil Sroka, "A Study of the Growing Importance of the Blogosphere in the U.S. Congress," Institute for Politics, Democracy and the Internet, April 2006, at http://www.ipdi.org/UploadedFiles/PoliticalInfluenceOfBlogs.pdf.

32. Bara Vaida, "Blogging On," *National Journal*, October 6, 2007, p. 26.

33. Vaida, "Blogging On," p. 30.

34. Howard Kurtz, "Mainstream Blogs Open Floodgates for Political Coverage," *Washington Post*, October 26, 2007, p. C1.

35. Jeffery Knight, "King of Bloggers," *American Lawyer*, September 2002, p. 18; "Wonkette in the Flesh: An Evening with Ana Marie Cox," Society of Professional Journalists, Columbia University Graduate School of Journalism, at http://spj.jrn.columbia.edu/wonkette.html.

36. Vaida, "Blogging On," p. 30.

37. Vaida, "Blogging On," p. 28.

38. Vaida, "Blogging On," p. 30.

39. Vaida,, "Blogging On," p. 30.

40. Vaida, "Blogging On," p. 30.

41. Vaida, "Blogging On," p. 30.

42. Quoted in Daniel W. Drezner and Henry Farrell, "The Power and Politics of Blogs," paper presented at the annual meeting of the American Political Science Association, Chicago, September 2–5, 2004.

43. Drezner and Farrell, "The Power and Politics of Blogs."

44. Drezner and Farrell, "The Power and Politics of Blogs."

45. Glenn, "The (Josh) Marshall Plan."

46. "John Edward Denies Affair with Campaign Worker," *Los Angeles Times*, October 13, 2007, at http://latimesblogs.latimes.com/washington/2007/10/breaking-news-j.html; "Tabloid's Affair Rumor Dispelled, Says John Edwards," (New York) *Daily News*, November 29, 2007, at http://www.nydailynews.com/gossip/2007/11/29/2007–11–29_tabloids_affair_rumor_dispelled_says_joh.html.

47. See Joseph Graf, "The Audience for Political Blogs: New Research on Blog Readership," Institute for Politics, Democracy, and the Internet, October 2006, at http://ipdi.org/UploadedFiles/Audience%20for%20Political%20Blogs.pdf.

48. Quoted in Vaida, "Blogging On," p. 29.

Chapter 2

1. Mark Leibovich, "Strom of the Century: The Hill Sings 'Happy Birthday' as Sen. Thurmond Turns 100," *Washington Post*, December 6, 2002, p. A1.

2. Joel David Bloom, "The Blogosphere: How a Once-Humble Medium Came to Drive Elite Media Discourse and Influence Public Policy and Elections," paper presented at the second annual pre-APSA Conference on Political Communication, Philadelphia, August 31, 2003.

3. See, for example, Leibovich, "Strom of the Century"; "Thurmond Honored on His 100th; Officials, Family Extend Birthday Greetings to the Nation's Oldest and Longest-Serving Senator," *Los Angeles Times*, December 6, 2002, p. A42.

4. Thomas B. Edsall, "Lott Stirs Criticism at Tribute to Senator; GOP Leader Praises Thurmond Stance," *Washington Post*, December 7, 2002, p. 9.

5. Interview with Joshua Micah Marshall, *Frontline*, PBS, April 24, 2006, at http://www.pbs.org/wgbh/pages/frontline/newswar.
6. Oliver Burkeman, "Bloggers Catch What Washington Post Missed," *The Guardian*, December 21, 2002, at http://www.guardian.co.uk/ technology/2002/dec/21/internetnews.usnews.
7. John Podhoretz, "The Internet's First Scalp," *New York Post*, December 13, 2002, p. 41.
8. Gail Russell, "Their Clout Rising, Blogs Are Courted by Washington's Elite," *Christian Science Monitor*, October 27, 2005, p. 1.
9. Matthew Scully, "The Harriet Miers I Know," *New York Times*, October 14, 2005, p. A25; Jim Geraghty, "The Growing Role of Bloggers; Democrats Continue to Decline," *Washington Times*, February 8, 2006, p. A19.
10. Geraghty, "The Growing Role of Bloggers"; Patti Waldmeir, "White House Fights Anti-Miers Bloggers," *Financial Times* (London), October 14, 2005.
11. Dick Polman, "Dodging a Fight May Fuel a Fight," *Philadelphia Inquirer*, October 4, 2005, p. A1.
12. U.S. Congress, Senate, "Senator Edward M. Kennedy Speaking on Nomination of Robert Bork," 100th Cong., 1st sess., *Congressional Record*, 133 no. 14, daily edition (July 1, 1987), p. S18518.
13. Nadine Cohodas, "Ginsburg Hurt Badly by Marijuana Admission," CQ *Weekly*, November 7, 1987, p. 2714.
14. David Glenn, "The (Josh) Marshall Plan," *Columbia Journalism Review*, September/October 2007, at http://www.cjr.org/feature/the_josh_marshall_ plan.php?page=all; Shawn Zeller, "Activists Belabor Secretary Chao," CQ *Weekly*, February 25, 2008, p. 475.
15. Katherine Q. Seelye, "Resignation at CNN Shows the Growing Influence of Blogs," *New York Times*, February 14, 2005, at http://www.nytimes. com/2005/02/14/technology/14cnn.html?ei=5088&en=23532a9b1f3dcf5c& ex=1266296400&adxnnl=1&partner=rssnyt&adxnnlx=1191261104-Q+kp/ P6wl6NMQtAxa/TItA.
16. Michael J. Miller, "The Year of the Blog," *PC Magazine*, December 28, 2004, p. 8.
17. David D. Perlmutter, "How Will the Clintons Harness the Political Force of the Blog," *USA Today*, October 2, 2006, p. 13A.
18. Chris Cillizza and Dan Balz, "On the Electronic Campaign Trail; Politicians Realize the Potential of Web Video," *Washington Post*, January 22, 2007, p. A1.
19. Howard Kurtz, "Mainstream Blogs Open Floodgates for Political Coverage," *Washington Post*, October 26, 2007, p. C1.
20. For previous discussions of these trends, see Richard Davis and Diana Owen, *New Media and American Politics*, New York: Oxford University Press, 1998; Bruce Bimber and Richard Davis, *Campaigning Online*, New York: Oxford University Press, 2003.
21. Monika Graff, "The Unmaking of a Senator: How Bloggers Pulled It Off," *Time*, August 9, 2006, at http://www.time.com/time/nation/

article/0,8599,1224538,00.html; "Grown Up and Buttoned-Down; Political Campaigning," *The Economist*, August 11, 2007, at http://www.economist.com/research/articlesBySubject/displaystory.cfm?subjectid=1291613&story_id=9621506.

22. Scott Helman, "Romney Connecting Quickly with Bloggers," *Boston Globe*, December 31, 2006, at http://www.boston.com/news/local/articles/2006/12/31/romney_connecting_quickly_with_bloggers/; Joe Garofoli, "Tech-Savvy Swarm of Bloggers Boosts Candidates' Online Presence," *San Francisco Chronicle*, November 3, 2007, at http://www.sfgate.com/cgi-bin/article.cgi?file=/c/a/2007/11/03/MNSFT5J6F.DTL; Katherine Q. Seelye, "Huckabee Thanks Bloggers," *New York Times*, January 1, 2008, at http://thecaucus.blogs.nytimes.com/2008/01/01/huckabee-thanks-bloggers/.

23. Chris Cillizza, "Clinton Courts Blogosphere," *The Fix*, June 26, 2006, at http://blog.washingtonpost.com/thefix/2006/06/sen_clintons_courts_blogospher.html; Jose Antonio Vargas, "'Net Roots' Event Becomes Democrats' Other National Convention," *Washington Post*, August 3, 2007, p. A4.

24. Chris Cillizza, "Campaigning in the Kos Primary," June 13, 2006, at http://blog.washingtonpost.com/thefix/2006/06/the_kos_primary.html.

25. See Benjamin R. Barber, "Draft Al Gore? Draft Al Gore!" The Huffington Post, June 7, 2007, at http://www.huffingtonpost.com/benjamin-r-barber/draft-al-gore-draft-al-g_b_51225.html, as well as www.algore.org and www.draftgore2008.org. For the Fred Thompson draft, see www.draftthompson08.blogspot.com and http://blogsforfredthompson.com/.

26. K. Daniel Glover and Mike Essl, "New on the Web: Politics as Usual," *New York Times*, December 3, 2006, Section 4, p. 13.

27. "Biden Explains Remarks on Indian-Americans," *CongressDaily*, July 10, 2006, p. 10.

28. See Mayhill Fowler, "Obama Exclusive (Audio): On V.P. and Foreign Policy, Courting the Working Class, and Hard-Pressed Pennsylvanians," The Huffington Post, April 11, 2008, at http://www.huffingtonpost.com/mayhill-fowler/obama-exclusive-audio-on_b_96333.html; Jim Kuhnhenn and Charles Babington, "Obama Concedes Remarks Were Ill Chosen," Associated Press, April 13, 2008, at http://ap.google.com/article/ALeqM5izQosMtCfjNjE1uAP6fQV2BZ_qWwD900GM0G0.

29. Greg Mitchell, "McCain: Sarah Palin's Daughter, Age 17, Is Pregnant—Alaska Press Did Not Know," *Editor and Publisher*, September 1, 2008, at http://www.editorandpublisher.com/eandp/news/article_display.jsp?vnu_content_id=1003844555; Steve Holland, "Palin Rebuts Rumors, Says Daughter Pregnant," ABC News, September 1, 2008, at http://abcnews.go.com/Politics/wireStory?id=5699565.

30. "Former Gillmor Aide, State Senator Opt Out of Special Election," *CongressDaily*, September 17, 2007, p. 14; Rachel Kapochunas, "Real Race in San Diego Is Courtesy of Scandal," CQ *Weekly*, April 3, 2006, p. 888.

31. Adam Nagourney, "Gathering Highlights Power of the Blog," *New York Times*, June 10, 2006, at http://www.nytimes.com/2006/06/10/us/10bloggers.html?fta=y.

32. Nagourney, "Gathering Highlights Power of the Blog."
33. Glover and Essl, "New on the Web."
34. Cari Lynn Hennessy and Paul S. Martin, "Blogs, the Mainstream Media, and the War in Iraq," paper prepared for presentation at the annual meeting of the American Political Science Association, Philadelphia, August 31–September 3, 2006.
35. Adam Nagourney, "A Mixed Bag of First Impressions by Democrats at Blog Rendezvous," *New York Times*, June 11, 2006, at http://www.nytimes.com/2006/06/11/us/11bloggers.html?scp=18&sq=politician+support+blog&st=nyt.
36. Jim VandeHei, "Blogs Attack from Left as Democrats Reach for the Center," *Washington Post*, January 29, 2006, p. A4; David D. Kirkpatrick, "Kerry Urges Alito Filibuster, but His Reception Is Cool," *New York Times*, January 27, 2006, p. A14.
37. David D. Perlmutter, *Blogwars*, New York: Oxford University Press, 2008, pp. 197–198.
38. Conn Carroll, "Parallel Party Pushes Democrats," *National Journal*, November 10, 2007, p. 69.
39. Carroll, "Parallel Party Pushes Democrats."
40. "Mukasey Judiciary Whip," November 2, 2007, at www.democrats.com; Dan Eggen, "Senate Democrats Boost Mukasey's Prospects," *Washington Post*, November 2, 2007, at www.washingtonpost.com.
41. For example, see "The Conservative Case against McCain," December 13, 2005, at http://thenextprez.blogspot.com/2005/12/conservative-case-against-mccain.html; John LeBoutillier, "Conservatives against McCain," February 6, 2008, at http://www.newsmax.com/john_leboutillier/romney_mccain/2008/02/06/70570.html.
42. Nicholas Lemann, "Right Hook: The Wayward Press," *New Yorker*, August 29, 2005, p. 34.
43. See Jerome Armstrong and Markos Moulitsas, *Crashing the Gate: Netroots, Grassroots, and the Rise of People-Powered Politics*, White River Junction, Vt.: Chelsea Green, 2006.
44. Quoted in Dan Balz, "Bloggers' Convention Draws Democrats," *Washington Post*, June 11, 2006, p. A5.
45. Quoted in Balz, "Bloggers' Convention Draws Democrats."
46. Matthew Mosk, "Donations Pooled Online Are Getting Candidates' Attention," *Washington Post*, March 11, 2007, p. A7.
47. Interview with Scott Johnson, *Frontline*, PBS, August 26, 2006, at http://ww48 Interview with Scott Johnson.
49. Stephen Humphries, "Blogs Look Burly after Kicking Sand on CBS," *Christian Science Monitor*, September 22, 2004, p. 1; "CBS Names Memo Probe Panel," CBS News, September 22, 2004, at http://www.cbsnews.com/stories/2004/09/06/politics/main641481.shtml; "Dropping the Anchorman," *Economist*, November 27, 2004, p. 36.
50. Andrew Sullivan, "A Blogger's Creed," *Time*, September 27, 2004, p. 37.

51. Quoted in Matt McKinney, "Bloggers Exult in Rather's Departure; They Call Internet Chatter New Political Force," *Star Tribune* (Minneapolis), March 10, 2005, p. 8A.
52. Humphries, "Blogs Look Burly."
53. Seelye, "Resignation at CNN."
54. Alex Williams, "Blogged in Boston: Politics Gets an Unruly Spin," *New York Times*, August 1, 2004, section 9, p. 1.
55. Matthew Klam, "Fear and Laptops on the Campaign Trail," *New York Times Magazine*, September 26, 2004, p. 43.
56. Quoted in Peter Johnson, "It's Prime Time for Blogs on CNN's 'Inside Politics'" *USA Today*, March 21, 2005, p. 4D.
57. Erica Iacono, "New Media Tactics Alter Face of Election," *PRWeek*, November 6, 2006, p. 14.
58. Stuart Allen, *Online News*, London: Open University Press, 2006, pp. 88–89.
59. See Andrew Paul Williams, "Self-Referential and Opponent-Based Framing: Candidate E-Mail Strategies in Campaign 2004," in *The Internet Election: Perspectives on the Web in Campaign 2004*, ed. Andrew Paul Williams and John C. Tedesco, Lanham, Md.: Rowman and Littlefield, 2006, pp. 83–98.

Chapter 3

1. Nikki Schwab, "Dems Are No-Shows at DLC," *U.S. News & World Report*, July 30, 2007, at http://www.usnews.com/usnews/news/articles/070730/30dlc.htm.
2. Matthew Klam, "Fear and Laptops on the Campaign Trail," *New York Times Magazine*, September 26, 2004, p. 43.
3. Matthew R. Kerbel and Joel David Bloom, "Blog for America and Civic Involvement," *Harvard International Journal of Press/Politics*, 10 (October 2005), pp. 3–27.
4. Jennifer Stromer-Galley and Andrea B. Baker, "Joy and Sorrow of Interactivity on the Campaign Trail: Blogs in the Primary Campaign of Howard Dean," in *The Internet Election: Perspectives on the Web in Campaign 2004*, ed. Andrew Paul Williams and John C. Tedesco, Lanham, Md.: Rowman and Littlefield, 2006, pp. 111–132.
5. See Kaye D. Trammell, "The Blogging of the President," in *The Internet Election: Perspectives on the Web in Campaign 2004*, ed. Andrew Paul Williams and John C. Tedesco, Lanham, Md.: Rowman and Littlefield, 2006, pp. 133–146.
6. Matthew Hindman, *The Myth of Digital Democracy*, Princeton, N.J.: Princeton University Press, forthcoming, chapter 6.
7. Michael J. Miller, "The Year of the Blog," *PC Magazine*, December 28, 2004, p. 8.
8. Jerome Armstrong, "A Victory for People-Powered Politics," *Christian Science Monitor*, November 9, 2006, p. 9.

9. Stephen Coleman, "Blogs and the New Politics of Listening," *Political Quarterly*, 76 (April 2005), p. 274.

10. Interview with *Frontline*, PBS, August 13, 2006, at http://www.pbs.org/wgbh/pages/frontline/newswar.

11. James Stanyer, "Levelling the Electoral Communication Playing Field? The Hype and Reality of Campaign Blogging," paper presented at the annual meeting of the American Political Science Association, Philadelphia, August 30–September 3, 2006.

12. Stanyer, "Levelling the Electoral Communication Playing Field?"

13. David Carr, "24-Hour Newspaper People," *New York Times*, January 15, 2007, p. C1.

14. Amanda Lenhart and Susannah Fox, "Bloggers: A Portrait of the Internet's New Storytellers," Pew Internet and American Life Project, July 19, 2006, at http://www.pewinternet.org/PPF/r/186/report_display.asp.

15. Lenhart and Fox, "Bloggers: A Portrait of the Internet's New Storytellers."

16. Paul Kane, "Lott Will Quit Senate Next Month; Resignation Is Seen as Blow to the GOP," *Washington Post*, November 27, 2007, p. A1.

17. See, for example, Richard Simon, "Lott to Quit Senate Only One Year into New Term," *Los Angeles Times*, November 27, 2007, at http://www.latimes.com/news/nationworld/nation/la-na-lott27nov27,1,1029406.story?ctrack=2&cset=true; Adam Nossiter and David M. Herszenhorn, "Mississippi's Lott to Leave Senate Seat," *New York Times*, November 27, 2007, at http://www.nytimes.com/2007/11/27/washington/27lott.html?_r=1&oref=slogin.

18. "Trent Lott 'Will Not Be Missed' by Bloggers," *Beltway Blogroll*, November 26, 2007, at http://beltwayblogroll.nationaljournal.com/archives/2007/11/trent_lott_will.php.

19. See, for example, Zizi Papacharissi, "Audiences as Media Producers: Content Analysis of 260 Blogs," in *Blogging, Citizenship, and the Future of Media*, ed. Mark Tremayne, New York: Routledge, 2007, pp. 21–38.

20. David. D. Perlmutter, *Blogwars*, New York: Oxford University Press, 2008, p. 18.

21. Hindman, *The Myth of Digital Democracy*.

22. Laura McKenna, "Getting the Word Out," paper prepared for presentation at the American Political Science Association annual meeting, Philadelphia, August 31–September 3, 2006.

23. Daniel W. Drezner and Henry Farrell, "The Power and Politics of Blogs," paper presented at the annual meeting of the American Political Science Association, Chicago, September 2–5, 2004.

24. Drezner and Farrell, "The Power and Politics of Blogs."

25. Drezner and Farrell, "The Power and Politics of Blogs."

26. Stanyer, "Levelling the Electoral Communication Playing Field?"

27. Interview with Scott Johnson, *Frontline*, PBS, August 26, 2006, at http://www.pbs.org/wgbh/pages/frontline/newswar.

28. Christine Rosen, "Technobabble," *New Republic*, June 26, 2006, p. 14; Klam, "Fear and Laptops," p. 43.

29. Gavin Edwards, "Inside the Huff Trade," *Rolling Stone*, December 14, 2006, p. 65; Howard Kurtz, "Dazzle, Yes. But Can They Blog? For Arianna Huffington, The Stars Come Out to Post," *Washington Post*, May 9, 2005, p. C1.
30. Norman Makatgo Su et al., "Politics as Usual in the Blogosphere," *Proceedings of the 4th International Workshop on Social Intelligence Design* (SID 2005), at http://cache.search.yahoo-ht2.akadns.net/search/cache?ei=UTF-8&p=politics+as+usual+in+the+blogosphere&fr=yfp-t-501&u=www.ics.uci.edu/%7Eyangwang/papers/SID05.pdf&w=politics+usual+blogosphere&d=Wiu2FjWxQzBd&icp=1&.intl=us.
31. Hindman, *The Myth of Digital Democracy*.
32. Perlmutter, *Blogwars*, pp. 28–29.
33. Bara Vaida, "Blogging On," *National Journal*, October 6, 2007, p. 25.
34. Kathy E. Gill, "How Can We Measure the Influence of the Blogosphere?" *WWW2004*, New York, May 17–22, 2004.
35. Armstrong, "A Victory for People-Powered Politics," p. 9
36. Interview with Markos Moulitsas, *Frontline*, PBS, August 13, 2006, at http://www.pbs.org/wgbh/pages/frontline/newswar.
37. Hindman, *The Myth of Digital Democracy*.
38. Hindman, *The Myth of Digital Democracy*.
39. Hindman, *The Myth of Digital Democracy*.
40. For a discussion of the dearth of female bloggers in the political blogosphere, see Dustin Harp and Mark Tremayne, "The Gendered Blogosphere: Examining Inequality Using Network and Feminist Theory," *Journalism and Mass Communication Quarterly*, 83 (Summer 2006), pp. 247–265.
41. Hindman, *The Myth of Digital Democracy*.
42. Antoinette Pole, "Hispanic Bloggers in the Blogosphere: Politics and Participation," paper presented at the annual meeting of the American Political Science Association, Chicago, August 30–September 2, 2007.
43. Lenhart and Fox, "Bloggers: A Portrait of the Internet's New Storytellers."
44. Noam Cohen, "Steven Gilliard Jr., 42, Dies; Founder of Liberal Political Blog," *New York Times*, June 6, 2007, at http://www.nytimes.com/2007/06/06/us/06gilliard.html?ex=1338782400&en=70afa45be93602cd&ei=5090&partner=rssuserland&emc=rss.
45. Antoinette Pole, "Black Bloggers and the Blogosphere," paper presented at the Second International Conference on Technology, Knowledge and Society, Hyderabad, India, December 12–15, 2005.
46. Hindman, *The Myth of Digital Democracy*.
47. Perlmutter, *Blogwars*, p. 36.
48. Hindman, *The Myth of Digital Democracy*.
49. For example, see Howard Kurtz, "Post.com Bloggers Quits Amid Furor," *Washington Post*, March 25, 2006, p. C1.
50. Liriel Higa, "United Bloggers? Depends on the Issue," CQ *Weekly*, October 16, 2006, p. 2745.

51. AdamB, "Electronic Disclosure Ready to Pass—We Just Need Senator Lott," September 29, 2006, at http://www.dailykos.com/storyonly/2006/9/29/14542/4378.

52. Vaida, "Blogging On," pp. 27–28.

53. Vaida, "Blogging On," pp. 24–25.

54. Interview with Jerome Armstrong, *Frontline*, PBS, August 13, 2006, at http://www.pbs.org/wgbh/pages/frontline/newswar.

55. Dan Balz, "Bloggers' Convention Draws Democrats," *Washington Post*, June 11, 2006, p. A5.

56. "Popular Blogs," January 7, 2008, at http://technorati.com/pop/blogs/.

57. Klam, "Fear and Laptops," p. 43; "Markos Moulitsas Zuniga," *Current Biography*, 58 (March 2007), pp. 61–68.

58. "Markos Moulitsas Zuniga," p. 65.

59. "About Daily Kos," at www.dailykos.com; Interview with Markos Moulitsas, *Frontline*, PBS, August 13, 2006, at http://www.pbs.org/wgbh/pages/frontline/newswar.

60. Holly Bailey, "Bloggers Log On," *Newsweek*, October 25, 2004, p. 10.

61. Interview with Markos Moulitsas.

62. Rachel Smolkin, "The Expanding Blogosphere," *American Journalism Review*, July 2004, at http://www.ajr.org/archive.asp?issue=66; Interview with Markos Moulitsas.

63. Balz, "Bloggers' Convention Draws Democrats."

64. Matt Bai, "Can Bloggers Get Real?" *New York Times Magazine*, May 28, 2006, p. 13; Dan Balz, "Bloggers' Convention Draws Democrats," *Washington Post*, June 11, 2006, p. A5.

65. Adam Nagourney, "Internet Injects Sweeping Change into U.S. Politics," *New York Times*, April 2, 2006, section 1, p. 1.

66. Balz, "Bloggers' Convention Draws Democrats."

67. Interview with Markos Moulitsas.

68. David Brooks, "Respect Must Be Paid," *New York Times*, June 25, 2006, section 4, p. 12.

69. Balz, "Bloggers' Convention Draws Democrats."

70. Chris Cillizza, "Kerry Rules Out 2008 Run for President," *Washington Post*, January 25, 2007, p. A4.

71. "Interview with Jerome Armstrong," *Mother Jones*, June 29, 2007, at http://www.motherjones.com/interview/2007/07/jerome_armstrong.html.

72. Armstrong, "A Victory for People-Powered Politics," p. 9.

73. "Huffington Withdraws from Recall Race," CNN, September 30, 2003, at http://www.cnn.com/2003/ALLPOLITICS/09/30/calif.recall/index.html.

74. Howard Kurtz, "A Blog That Made It Big: The Huffington Post, Trending Up and Left," *Washington Post*, July 9, 2007, p. C1.

75. Kurtz, "Dazzle, Yes."

76. Edwards, "Inside the Huff Trade"; Kurtz, "A Blog That Made It Big."

77. Kurtz, "A Blog That Made It Big."

78. Jason Fagone, "The Unknown Blogger," *Philadelphia Magazine*, March 2004, p. 14; Hindman, *The Myth of Digital Democracy.*

79. "'Big Media' Meets the 'Bloggers': Coverage of Trent Lott's Remarks at Strom Thurmond's Birthday Party," Kennedy School of Government Case Program, C14–04–1731.0, at http://www.ksg.harvard.edu/presspol/research_publications/case_studies/1731_0.pdf.

80. Quoted in Gregg Sangillo, "Bloggers: A Who's Who," *National Journal*, January 21, 2006, pp. 37–39.

81. "Selling Out or Growing Up," *The Hotline*, September 5, 2006; "18 Blogs Responsible for the 100 Most Popular Posts of 2006," *Market Wire*, December 28, 2006; Esther Walker, "Bloggers' Who's Who," *Toronto Star*, December 29, 2007, p. D12.

82. Tom Zeller Jr., "Blogs Take Lead in Reporting Polling Problems, with Supporting Evidence on YouTube," *New York Times*, November 8, 2006, p. P11; "Crooks and Liars: C&L's John Amato Joins Keith Olbermann for Post Debate Analysis," January 31, 2008, at http://blog.newsweek.com/blogs/theruckus/archive/2008/01/31/crooks-and-liars-c-l-s-john-amato-joins-keith-olbermann-for-post-debate-analysis.aspx; "Crooks and Liars: John Amato and Rachel Maddow Talk about Indiana's Voter ID Case," January 18, 2008, at http://www.blog.newsweek.com/blogs/theruckus/archive/2008/01/18/crooks-and-liars-john-amato-and-rachel-maddow-talk-about-indiana-s-voter-id-case.aspx.

83. "Blogger: Joshua Micah Marshall, 34, Editor, Talking Points Memo," *Washington Post*, December 21, 2003, p. M3.

84. "Blogger: Joshua Micah Marshall."

85. Hindman, *The Myth of Digital Democracy*; Interview with Joshua Micah Marshall, *Frontline*, PBS, April 24, 2006, at http://www.pbs.org/wgbh/pages/frontline/newswar.

86. Sangillo, "Bloggers: A Who's Who," pp. 37–39.

87. Julie Bosman, "First with the Scoop, If Not the Truth," *New York Times*, April 18, 2004, section 9, p. 10.

88. Klam, "Fear and Laptops," p. 43.

89. Klam, "Fear and Laptops," p. 43.

90. Bosman, "First with the Scoop, If Not the Truth."

91. Bosman, "First with the Scoop, If Not the Truth."

92. "Wonkette in the Flesh: An Evening with Ana Marie Cox," Society of Professional Journalists, Columbia University Graduate School of Journalism, at http://spj.jrn.columbia.edu/wonkette.html.

93. Jonathan Miller, "He Fought the Law. They Both Won," *New York Times*, January 22, 2006, section 14NJ, p. 1.

94. Bosman, "First with the Scoop, If Not the Truth."

95. Bosman, "First with the Scoop, If Not the Truth."

96. Jeffrey Toobin, "SCOTUS WATCH: Jeffrey Toobin on a Federal-Judge Fan Blog," *New Yorker*, November 21, 2005, p. 44; Adam Liptak, "Mystery of Gossipy Blog on the Judiciary Is Solved," *New York Times*, November 16, 2005, p. A14.

97. J. Miller, "He Fought the Law."

98. Steven Levy, "Living in the Blog-osphere," *Newsweek*, August 26, 2002, p. 42.

99. "Glenn Harlan Reynolds," *Current Biography*, October 2007, pp. 76–79.

100. Jeffery Knight, "King of Bloggers," *American Lawyer*, September 2002, p. 18; Sangillo, "Bloggers: A Who's Who," pp. 37–39; "Glenn Harlan Reynolds," pp. 76–79.

101. Smolkin, "The Expanding Blogosphere."

102. "A Blog's Bark Has Bite," *U.S. News & World Report*, May 5, 2002, at http://www.usnews.com/usnews/opinion/articles/020513/archive_020772.htm.

103. Glenn Reynolds, *An Army of Davids: How Markets and Technology Empower Ordinary People to Beat Big Media, Big Government, and Other Goliaths*, Nashville, Tenn.: Thomas Nelson, 2006.

104. Sangillo, "Bloggers: A Who's Who," pp. 37–39.

105. Howard Kurtz, "The Comeback Columnist: Andrew Sullivan Continues to Defy All Expectations," *Washington Post*, April 19, 2001, p. C1; Gill, "How Can We Measure the Influence of the Blogosphere?"

106. Kurtz, "Columnist Andrew Sullivan Bites Paper; Paper Bites Back," *Washington Post*, May 14, 2002, p. C1.

107. Sangillo, "Bloggers: A Who's Who," pp. 37–39.

108. Andrew Sullivan, "Ron Paul for the Republican Nomination," *The Atlantic*, December 17, 2007, at http://andrewsullivan.theatlantic.com/the_daily_dish/2007/12/ron-paul-for-th.html; Andrew Sullivan, "Goodbye to All That: Why Obama Matters," *The Atlantic*, December 2007, at http://www.theatlantic.com/doc/200712/obama.

109. Howard Kurtz, "A Hard Right Punch: Michelle Malkin's Conservative Fight Has Others Coming Out Swinging," *Washington Post*, February 16, 2007, p. C1; Sangillo, "Bloggers: A Who's Who," pp. 37–39.

110. Kurtz, "A Hard Right Punch."

111. Kurtz, "A Hard Right Punch."

112. Kurtz, "A Hard Right Punch."

113. Kurtz, "A Hard Right Punch."

114. Kurtz, "A Hard Right Punch."

115. Paul Farhi, "Blogger Takes Aim at News Media and Makes a Direct Hit," *Washington Post*, August 9, 2006, p. C1.

116. Farhi, "Blogger Takes Aim at News Media."

117. Randy Doting, "A Blogger Shines When News Media Get It Wrong," *Christian Science Monitor*, August 9, 2006, p. 1.

118. Nicholas Lemann, "Right Hook: The Wayward Press," *New Yorker*, August 29, 2005, p. 34.

119. Carl Bialik and Elizabeth Weinstein, "Meet Bloggers, Part Two," *Wall Street Journal*, August 26, 2004, at http://online.wsj.com/article_email/SB109278109869594104-INjeoNhlaR3o52raoKIbquIm5.html.

120. Hindman, *The Myth of Digital Democracy*; Bialik and Weinstein, "Meet Bloggers, Part Two."

121. Interview with Scott Johnson.

122. Stephen Humphries, "Blogs Look Burly after Kicking Sand on CBS," *Christian Science Monitor*, September 22, 2004, p. 1; quoted in Matt McKinney, "Bloggers Exult in Rather's Departure; They Call Internet Chatter New Political Force," *Star Tribune* (Minneapolis), March 10, 2005, p. 8A.

123. Quoted in Sangillo, "Bloggers: A Who's Who," pp. 37–39.

124. Bialik and Weinstein, "Meet Bloggers, Part Two."

125. Eric Zorn, "Change of Subject: Political Site Polls Well with Election Junkies," *Chicago Tribune*, April 11, 2006, at http://blogs.chicagotribune.com/news_columnists_ezorn/2006/04/good_riddance_t.html.

126. Rob MacKay, "Political Junkies Create Web Site for Opinion and Analysis," *Princeton Alumni Weekly*, June 6, 2001, at http://www.princeton.edu/paw/web_exclusives/more/more_20.html.

127. Sangillo, "Bloggers: A Who's Who," pp. 37–39.

128. Howard Kurtz, "Eason Jordan, Quote, Unquote," *Washington Post*, February 8, 2005, p. C1; Katherine Q. Seelye, "Resignation at CNN Shows the Growing Influence of Blogs," *New York Times*, February 14, 2005, at http://www.nytimes.com/2005/02/14/technology/14cnn.html.

129. Mike Mills, "The Futurist: Rise of the Citizen Auditor," CQ *Weekly Online*, October 9, 2006, p. 2689, at http://library.cqpress.com/cqweekly/weeklyreport109–000002387425.

Chapter 4

1. Kaye D. Trammell, "Celebrity Blogs: Investigation in the Persuasive Nature of Two-Way Communication Regarding Politics," Ph.D. dissertation, University of Florida, 2004; Michael Keren, "Blogging and the Politics of Melancholy," *Canadian Journal of Communication*, 29 (2004), pp. 5–23.

2. Svetlana V. Kulikova and David D. Perlmutter, "Blogging Down the Dictator? The Kyrgyz Revolution and Samizdat Websites," *International Communication Gazette*, 69 (2007), pp. 29–50; Antoinette Pole, "Hispanic Bloggers in the Blogosphere: Politics and Participation," paper presented at the annual meeting of the American Political Science Association, Chicago, August 30–September 2, 2007.

3. Susan C. Herring et al., "Longitudinal Content Analysis of Blogs: 2003–2004," in *Blogging, Citizenship, and the Future of Media*, ed. Mark Tremayne, New York: Routledge, 2007, pp. 3–20.

4. David Glenn, "The (Josh) Marshall Plan," *Columbia Journalism Review*, September/October 2007, at http://www.cjr.org/feature/the_josh_marshall_plan.php?page=all.

5. D. Travers Scott, "Pundits in Muckracker's Clothing: Political Blogs and the 2004 U.S. Presidential Election," in *Blogging, Citizenship, and the Future of Media*, ed. Mark Tremayne, New York: Routledge, 2007, pp. 39–57.

6. For more treatment of this, see Scott, "Pundits in Muckracker's Clothing."

7. "What Does Your Blog Mean to You?" Pew Internet and American Life Project, July 19, 2006, at http://www.pewinternet.org/PPF/p/1136/

pipcomments.asp; Brian Ekdale et al., "From Expression to Influence: Understanding the Change in Blogger Motivations over the Blogspan," paper presented at the annual meeting of the Association for Education in Journalism and Mass Communication, Washington, D.C., August 9–12, 2007.

8. Herring et al., "Longitudinal Content Analysis of Blogs: 2003–2004," pp. 3–20.

9. Scott, "Pundits in Muckracker's Clothing," p. 54.

10. Pole, "Hispanic Bloggers in the Blogosphere." However, Laura McKenna found the opposite in her study of nine policy bloggers: they rarely encouraged readers to take political action. See Laura McKenna, "Getting the Word Out," paper prepared for presentation at the American Political Science Association annual meeting, Philadelphia, August 31–September 3, 2006.

Chapter 5

1. Mayhill Fowler, "Obama: No Surprise That Hard-Pressed Pennsylvanians Turn Bitter," *The Huffington Post*, April 11, 2008, at http://www.huffingtonpost.com/mayhill-fowler/obama-no-surprise-that-ha_b_96188.html.

2. Katherine Q. Seelye, "Blogger Is Surprised by Uproar over Obama Story, but Not Bitter," *New York Times*, April 14, 2008, at http://www.nytimes.com/2008/04/14/us/politics/14web-seelye.html?_r=1&scp=3&sq=seelye&st=nyt&oref=slogin.

3. Jeff Zeleny, "Opponents Call Obama Remarks 'Out of Touch,' " *New York Times*, April 12, 2008, at http://www.nytimes.com/2008/04/12/us/politics/12campaign.html?scp=2&sq=mccain+obama+elitism&st=nyt.

4. Elisabeth Bumiller, "Family Recipes, Passed Down from One Site to Another," *New York Times*, April 16, 2008, at http://www.nytimes.com/2008/04/16/us/politics/16recipes.html?scp=24&sq=mccain&st=nyt.

5. Ian Urbina, "Kentucky Governor Draws Fire from a New Quarter," *New York Times*, June 23, 2006, p. A24.

6. Terry Ganey, "Blunt Reaction: Governor Removes Blogger from Press Event," *St. Louis Journalism Review*, July/August 2006, pp. 16–17.

7. "The Blog in the Corporate Machine: Corporate Reputations," *The Economist*, February 11, 2006; Matthew Creamer and James B. Arndorfer, "The Art of the PR Schmooze, Translated for the Blogosphere," *Advertising Age*, April 4, 2005, p. 3.

8. Raymond Hernandez, "A Well-Known Political Blogger Is Hired by the Clinton Campaign," *New York Times*, June 27, 2006, p. B4.

9. Michael D. Shear and Tim Craig, "Paid Bloggers Stoke Senate Battle in Va.; Campaigns Test Limits of Finance Laws," *Washington Post*, September 17, 2006, p. A1; K. Daniel Glover, "Bloggers Proliferate on Campaign Payroll," *National Journal*, October 31, 2006, at http://www.msnbc.msn.com/id/15498843/; K. Daniel Glover and Mike Essl, "New on the Web: Politics as Usual," *New York Times*, December 3, 2006, section 4, p. 13; Scott Helman, "Romney Connecting Quickly with Bloggers," Boston Globe, December 31,

2006, at http://www.boston.com/news/local/articles/2006/12/31/romney_connecting_quickly_with_bloggers/.

10. Adam Nagourney, "Internet Injects Sweeping Change into U.S. Politics," *New York Times*, April 2, 2006, section 1, p. 1.

11. Glover and Essl, "New on the Web."

12. Alex Williams, "Blogged in Boston: Politics Gets an Unruly Spin," *New York Times*, August 1, 2004, section 9, p. 1.

13. Quoted in Dan Balz, "Bloggers' Convention Draws Democrats," *Washington Post*, June 11, 2006, p. A5.

14. Brian Faler, "A Capitol Hill Presence in the Blogosphere," *Washington Post*, October 11, 2005, p. A15.

15. David D. Perlmutter and Emily Metzgar, "Could Blogs Trump Stumping in Iowa?" *Christian Science Monitor*, November 3, 2005, p. 9.

16. Taylor Ansley and Patrick Sellers, "Framing, Indexing, and Blogs in the Alito Nomination Debate," paper presented at the annual meeting of the Midwest Political Science Association, Chicago, April 12–15, 2007.

17. Eric Pfeiffer, "Bloggers Emerge as Force on Right; Briefings Pull Heavy-Hitters," *Washington Times*, August 15, 2007, p. A3.

18. Gail Russell, "Their Clout Rising, Blogs Are Courted by Washington's Elite," *Christian Science Monitor*, October 27, 2005, p. 1.

19. Russell, "Their Clout Rising."

20. Matthew Hindman, *The Myth of Digital Democracy*, Princeton, N.J.: Princeton University Press, forthcoming, chapter 6; Carl Bialik and Elizabeth Weinstein, "Meet Bloggers, Part Two," *Wall Street Journal*, August 26, 2004, at http://online.wsj.com/article_email/SB109278109869594104-INjeoNhlaR3o52rao"AKIbquIm5.html.

21. "White House Conference Call on Executive Privilege," July 27, 2007, at http://www.captainsquartersblog.com/mt/archives/010651.php; "A Warning about Blogger Conference Calls," February 4, 2006, at http://beltwayblogroll.nationaljournal.com/archives/2006/02/a_warning_about.php; "GOP's Direct Appeal to Bloggers Falls Flat," October 13, 2005, at http://beltwayblogroll.nationaljournal.com/archives/2005/10/gops_direct_app.php; David D. Perlmutter, *Blogwars*, New York: Oxford University Press, 2008, p. xiv; Ana Marie Cox, "McCain Fires Back," May 21, 2007, at http://time-blog.com/swampland/2007/05/mccain_fires_back.html; Leon D. Wolf, "McCain Blogger Conference Call," *RedState*, at http://www.redstate.com/stories/elections/2008/mccain_blogger_conference_call; Shear and Craig, "Paid Bloggers Stoke Senate Battle in Va."; Mark Brunswick, "Bloggers, Governor Hobnob; Right-of-Center Cyberspace Came to Summit Avenue at Pawlenty's Invitation," *Minneapolis Star Tribune*, May 21, 2005, p. 4B; Dwight Silverman, "Updated: Playing to the Blogosphere," May 15, 2006, at http://blogs.chron.com/techblog/archives/2006/05/playing_to_the_1.html.

22. Brunswick, "Bloggers, Governor Hobnob."

23. "Bill Clinton Meets Bloggers," *TalkLeft*, September 12, 2006, at http://www.talkleft.com/story/2006/09/12/091/72051.

24. "Bill Clinton Meeting," *Crooks and Liars*, September 13, 2006, at http://www.crooksandliars.com/2006/09/13/bill-clinton-meeting/.

25. Shawn Zeller, "Blogs Bulk Up in Beltway," CQ *Weekly*, November 14, 2005, p. 3028.

26. Joelle Tessler, "Some Faces behind the Blogs," CQ *Weekly*, August 8, 2005, p. 2172.

27. S. Zeller, "Blogs Bulk Up in Beltway," p. 3028.

28. Thomas B. Edsall, "FEC Rules Exempt Blogs from Internet Political Limits," *Washington Post*, March 28, 2006, p. A3.

29. Rebecca Neal, "Bloggers vs. Journalists," *Quill*, December 2007, pp. 22–23; James Baetke, "Quest for Credibility: Leader of Blogging Association Tours Country in Hopes of Bringing Legitimacy to Craft," *Quill*, October/November 2006, pp. 24–25.

30. Matthew R. Kerbel and Joel David Bloom, "Blog for America and Civic Involvement," *Harvard International Journal of Press/Politics*, 10 (4), pp. 3–27; Sue MacDonald, "Drudge Report, DailyKos, and Instapundit Grab Most 'Buzz' among Political Blogs, Says Intelliseek," *Business Wire*, October 27, 2004, p. 1.

31. Howard Kurtz, "Dazzle, Yes. But Can They Blog? For Arianna Huffington, the Stars Come Out to Post," *Washington Post*, May 9, 2005, p. C1.

32. J. D. Lasica, "Weblogs: A New Source of News," *USC Annenberg Online Journalism Review*, May 24, 2001, at http://www.ojr.org/ojr/workplace/1017958782.php.

33. Jacques Steinberg, "An Anchor by Evening, a Blogger Any Time," *New York Times*, August 25, 2005, p. 1.

34. Susan Young, "News Viewers Chat Back: Broadcasts Move from Monologue to Dialogue," *McClatchy-Tribune Business News*, November 17, 2007.

35. Joe Strupp, "Voting for the Web," *Editor & Publisher*, October 2006, p. 62.

36. Nat Ives, "Madison Avenue Ponders the Potential, and the Perils, of the Web Logs Being Set Up by Agencies," *New York Times*, October 27, 2004, p. C9; James Stanyer, "Levelling the Electoral Communication Playing Field? The Hype and Reality of Campaign Blogging," paper presented at the annual meeting of the American Political Science Association, Philadelphia, August 30–September 3, 2006.

37. Rachel Smolkin, "The Expanding Blogosphere," *American Journalism Review*, July 2004, at http://www.ajr.org/archive.asp?issue=66.

38. Matthew Karnitschnig, "Time Inc. Makes New Bid to Be Big Web Player," *Wall Street Journal*, March 29, 2006, p. B1.

39. Smolkin, "The Expanding Blogosphere": Glenn Reynolds, "So Long, and Thanks for All the Pageviews," MSNBC, July 31, 2006, at http://www.msnbc.com/id/3395977/.

40. *Kausfiles*, at http://www.slate.com/id/2182569/.

41. Daniel Terdiman, "On Fridays, Bloggers Sometimes Retract Their Claws," *New York Times*, October 28, 2004, p. G6.

42. John Cochran, "Surrendering to the 'Blogosphere,'" CQ *Weekly*, March 13, 2006, p. 655.

43. Bara Vaida, "Blogging On," *National Journal*, October 6, 2007, p. 27.

44. Jill Barshay, "Chamber Stakes Out Right End of the Blogosphere," CQ *Weekly*, October 16, 2006, p. 2738.

45. David Kirkpatrick, "Why There's No Escaping the Blog," *Fortune*, January 10, 2005, pp. 44–50.

46. "The Blog in the Corporate Machine: Corporate Reputations," *The Economist*, February 11, 2006.

47. Tania Ralli, "Brand Blogs Capture the Attention of Some Companies," *New York Times*, October 24, 2005, p. C1.

48. Marc Gunther, "Corporate Blogging: Wal-Mart's Fumbles," *Fortune*, October 18, 2006, at http://money.cnn.com/2006/10/17/technology/pluggedin_gunther_blog.fortune/index.htm.

49. Daniel Rubin, "In the Blink of an Eye, Blogs Became Big," *Philadelphia Inquirer*, December 20, 2005, p. A1.

50. Vaida, "Blogging On," p. 28.

51. Vaida, "Blogging On," p. 27.

52. Matt Bai, "Can Bloggers Get Real?" *New York Times Magazine*, May 28, 2006, p. 14.

53. *BlogHer*, July 17, 2008, at http://www.blogher.com/lets-talk.

54. Kaye D. Trammell, "Blog Offensive: An Exploratory Analysis of Attacks Published on Campaign Blog Posts from a Political Public Relations Perspective," *Public Relations Review*, 32 (2006): 402–406.

55. Kerbel and Bloom, "Blog for America and Civic Involvement," p. 4.

56. Gracie Lawson-Borders and Rita Kirk, "Blogs in Campaign Communication," *American Behavioral Scientist*, 49 (December 2005), p. 555.

57. Joan Conners, "Meetup, Blogs, and Online Involvement: U.S. Senate Campaign Websites of 2004," paper delivered at the annual meeting of the American Political Science Association, Washington, D.C., September 1–4, 2005.

58. Kerbel and Bloom, "Blog for America and Civic Involvement," pp. 3–27.

59. Matthew Klam, "Fear and Laptops on the Campaign Trail," *New York Times Magazine*, September 26, 2004, p. 43.

60. Matt Gross, at http://mathewgross.com/node/1327.

61. Kerbel and Bloom, "Blog for America and Civic Involvement," pp. 6–7.

62. Kerbel and Bloom, "Blog for America and Civic Involvement," p. 7.

63. Kerbel and Bloom, "Blog for America and Civic Involvement," p. 24.

64. Sharon Meraz, "Analyzing Political Conversation on the Howard Dean Candidate Blog," in *Blogging, Citizenship, and the Future of Media*, ed. Mark Tremayne, New York: Routledge, 2007, pp. 59–82.

65. Lawson-Borders and Kirk, "Blogs in Campaign Communication," pp. 548–559.

66. Quoted in Miles Maguire, "Online Debates: Using the Blog to Promote an Engaged Electorate," paper presented at the annual meeting of the Midwest Political Science Association, Chicago, April 20–23, 2006.

67. Andrea Stone, "Blogs—The Hill's Version of Talk Radio; More Lawmakers Using Interactive Websites to Engage Constituents," *USA Today*, June 1, 2006, p. 2A.

68. David R. Mayhew, *Congress: The Electoral Connection*, New Haven: Yale University Press, 1974.

69. Antoinette Pole, "Congressional Blogging: Advertising, Credit Claiming, and Position Taking," paper presented at the annual meeting of the American Political Science Association, Philadelphia, August 30– September 3, 2006.

70. Pole, "Congressional Blogging."

71. Pole, "Congressional Blogging."

72. John Kerry, "Filibuster Alito," *Daily Kos*, January 26, 2006, at http://www. dailykos.com/storyonly/2006/1/26/192843/363; Nancy Pelosi, "Progress Is Possible Again," *Huffington Post*, January 18, 2007, at http://www. huffingtonpost.com/rep-nancy-pelosi/progress-is-possible-agai_b_39019. html; Nancy Pelosi, "Bringing the War to an End Is My Highest Priority as Speaker," *Huffington Post*, November 17, 2006, at http://www.huffingtonpost. com/rep-nancy-pelosi/bringing-the-war-to-an-en_b_34393.html; Howard Kurtz, "A Blog That Made It Big; The Huffington Post, Trending Up and Left," *Washington Post*, July 9, 2007, p. C1; Gregg Sangillo, "Bloggers: A Who's Who," *National Journal*, January 21, 2006, pp. 37–39.

73. Russell, "Their Clout Rising"; Eric Pfieffer, "Conservative Bloggers Seek a Place on the Political Web," *Washington Times*, June 29, 2006, p. A3.

74. A. Stone, "Blogs—The Hill's Version of Talk Radio."

75. David Nather, "The Soft Murmur of Congressional Blogging," CQ *Weekly*, April 3, 2006, p. 880.

76. Ross Ferguson and Barry Griffiths, "Thin Democracy? Parliamentarians, Citizens and the Influence of Blogging on Political Engagement," *Parliamentary Affairs*, 59 (2006), pp. 4.

77. A. Stone, "Blogs—The Hill's Version of Talk Radio."

78. See Perlmutter, *Blogwars*, p. 84

79. Nather, "The Soft Murmur of Congressional Blogging," p. 880.

80. A. Stone, "Blogs—The Hill's Version of Talk Radio."

81. Pam Greenberg, "I Blog, You Blog, We All Blog," *State Legislatures*, March 2005, pp. 22–25.

82. Mark Sappenfield, "More Politicians Write Blogs to Bypass Mainstream Media," *Christian Science Monitor*, March 24, 2005, p. 2.

83. Sappenfield, "More Politicians Write Blogs," p. 2.

84. Greenberg, "I Blog, You Blog," pp. 22–25.

85. Greenberg, "I Blog, You Blog," pp. 22–25.

86. "A Readers' Pick of the British Political Blogs," *Daily Telegraph*, September 22, 2007.

87. Pole, "Congressional Blogging."

88. "A Readers' Pick of the British Political Blogs."

89. Jill Aitoro, "Keeping It Real," *Government Executive*, December 2007, p. 47.

90. "Dipnote: U.S. Department of State Official Blog," at http://blogs.state. gov/index.php.

91. See "InfoFarm: The NAL Blog," at http://weblogs.nal.usda.gov/infofarm/; "Peace Corps: About the Peace Corps," at http://www.peacecorps.gov/ index.cfm?shell=learn.whatlike.voljournal.

92. "Rhode Island State Council on the Arts," at http://www.arts. ri.gov/blogs/index.php/?p=3200; "Talking Trash," at http://www. montgomerycountymd.gov/apps/News/Blog/solidwasteBlog. asp?BlogID=2; "Ag Blog," at http://www.mrcog-nm.gov/content/ blogcategory/33/241/.

93. For example, see the blog of the Consumer Protection Division of the Missouri Attorney General's Office, at ago.mo.gov/ConsumerCorner.

94. Aitoro, "Keeping It Real," p. 47.

95. Nagourney, "Internet Injects Sweeping Change into U.S. Politics."

96. Quoted in Michael Skube, "Blogs: All the Noise That Fits," *Los Angeles Times*, August 19, 2007, p. M5.

97. Ari Melber, "Bloggers on the Trail," *The Nation*, March 12, 2007, p. 5.

98. Daniel J. Solove, *The Future of Reputation: Gossip, Rumor, and Privacy on the Internet*, New Haven, Conn.: Yale University Press, 2007, p. 5.

99. Cass Sunstein, republic.com, Princeton, N.J.: Princeton University Press, 2001; John Maynor, "Blogging for Democracy: Deliberation, Autonomy, and Reasonableness in the Blogosphere," paper presented at the annual meeting of the American Political Science Association, Chicago, August 30–September 2, 2007.

100. Perlmutter, *Blogwars*, p. 56.

101. Klam, "Fear and Laptops," p. 43.

102. "Selling Out or Growing Up," *The Hotline*, September 5, 2006.

103. Interview with Joshua Micah Marshall, *Frontline*, PBS, April 24, 2006, at http://www.pbs.org/wgbh/pages/frontline/newswar.

104. Julie Flaherty, "Many Started Web Logs for Fun, but Bloggers Need Money, Too," *New York Times*, April 19, 2004, p. C4.

105. "Adver-Blogging," *The Hotline*, February 14, 2007.

106. Interview with Markos Moulitsas, *Frontline*, PBS, August 13, 2006, at http:// www.pbs.org/wgbh/pages/frontline/newswar.

107. Interview with Joshua Micah Marshall.

108. Andrew Ross Sorkin, "Building a Web Media Empire on a Daily Dose of Fresh Links," *New York Times*, November 17, 2003, at http://www.nytimes. com/2003/11/17/technology/17blog.html?ex=1384491600&en=d14f43fbe 25dcfd4&ei=5007&partner=USERLAND.

109. Interview with Markos Moulitsas.

110. Stephen Coleman, "Blogs and the New Politics of Listening," *Political Quarterly*, 76 (April 2005), pp. 272–280.

111. John M. Broder, "Edwards Learns Campaign Blogs Can Cut 2 Ways," *New York Times*, February 9, 2007, p. A1; "Non-Paper Trail: Bloggers May Sometimes Regret What They Write—And Now Presidential Candidates

Who Hire Them May Too," *Los Angeles Times*, February 11, 2007, p. M5; Melber, "Bloggers on the Trail."

112. Shear and Craig, "Paid Bloggers Stoke Senate Battle in Va."
113. Broder, "Edwards Learns Campaign Blogs Can Cut 2 Ways."
114. Gavin O'Malley, "Why Bloggers Can't Win White House; Lamont Gives Netroots a Rare Win, but Race Isn't Likely to Be a Bellwether," *Advertising Age*, August 14, 2006, p. 3.
115. Smolkin, "The Expanding Blogosphere."
116. Broder, "Edwards Learns Campaign Blogs Can Cut 2 Ways."
117. Ives, "Madison Avenue Ponders the Potential."
118. Pole, "Congressional Blogging."
119. Ferguson and Griffiths, "Thin Democracy?" p. 6.
120. Sunstein, republic.com; Maynor, "Blogging for Democracy."
121. Antoinette Pole, "Hispanic Bloggers in the Blogosphere: Politics and Participation," paper presented at the annual meeting of the American Political Science Association, Chicago, August 30–September 2, 2007.
122. Daniel Burke, "To Congregate or Confess, Believers Turning to Blogs," *Washington Post*, October 2, 2004, p. B9; Daniel Terdiman, "A Blog for Baseball Fans Builds a League of Sites," *New York Times*, April 18, 2005, p. C8; Susan Kinzie, "Blogging Clicks with Colleges; Interactive Web Pages Changing Class Participation," *Washington Post*, March 11, 2005, p. B1; Sine Anahita, "Blogging the Borders: Virtual Skinheads, Hypermasculinity, and Heteronormativity," *Journal of Political and Military Sociology*, 34 (Summer 2006), pp. 143–169.
123. Amanda Lenhart and Susannah Fox, "Bloggers: A Portrait of the Internet's New Storytellers," Pew Internet and American Life Project, July 19, 2006, at http://www.pewinternet.org/PPF/r/186/report_display.asp.
124. Brad Stone, "A Call for Manners in the World of Nasty Blogs," *New York Times*, April 9, 2007, at http://www.nytimes.com/2007/04/09/technology/09blog.html?pagewanted=1&_r=2&hp.
125. Solove, *The Future of Reputation*, pp. 140–141.
126. Alan Wirzbicki, "Political Bloggers Fear Publicists Will Infiltrate Sites," *Boston Globe*, February 23, 2007, p. A1.
127. Wirzbicki, "Political Bloggers Fear Publicists Will Infiltrate Sites."
128. Nagourney, "Internet Injects Sweeping Change into U.S. Politics."
129. For a general discussion of this dilemma, see J. D. Lasica, "The Cost of Ethics: Influence Peddling in the Blogosphere," *USC Annenberg Online Journalism Review*, February 17, 2005, at http://www.ojr.org/ojr/stories/050217lasica/.
130. "Markos Moulitsas Zuniga," *Current Biography*, 58 (March 2007), p. 67.
131. Greg Pierce, "McCain's Blogola," *Washington Times*, July 28, 2006, p. A6; Daniel Schulman, "Meet the New Bosses," *Mother Jones*, June 20, 2007, at http://www.motherjones.com/news/feature/2007/07/meet_the_new_bosses.html.
132. David D. Perlmutter, "'If I Break a Rule, What Do I Do, Fire Myself?' Ethics Codes of Independent Blogs," *Journal of Mass Media Ethics*, 22 (2007), pp. 37–48.

133. Stone, "A Call for Manners."
134. Perlmutter, "'If I Break a Rule"; Adam Cohen, "The Latest Rumbling in the Blogosphere: Questions about Ethics," *New York Times*, May 8, 2005, section 4, p. 11.
135. "Draft Blogger's Code of Conduct," at http://radar.oreilly.com/archives/2007/04/draft_bloggers_1.html.
136. Lasica, "The Cost of Ethics."
137. Chris Suellentrop, "Blogger to Pay $30,000 in S.E.C. Case," *The Opinionator*, at http://opinionator.blogs.nytimes.com/tag/jerome-armstrong/.
138. Lasica, "The Cost of Ethics."
139. Chris Suellentrop, "Blogging for Dollars," *Slate*, January 14, 2005, at http://www.slate.com/id/2112314.
140. Smolkin, "The Expanding Blogosphere."
141. See, for example, Suellentrop, "Blogging for Dollars."

Chapter 6

1. Howard Kurtz, "Web Site Rushes to Crack the Story and Ends Up with Egg on Its Face," *Washington Post*, March 23, 2007, p. C1.
2. Stephen Coleman, "Blogs and the New Politics of Listening," *Political Quarterly*, 76 (April 2005), pp. 272–280.
3. Daniel Schulman, "Meet the New Bosses," *Mother Jones*, June 20, 2007, at http://www.motherjones.com/news/feature/2007/07/meet_the_new_bosses.html; David Brooks, "Respect Must Be Paid," *New York Times*, June 25, 2006, section 4, p. 12.
4. Antoinette Pole, "Hispanic Bloggers in the Blogosphere: Politics and Participation," paper presented at the annual meeting of the American Political Science Association, Chicago, August 30–September 2, 2007.
5. Alex Williams, "Blogged in Boston: Politics Gets an Unruly Spin," *New York Times*, August 1, 2004, section 9, p. 1.
6. Jim Rutenberg, "Web Offers Hefty Voice to Critics of Mainstream Journalists," *New York Times*, October 28, 2004, p. A26.
7. Rutenberg, "Web Offers Hefty Voice."
8. David Vaina, "Newspapers and Blogs: Closer Than We Think?" *USC Annenberg Online Journalism Review*, April 23 2007, at http://www.ojr.org/ojr/stories/070423_vaina/.
9. David D. Perlmutter, "'If I Break a Rule, What Do I Do, Fire Myself?' Ethics Codes of Independent Blogs," *Journal of Mass Media Ethics*, 22 (2007), pp. 37–48.
10. David Glenn, "The (Josh) Marshall Plan," *Columbia Journalism Review*, September/October 2007, at http://www.cjr.org/feature/the_josh_marshall_plan.php?page=all.
11. Quoted in Paul Burka, "That Blog Won't Hunt," *Texas Monthly*, March 2005, p. 12.
12. Rachel Smolkin, "The Expanding Blogosphere," *American Journalism Review*, July 2004, at http://www.ajr.org/archive.asp?issue=66.

13. Quoted in Burka, "That Blog Won't Hunt," p. 12.
14. Interview with Joshua Micah Marshall, *Frontline*, PBS, April 24, 2006, at http://www.pbs.org/wgbh/pages/frontline/newswar.
15. Nicholas Lemann, "Right Hook: The Wayward Press," *New Yorker*, August 29, 2005, p. 34.
16. Rutenberg, "Web Offers Hefty Voice."
17. "Outreach and Outrage; Blogging," *The Economist*, March 11, 2006.
18. Rem Reider, "Hold That Obit," *American Journalism Review*, April/May 2005, p. 6.
19. J. D. Lasica, "Blogging as a Form of Journalism," *USC Annenberg Online Journalism Review*, April 29, 2001, at http://www.ojr.org/ojr/lasica/1019166956.php.
20. Jennifer Dorroh, "Knocking Down the Stonewall," *American Journalism Review*, December 2004/January 2005, p. 48.
21. Ryan Chittum and Joe Hagain, "Student's Suicide Sets Off Explosion of Theories by Blogs," *Wall Street Journal*, October 13, 2005, p. B1.
22. Dorroh, "Knocking Down the Stonewall," p. 48.
23. See Michelle Dammon Loyalka, "Blog Alert: Battalion of Citizen Investigative Reporters Cannot Be Ignored by Mainstream Media," *IRE Journal*, July/August 2005, p. 19; Alexandra Starr, "Open-Source Reporting," *New York Times Magazine*, December 11, 2005, p. 82; Suzanne Perry, "Seeking Online Exposure," The Sunlight Foundation, January 10, 2008, at http://www.sunlightfoundation.com/node/4354; David D. Perlmutter, *Blogwars*, New York: Oxford University Press, 2008, pp. 124–125.
24. Melissa Wall, "'Blogs of War': Weblogs as News," *Journalism*, 6 (2005), pp. 157–158.
25. Interview with John Hinderaker, *Frontline*, PBS, August 26, 2006, at http://www.pbs.org/wgbh/pages/frontline/newswar.
26. Quoted in Daniel W. Drezner and Henry Farrell, "The Power and Politics of Blogs," paper presented at the annual meeting of the American Political Science Association, Chicago, September 2–5, 2004.
27. Quoted in Drezner and Farrell, "The Power and Politics of Blogs."
28. Matthew Klam, "Fear and Laptops on the Campaign Trail," *New York Times Magazine*, September 26, 2004, p. 43.
29. D. Travers Scott, "Pundits in Muckracker's Clothing: Political Blogs and the 2004 U.S. Presidential Election," in *Blogging, Citizenship, and the Future of Media*, ed. Mark Tremayne, New York: Routledge, 2007, p. 54.
30. Interview with Joshua Micah Marshall; Interview with Markos Moulitsas, *Frontline*, PBS, August 13, 2006, at http://www.pbs.org/wgbh/pages/frontline/newswar.
31. Scott, "Pundits in Muckracker's Clothing," p. 54.
32. Interview with Markos Moulitsas.
33. Michael Skube, "Blogs: All the Noise That Fits," *Los Angeles Times*, August 19, 2007, p. M5.
34. Wall, "'Blogs of War,'" pp. 153–172.

35. See Bernard Bailyn and John B. Hench, eds., *The Press and the American Revolution*, Worcester, Mass.: American Antiquarian Society, 1980; John Byrne Cooke, *Reporting the War: Freedom of the Press from the American Revolution to the War on Terrorism*, New York: Palgrave Macmillan, 2007; Culver Smith, *The Press, Politics, and Patronage: The American Government's Use of Newspapers, 1789–1875*, Athens: University of Georgia Press, 1977.

36. See Michael Schudson, *Discovering the News*, New York: Basic Books, 1980.

37. "News Audiences Increasingly Polarized: Online News Audience Larger, More Diverse," Pew Research Center for the People and the Press, June 8, 2004, at http://people-press.org/reports/pdf/215.pdf.

38. Jane B. Singer, "Still Guarding the Gate? The Newspaper Journalist's Role in an On-line World," *Convergence*, 3 (1997), pp. 72–89.

39. Williams, "Blogged in Boston."

40. Nicole Moore, "A Victory for Bloggers," *The Thicket at State Legislatures*, March 9, 2007, at http://ncsl.typepad.com/the_thicket/2007/03/another_blogger.html.

41. Alan Sipress, "Too Casual to Sit on Press Row? Bloggers' Credentials Boosted with Seats at the Libby Trial," *Washington Post*, January 11, 2007, p. D1.

42. Williams, "Blogged in Boston."

43. Frank Luther Mott, *American Journalism: A History: 1690–1960*, New York: Macmillan, 1962, pp. 446–458; Edwin Emery, *The Press and America: An Interpretive History of the Mass Media*, 5th edition, Englewood Cliffs, N.J.: Prentice-Hall, 1984, p. 238.

44. Drezner and Farrell, "The Power and Politics of Blogs."

45. Howard Kurtz, "The Comeback Columnist: Andrew Sullivan Continues to Defy All Expectations," *Washington Post*, April 19, 2001, p. C1.

46. Julie Bosman, "First with the Scoop, If Not the Truth," *New York Times*, April 18, 2004, section 9, p. 10.

47. "Wonkette in the Flesh: An Evening with Ana Marie Cox," Society of Professional Journalists, Columbia University Graduate School of Journalism, at http://spj.jrn.columbia.edu/wonkette.html.

48. Rachel Smolkin, "Lessons Learned," *American Journalism Review*, December 2004/January 2005, p. 44.

49. Interview with Markos Moulitsas.

50. Peter Johnson, "Web Becomes Source—Not Outlet—for News," *USA Today*, March 26, 2007, p. 7D.

51. Rhodes Cook, "The Nomination Process," in *The Elections of 1988*, ed. Michael Nelson, Washington, D.C.: CQ Press, 1989, pp. 45–46.

52. See Marvin Kalb, *One Scandalous Story: Clinton, Lewinsky, and Thirteen Days That Tarnished American Journalism*, New York: Free Press, 2001.

53. Smolkin, "The Expanding Blogosphere."

54. Alexandra Polier, "The Education of Alexandra Polier," *New York Magazine*, June 7, 2004, at http://nymag.com/nymag/features/coverstory/9221.

55. Quoted in Stephen Humphries, "Blogs Look Burly after Kicking Sand on CBS," *Christian Science Monitor*, September 22, 2004, p. 1.

56. Interview with Joshua Micah Marshall.

57. For a discussion of this problem, see Lori Robertson, "Romancing the Source," *American Journalism Review*, May 2002, at http://www.ajr.org/Article.asp?id=2520.

58. Dammon Loyalka, "Blog Alert," p. 19.

59. Humphries, "Blogs Look Burly."

60. John Milburn and Ellen Simon, "Army Denounces Articles Written by GI," *USA Today*, August 9, 2007, at http://www.usatoday.com/tech/news/2007–08–09-soldier-blogger-denounced_N.htm.

61. Howard Kurtz, "New Republic Disavows Iraq Diarist Reports," *Washington Post*, December 4, 2007, p. C1.

62. "The Short Happy Life of Scott Beauchamp, Fabulist," August 6, 2007, at http://www.powerlineblog.com/archives/2007/08/018142.php.

63. Bob Owens, "The Never-Ending Story," October 26, 2007, at http://mediamythbusters.com/blog/?p=127.

64. Greg Mitchell, "The 'Gannon' Case: Blogs Roll Again," *Editor & Publisher*, March 2005, p. 26.

65. Kurtz, "New Republic Disavows Iraq Diarist Reports."

66. Drezner and Farrell, "The Power and Politics of Blogs."

67. Jennifer Huberdeau, "Clark Trustee Resigns after Blogger Criticism," *North Adams Transcript* (Massachusetts), June 15, 2006.

68. Pajamasmedia.com.

69. Neil Reisner, "The Accidental Blogger," *American Journalism Review*, April/May 2005, p. 10.

70. For a discussion of the controversy, see Daniel Drezner, February 18, 2005, at http://www.danieldrezner.com/archives/001898.html.

71. Reisner, "The Accidental Blogger"; Howard Kurtz, "Eason Jordan, Quote, Unquote," *Washington Post*, February 8, 2005, p. C1; "CNN Executive Resigns after Controversial Remarks," CNN.com, February 11, 2005, at http://www.cnn.com/2005/SHOWBIZ/TV/02/11/easonjordan.cnn/index.html.

72. Michelle Malkin, February 11, 2005, at http://michellemalkin.com/2005/02/11/breaking-news-eason-jordan-resigns.

73. Interview with John Hinderaker.

74. See, for example, Barb Palser, "No More Name-Calling," *American Journalism Review*, May 2005, p. 70.

75. Interview with Joshua Micah Marshall.

76. Interview with Markos Moulitsas.

77. Interview with Markos Moulitsas, *Frontline*, PBS, August 13, 2006, at http://www.pbs.org/wgbh/pages/frontline/newswar.

78. Vaina, "Newspapers and Blogs: Closer Than We Think?"

79. Scott Martelle and Seema Mehta, "John Edwards Admits to Affair, Repeated Lies," *Los Angeles Times*, August 9, 2008, at http://www.latimes.com/news/politics/la-na-edwards9-2008aug09,0,4492173.story.

80. Joel David Bloom, "The Blogosphere: How a Once-Humble Medium Came to Drive Elite Media Discourse and Influence Public Policy and Elections," paper presented at the 2nd annual pre-APSA Conference on Political Communication, Philadelphia, August 31, 2003.

81. Quoted in Schulman, "Meet the New Bosses," June 20, 2007, at http://www.motherjones.com/news/feature/2007/07/meet_the_new_bosses.html.

82. J. D. Lasica, "Weblogs: A New Source of News," *USC Annenberg Online Journalism Review*, May 24, 2001, at http://www.ojr.org/ojr/workplace/1017958782.php.

83. Gracie Lawson-Borders and Rita Kirk, "Blogs in Campaign Communication," *American Behavioral Scientist*, 49 (December 2005), p. 549.

84. Joe Strupp, "Voting for the Web," *Editor & Publisher*, October 2006, p. 62.

85. Howard Kurtz, "Mainstream Blogs Open Floodgates for Political Coverage," *Washington Post*, October 26, 2007, p. C1.

86. Lawson-Borders and Kirk, "Blogs in Campaign Communication," p. 550.

87. J. D. Lasica, "Blogs and Journalism Need Each Other," *Nieman Reports*, Fall 2003, p. 71.

88. Perlmutter, *Blogwars*, p. 17.

89. Lasica, "Weblogs: A New Source of News."

90. Michael Falcone, "Does an Editor's Pencil Ruin a Web Log?" *New York Times*, September 29, 2003, C9; Daniel Weintraub, "Scuttlebutt and Speculation Fill a Political Weblog," *Nieman Reports*, Winter 2003, pp. 58–59.

91. Smolkin, "The Expanding Blogosphere."

92. Smolkin, "The Expanding Blogosphere."

93. Falcone, "Does an Editor's Pencil Ruin a Web Log?"

94. Quoted in Lasica, "Weblogs: A New Source of News."

95. Matthew Hindman, *The Myth of Digital Democracy*, Princeton, N.J.: Princeton University Press, forthcoming, chapter 6.

96. Strupp, "Voting for the Web," p. 62.

97. Jay Rosen et al., "The Best Blogging Newspapers in the U.S.," *BluePlateSpecial.Net*, March 1, 2006, at http://journalism.nyu.edu/pubzone/blueplate/issue1/best_nwsps/.

98. Quoted in Perlmutter, *Blogwars*, p. 33.

99. David Carr, "24-Hour Newspaper People," *New York Times*, January 15, 2007, p. C1.

100. Lasica, "Weblogs: A New Source of News."

101. Amanda Lenhart and Susannah Fox, "Bloggers: A Portrait of the Internet's New Storytellers," Pew Internet and American Life Project, July 19, 2006, at http://www.pewinternet.org/PPF/r/186/report_display.asp.

102. "Blogger: Joshua Micah Marshall, 34, Editor, Talking Points Memo," *Washington Post*, December 21, 2003, p. M3.

103. "Internet's Broader Role in Campaign 2008: Social Networking and Online Videos Take Off," Pew Research Center, January 11, 2008, at http://people-press.org/reports/pdf/384.pdf; "Internet News Audience Highly Critical of News Organizations," Pew Research Center, August 9, 2007, at http://people-press.org/reports/pdf/348.pdf.

104. Lasica, "Weblogs: A New Source of News."

105. "Internet's Broader Role in Campaign 2008."

106. "Public More Critical of Press, but Goodwill Persists," Pew Research Center, June 26, 2005, at http://people-press.org/reports/pdf/248.pdf.

107. Bloom, "The Blogosphere."

108. Quoted in Smolkin, "The Expanding Blogosphere."

109. J. D. Lasica, "Blogging as a Form of Journalism," *USC Annenberg Online Journalism Review*, April 29, 2001, at http://www.ojr.org/ojr/lasica/1019166956.php.

110. Paul McLeary, "Franklin Foer on the Blogosphere's War on the Media," *Columbia Journalism Review*, January 6, 2006, at http://www.cjr.org/the_water_cooler/franklin_foer_on_the_blogosphe.php.

111. Sue MacDonald, "Drudge Report, DailyKos, and Instapundit Grab Most 'Buzz' among Political Blogs, Says Intelliseek," *Business Wire*, October 27, 2004, p. 1.

112. Interview with Markos Moulitsas.

113. Interview with John Hinderaker.

114. Interview with Markos Moulitsas.

115. "Blogger: Joshua Micah Marshall, 34, Editor, Talking Points Memo."

116. Glenn, "The (Josh) Marshall Plan."

117. Drezner and Farrell, "The Power and Politics of Blogs."

118. Wilson Lowrey, "Mapping the Journalism-Blogging Relationship," *Journalism*, 7 (2006), p. 487.

119. Drezner and Farrell, "The Power and Politics of Blogs."

120. Smolkin, "The Expanding Blogosphere."

121. Smolkin, "The Expanding Blogosphere."

122. Marci McCoy Roth, "How Journalists See the Blogosphere," Annenberg School of Communication, University of Pennsylvania, December 2004, at http://java.cs.vt.edu/public/projects/digitalgov/papers/blogs.pdf.

123. See, for example, Adam Reilly, "The Allure of the Web," *Nieman Reports*, Spring 2004, pp. 27–28.

124. These blogs were determined as most popular by their presence on the top of both lists of influence (number of links from other blogs) and readership (the number of daily visits).

125. Hindman, *The Myth of Digital Democracy*.

126. Glenn, "The (Josh) Marshall Plan."

127. Kevin Wallsten, "Political Blogs and Bloggers Who Blog Them: Is the Political Blogosphere an Echo Chamber?" paper presented at the annual meeting of the American Political Science Association, Washington, D.C., September 1–4, 2005.

128. Rebecca Reynolds, "Political News Blog and Newspaper Coverage of Democratic Candidates in the 2004 U.S. Presidential Election," paper presented at the annual meeting of the International Communication Association, New York, May 26–30, 2005.

129. Inclusion of the day before allowed for the possibility that the online version of the next day's front-page story may have appeared sometime during the previous day.

Chapter 7

1. Carl Stempel, Thomas Hargrove, and Guido H. Stempel III, "Media Use, Social Structure, and Belief in 9/11 Conspiracy Theories," *Journalism and Mass Communication Quarterly*, 84 (November 2007), pp. 353–372; Thomas J. Johnson et al., "Every Blog Has Its Day: Politically-Interested Internet Users' Perceptions of Blog Credibility," *Journal of Computer-Mediated Communication*, 13 (October 2007), pp. 100–122; Amanda Lenhart and Susannah Fox, "Bloggers: A Portrait of the Internet's New Storytellers," Pew Internet and American Life Project, July 19, 2006, at http://www.pewinternet.org/PPF/r/186/report_display.asp; Joseph Graf, "The Audience for Political Blogs: New Research on Blog Readership," Institute for Politics, Democracy, & the Internet, October 2006, at http://ipdi.org/UploadedFiles/Audience%20for%20Political%20Blogs.pdf; Kaye D. Trammell, "Celebrity Blogs: Investigation in the Persuasive Nature of Two-Way Communication Regarding Politics," PhD dissertation, University of Florida, 2004.

2. See Graf, "The Audience for Political Blogs"; Amanda Lenhart and Mary Madden, "Teen Content Creators and Consumers," Pew Internet and American Life Project, November 2005, at http://www.pewinternet.org/pdfs/PIP_Teens_Content_Creation.pdf; Lee Rainie, "The State of Blogging," Pew Internet & American Life Project, January 2005, at http://www.pewinternet.org/pdfs/PIP_blogging_data.pdf; "More Than Half of Americans Never Read Political Blogs," The Harris Poll no. 25, March 10, 2008; "Two-Fifths of U.S. Adults Who Are Online Have Read Political Blogs," The Harris Poll no. 27, April 13, 2005, at http://www.harrisinteractive.com/harris_poll/index.asp?PID=556.

3. "More Than Half of Americans Never Read Political Blogs."

4. Marjorie Connelly, "The Blogs," *New York Times*, March 13, 2007, p. A16; "More Than Half of Americans Never Read Political Blogs."

5. "Internet Penetration and Impact," Pew Internet and American Life Project, April 26, 2006, at http://www.pewinternet.org/PPF/r/182/report_display.asp.

6. "Public Knowledge of Current Affairs Little Changed by News and Information Revolutions," Pew Research Center for the People and the Press, April 15, 2007, at http://people-press.org/reports/display.php3?ReportID=319.

7. Rainie, "The State of Blogging."

8. "Public Knowledge of Current Affairs Little Changed by News and Information Revolutions."

9. "Public Knowledge of Current Affairs Little Changed by News and Information Revolutions."

10. "Public Knowledge of Current Affairs Little Changed by News and Information Revolutions."

11. See "More Than Half of Americans Never Read Political Blogs"; Graf, "The Audience for Political Blogs"; Rainie, "The State of Blogging."

12. For similar findings, see William P. Eveland Jr. and Ivan Dylko, "Reading Political Blogs during the 2004 Election Campaign: Correlates and Political

Consequences," in *Blogging, Citizenship, and the Future of Media*, ed. Mark Tremayne, New York: Routledge, 2007, pp. 105–126.

13. Dustin Harp and Mark Tremayne, "The Gendered Blogosphere: Examining Inequality Using Network and Feminist Theory," *Journalism and Mass Communication Quarterly*, 83 (Summer 2006), pp. 247–264.

14. Matthew Hindman, *The Myth of Digital Democracy*, Princeton, N.J.: Princeton University Press, forthcoming, chapter 6.

15. See, for example, Susan Herring, "Posting in a Different Voice: Voice, Gender and Ethics in Computer-Mediated Communication," in *Philosophical Perspectives in Computer-Mediated Communication*, ed. Charles Ess, Albany: State University of New York Press, 1996, pp. 115–146; Richard Davis, *Politics Online: Blogs, Chatrooms, and Discussion Groups in American Democracy*, New York: Routledge, 2005, chapter 3; Richard Davis, *The Web of Politics: The Internet's Impact on the American Political System*, New York: Oxford University Press, 1999, chapter 6.

16. Rainie, "The State of Blogging"; Lenhart and Fox, "Bloggers: A Portrait of the Internet's New Storytellers."

17. Hindman, *The Myth of Digital Democracy*; "More Than Half of Americans Never Read Political Blogs."

18. Lenhart and Fox, "Bloggers: A Portrait of the Internet's New Storytellers."

19. See Martin P. Wattenberg, *Is Voting for Young People*, New York: Longman, 2007, pp. 9–16.

20. See, for example, Eveland and Dylko, "Reading Political Blogs during the 2004 Election Campaign," pp. 105–126; Davis, *Politics Online*.

21. Jeffrey M. Jones, "GOP Identification in 2007 Lowest in Last Two Decades," January 14, 2008, at http://www.gallup.com/poll/103732/GOP-Identification-2007-Lowest-Last-Two-Decades.aspx.

22. Rainie, "The State of Blogging."

23. "Public Knowledge of Current Affairs Little Changed by News and Information Revolutions."

24. American National Election Studies, at www.electionstudies.org.

25. Stempel, Hargrove, and Stempel, "Media Use, Social Structure, and Belief in 9/11 Conspiracy Theories."

26. For a discussion of this thesis, see Barbara K. Kaye, "Blog Use Motivations: An Exploratory Study," in *Blogging, Citizenship, and the Future of Media*, ed. Mark Tremayne, New York: Routledge, 2007, pp. 127–148.

27. Kaye, "Blog Use Motivations."

28. Johnson et al., "Every Blog Has Its Day"; Thomas J. Johnson and Barbara K. Kaye, "Wag the Blog: How Reliance on Traditional Media and the Internet Influence Credibility Perceptions of Weblogs among Blog Users," *Journalism & Mass Communication Quarterly*, 81 (Autumn 2004), pp. 622–642.

29. Quoted in David. D. Perlmutter, *Blogwars*, New York: Oxford University Press, 2008, p. 32.

30. Richard Siklos, "Meet Arianna Huffington 2.0," *Fortune*, October 29, 2007, at http://money.cnn.com/2007/10/26/magazines/fortune/huffington.fortune/.

31. Matthew Klam, "Fear and Laptops on the Campaign Trail," *New York Times Magazine*, September 26, 2004, p. 43; Rachel Smolkin, "The Expanding Blogosphere," *American Journalism Review*, July 2004, at http://www.ajr.org/archive.asp?issue=66.

32. Siklos, "Meet Arianna Huffington 2.0."

33. Rainie, "The State of Blogging."

34. Alister Cameron, "Blogging in the Eye of the Storm," April 27, 2007, at http://www.alistercameron.com/2007/04/27/blogging-in-the-eye-of-the-storm/.

35. Liriel Higa, "United Bloggers? Depends on the Issue," CQ *Weekly*, October 16, 2006, p. 2745.

36. Lorelle VanFossen, "Are You Losing Readers? Why?" *Blog Herald*, July 17, 2007, at http://www.blogherald.com/2007/07/17/are-you-losing-readers-why/.

Conclusion

1. Rachel Smolkin, "The Expanding Blogosphere," *American Journalism Review*, July 2004, at http://www.ajr.org/archive.asp?issue=66.

2. Gracie Lawson-Borders and Rita Kirk, "Blogs in Campaign Communication," *American Behavioral Scientist*, 49 (December 2005), p. 557.

3. Rebecca Reynolds, "Political News Blog and Newspaper Coverage of Democratic Candidates in the 2004 U.S. Presidential Election," paper presented at the annual meeting of the International Communication Association, New York, May 26–30, 2005.

4. Lada Adamic and Natalie Glance, "The Political Blogosphere and the 2004 U.S. Election: Divided They Blog," paper presented at the 2nd Annual Workshop on the Weblogging Ecosystem: Aggregation, Analysis and Dynamics, Chiba, Japan, May 10, 2005.

5. "Journalist Q & A—Andrew Sullivan, Time.com," *PR Week*, January 15, 2007, p. 14.

6. See J. D. Lasica, "Blogs and Journalism Need Each Other," *Nieman Reports*, Fall 2003, p. 71; Shawn McIntosh, "Web Review: Blogs: Has Their Time Finally Come—or Gone?" *Global Media and Communication*, 1 (2005), pp. 385–388.

7. Andrew Sullivan, "A Blogger's Creed," *Time*, September 27, 2004, p. 37.

8. Smolkin, "The Expanding Blogosphere."

9. Smolkin, "The Expanding Blogosphere."

10. Joe Trippi, *The Revolution Will Not Be Televised: Democracy, the Internet, and the Overthrow of Everything*, New York: Regan Books, 2004.

11. Jerome Armstrong and Markos Moulitsas Zuniga, *Crashing the Gate: Netroots, Grassroots, and the Rise of People-Powered Politics*, White River Junction, Vt.: Chelsea Green Publishing, 2006; David Kline et al., eds., *Blog! How the Newest Media Revolution Is Changing Politics, Business, and Culture*, Durham, N.C.: CDS Books, 2005.

12. David Glenn, "The (Josh) Marshall Plan," *Columbia Journalism Review*, September/October 2007, at http://www.cjr.org/feature/the_josh_marshall_plan.php?page=all.

13. Quoted in Scott Helman, "Romney Connecting Quickly with Bloggers," *Boston Globe*, December 31, 2006, at http://www.boston.com/news/local/articles/2006/12/31/romney_connecting_quickly_with_bloggers/.

14. Daniel Schulman, "Meet the New Bosses," *Mother Jones*, June 20, 2007, at http://www.motherjones.com/news/feature/2007/07/meet_the_new_bosses.html.

15. Antoinette Pole, "Hispanic Bloggers in the Blogosphere: Politics and Participation," paper presented at the annual meeting of the American Political Science Association, Chicago, August 30–September 2, 2007.

16. Antoinette Pole, "Black Bloggers and the Blogosphere," paper presented at the second International Conference on Technology, Knowledge and Society, Hyderabad, India, December 12–15, 2005.

17. Mark D. Brewer, "The Rise of Partisanship and the Expansion of Partisan Conflict within the American Electorate," *Political Research Quarterly*, 58 (June 2005), pp. 219–229. For a contrasting view, see Morris P. Fiorina et al., *Culture War? The Myth of a Polarized America*, New York: Longman, 2004.

18. John Leo, "A Blog's Bark Has Bite," *U.S. News and World Report*, May 5, 2002, at http://www.usnews.com/usnews/opinion/articles/020513/archive_020772.htm.

19. Christine Rosen, "Technobabble," *New Republic*, June 26, 2006, p. 15.

20. Michael Skube, "Blogs: All the Noise That Fits," *Los Angeles Times*, August 19, 2007, p. M5.

21. Thomas C. Leonard, *News for All: America's Coming-of-Age with the Press*, New York: Oxford University Press, 1995, pp. 177–181.

22. Brian Stelter, "Citizen Huff," *New York Times*, March 31, 2008, p. C1.

23. Stelter, "Citizen Huff."

24. Skube, "Blogs: All the Noise That Fits."

25. Richard L. Rubin, *Press, Party, and Presidency*, New York: Norton, 1981; James E. Pollard, *The Presidents and the Press*, New York: Octagon Books, 1973.

26. Martin P. Wattenberg, *Is Voting for Young People?* New York: Pearson Longman, 2007, pp. 9–16.

Appendix

1. For content analyses, see Susan C. Herring et al., "Longitudinal Content Analysis of Blogs: 2003–2004," in *Blogging, Citizenship, and the Future of Media*, ed. Mark Tremayne, New York: Routledge, 2007, pp. 3–20; Zizi Papacharissi, "Audiences as Media Producers: Content Analysis of 260 Blogs," in *Blogging, Citizenship, and the Future of Media*, ed. Mark Tremayne, New York: Routledge, 2007, pp. 21–38; Svetlana V. Kulikova and David D. Perlmutter, "Blogging Down the Dictator? The Kyrgyz Revolution and Samizdat Websites," *International Communication Gazette*, 69 (2007), pp. 29–50; Melissa Wall, "'Blogs of War': Weblogs as News," *Journalism*, 6 (2005), pp. 153–172; Rebecca Reynolds, "Political News Blog and Newspaper Coverage of Democratic Candidates in the 2004 U.S. Presidential

Election," paper presented at the annual meeting of the International Communication Association, New York, May 26–30, 2005; Michael Keren, "Blogging and the Politics of Melancholy," *Canadian Journal of Communication,* 29 (2004), pp. 5–23.

2. For audience surveys, see Mark Tremayne, ed., *Blogging, Citizenship, and the Future of Media,* New York: Routledge, 2007; Carl Stempel, Thomas Hargrove, and Guido H. Stempel III, "Media Use, Social Structure, and Belief in 9/11 Conspiracy Theories," *Journalism and Mass Communication Quarterly,* 84 (November 2007), pp. 353–372; Joseph Graf, "The Audience for Political Blogs: New Research on Blog Readership," Institute for Politics, Democracy, and the Internet, October 2006, at http://ipdi.org/ UploadedFiles/Audience%20for%20Political%20Blogs.pdf; Amada Lenhart, "Bloggers: A Portrait of the Internet's New Storytellers," Pew Internet and American Life Project, July 19, 2006, at http://www.pewinternet.org/pdfs/ PIP%20Bloggers%20Report%20July%2019%202006.pdf; Lee Rainie, "The Stage of Blogging," Pew Internet and American Life Project, January 2005, at http://www.pewinternet.org/pdfs/PIP_blogging_data.pdf; Thomas J. Johnson and Barbara K. Kaye, "Wag the Blog: How Reliance on Traditional Media and the Internet Influence Credibility Perceptions of Weblogs among Blog Users," *Journalism and Mass Communication Quarterly,* 81 (Autumn 2004), pp. 622–642.

3. For studies incorporating both, see Kaye D. Trammell, "Celebrity Blogs: Investigation in the Persuasive Nature of Two-Way Communication Regarding Politics," PhD dissertation, University of Florida, 2004; Kulikova and Perlmutter, "Blogging Down the Dictator?"

4. Kevin Wallsten, "Agenda Setting and the Blogosphere: An Analysis of the Relationship between Mainstream Media and Political Blogs," *Review of Policy Research,* 24 (2007), pp. 567–587.

5. For a discussion of content analysis as a social science technique, see Ole R. Holsti, *Content Analysis for the Social Sciences and Humanities,* Reading, Mass.: Addison-Wesley, 1969; Klaus Krippendorf, *Content Analysis,* Beverly Hills, Calif.: Sage, 1980.

6. Determining measures of influence in the blogosphere is a challenge for blog researchers. See Kathy E. Gill, "How Can We Measure the Influence of the Blogosphere?" *WWW2004,* New York, May 17–22, 2004.

Index